Managing the Entrepreneurial University

Managing the Entrepreneurial University is essential reading for both higher education administrators and those studying to enter the field. As universities have become more market focused, they have changed dramatically. But has the law kept up? This book explains fundamental legal concepts in clear, non-technical language and grounds them in practical management situations, indicating where doctrines and standards have evolved, identifying where legal difficulties may be more likely to arise, and suggesting where change may be merited.

In its chapters on process, discrimination, employment, students, and regulation, the book:

- Provides lively case studies applicable to every type of institution
- Includes a simulation exercise at the end of each chapter for use in teaching or training
- Draws on an over 550-source bibliography

A hypothetical case spans each chapter, addressing not only research universities and elite liberal arts colleges, but also community colleges, small private colleges, and regional comprehensive universities. Readers working across functional areas and at various institution types will find the book directly relevant in clarifying and deepening their understanding of the legal environment associated with their responsibilities within the entrepreneurial university.

J. Douglas Toma is associate professor at the Institute of Higher Education at the University of Georgia and has an appointment on the School of Law faculty.

Managing the Entrepreneurial University

Legal Issues and Commercial Realities

J. Douglas Toma

Routledge
Taylor & Francis Group

NEW YORK AND LONDON

First published 2011
by Routledge
711 Third Avenue, New York, NY 10017

Simultaneously published in the UK
by Routledge
2 Park Square, Milton Park, Abingdon, Oxon OX14 4RN

Routledge is an imprint of the Taylor & Francis Group, an informa business

Library of Congress Cataloging in Publication Data
Toma, J. Douglas.
    Managing the entrepreneurial university : legal issues and commercial realities / J. Douglas Toma.
    p. cm.
    Includes bibliographical references and index.
    1. Education, Higher—Law and legislation—United States. 2. Universities and colleges—Law and legislation—United States. I. Title.
    KF4225.T66 2011
    344.73'073—dc22
    2010033201

ISBN13: 978-0-415-87242-3 (hbk)
ISBN13: 978-0-415-87245-4 (pbk)
ISBN13: 978-0-203-83123-6 (ebk)

Typeset in Caslon, Trade Gothic, and Copperplate by
EvS Communication Networx, Inc.

Printed and bound in the United States of America on acid-free paper by
Walsworth Publishing Company, Marceline, MO

Contents

ACKNOWLEDGMENTS   VII

INTRODUCTION   1

1   PROCESS   9

2   DISCRIMINATION   41

3   EMPLOYMENT   69

4   STUDENTS   121

5   REGULATION   167

CONCLUSION   195

REFERENCES   201

INDEX   231

Acknowledgments

In addition to those who worked directly on the book, I would like to acknowledge two other groups and two individuals in particular, before adding a final personal note.

I have been fortunate to have extraordinary mentors throughout my academic career, beginning in the early 1990s with Joan Stark and Marv Peterson while I was a graduate student at the University of Michigan. As I assumed my first faculty position at the University of Missouri-Kansas City, Joan Gallos taught me that an academic career is a marathon and not a sprint. At the University of Pennsylvania, Bob Zemsky modeled a faculty career that involved offering bold ideas and being connected worldwide, while Marvin Lazerson personified how traditional values and entrepreneurial behavior could operate in tandem.

Upon arriving at my home at the Institute of Higher Education at the University of Georgia, I learned through Tom Dyer the meaning of devotion to an institution and the importance of civility within any academic community—and how both could be leveraged in building an academic unit. At the Institute, I have also had the privilege of working with Sheila Slaughter and Jim Hearn, two of the very best. I dedicate this book to one last mentor, Libby Morris, the current director of the Institute and vice provost of the University. Libby is the most creative and effective problem-solver I have ever encountered. On scholarly, instructional, advising, and administrative questions alike, Libby's counsel has always enabled me not to lose momentum.

Acknowledging another group of colleagues, nothing has brought me more pleasure during my career than working with a set of collaborators, who are also among my closest friends. Greg Dubrow, Matt Hartley, Adrianna Kezar, Kevin Kinser, Chris Morphew, Kelly Ward, Lisa Wolf-Wendel, and I have been partners on various projects, as well as being evening companions at conferences, essentially growing up together over the past 15 years. Beyond our seemingly endless capacity to discuss sports, politics, and travel, Chris especially has had an important impact on my work, challenging me to stretch my thinking. I also dedicate this book to him, both individually and as a representative of the group.

I would also like to thank Karen Miller, Scott Rizzo, Micki Waldrop, and Adam Wyatt of the Institute for their direct work on this volume. Finally, my wife, Linda, and our seven-year-old son, Jack, are the most important people in my life. They, as always, supported my late nights and weekends away reading and writing. I also dedicate this book to them.

Introduction

American higher education has increasingly become a commodity, its environment marked by intense competition and rhetoric associated with markets and efficiency, and its purposes have increasingly become connected more with individual gain than societal good. In the interest of generating more resources, institutions across types have defined "getting to the next level" as their primary aspiration, pursuing a rather generic set of strategies toward rising in the reputational rankings (O'Meara, 2007; Toma, 2010a). Institutions tend to approach positioning similarly despite the significant stratification in available resources and similar disparities otherwise between and among them. The perception across higher education is that prestige is linked with resources, because the wealthiest institutions head the rankings, whether annually in *U.S. News and World Report* directed toward popular audiences or the decennial National Research Council tables that rate various graduate programs (Ehrenberg, 2003; Meredith, 2004).

The most direct means to increase an institution's ranking is through enrolling more accomplished students, raising variables such as average standardized test scores, with institutions willing to discount tuition to attract them (Golden, 2007; McPherson and Shapiro, 1998; Schmidt, 2007). Research universities can also gain prestige through building endowments and developing funded research. The former enables them to fund scholarships, construct facilities, and endow professorships, which all advance strategic ends. The latter often involves recruiting or retaining faculty members—or even groups of researchers—considered to be able to attract funding, offering them attractive packages combining salaries, support, and facilities. Toward attracting undergraduate students, institutions are launching popular undergraduate majors, encouraging faculty-student research collaborations, and emphasizing honors programs to mimic the elite liberal arts college at a large university, and enhancing study abroad opportunities. They are also adding or augmenting graduate programs, whether to directly generate resources or indirectly enhance prestige—or both. These can be highly specialized doctoral programs or more generic master's degree efforts, as an education school might offer at a satellite campus—or anything in between.

Also in support of attracting those students who promise to raise institutional profile, universities and colleges are investing in luxurious collegiate infrastructure—student residences, dining commons, fitness centers, and even commercial districts. They are also investing in such academic facilities as science buildings, being increasingly creative in how they finance such activities, as in the use of bonds and debt. Institutions have also become more identity conscious, establishing more sophisticated approaches to branding and marketing. Athletics is also a strategy, perceived to be useful in building community and connecting with external constituents at larger institutions, and more directly in recruiting athletes as needed students at more financially fragile institutions.

The pursuit of prestige provides a useful surrogate for increasing shareholder value or bottom line profits as an outcome consistent with neoliberal ideas that privilege competition within markets. But doing so can exacerbate the mission inflation or academic drift that comes with institutions being naturally isomorphic, seeking legitimacy through replicating market leaders and security by staying with the herd. Through increasing their prestige, universities and colleges also attempt to minimize the influence of external entities on which they rely for support, thus enhancing their independent resource base (DiMaggio and Powell, 1983; DiMaggio and Powell, 1991; Greenwood et al., 2008; Kraatz and Zajac, 1996; Meyer and Rowan, 1977; Pfeffer and Salancik, 1978). Public institutions must diversify their resources, as states are providing a diminishing proportion of budgets and tuition and fund raising an even greater one. State financing of public higher education has increased, but not to the degree necessary to match escalating costs. These increased costs are not only associated with entrepreneurial activities related to institutional aspirations, but also fixed expenses for basic services such as health benefits, information technology, and deferred maintenance, as well as on items such as energy and building construction.

There are pressures on public institutions to maintain access and affordability, with effective limits on the increases in annual tuition that politicians and others can tolerate. These are sometimes associated with the merit-based scholarships that some states have adopted as a means to keep students in state, but the broader trend over the past two decades has been a dramatic shift from grants to loans. States also are increasingly expressing their expectations that institutions demonstrate quality and contribute to local, state, and national economic development, although such concepts remain poorly defined (McGuinness, 2005; Zumeta, 2001). In response, institutions have increasingly moved to employing return on investment rhetoric to justify their state support and frame their relationships with students, as opposed to framing higher education as a public good. The neoliberal environment also more directly influences students, both traditional and nontraditional, who are increasingly pursuing degrees in professional fields, both at the undergraduate and graduate levels, seeking more direct returns on their investment in higher education.

In order to economize, institutions across types are shifting, especially as retirements and departures occur, from faculty in tenure-significant lines to contingent faculty (those in temporary appointments). Graduate programs continue to overproduce, providing a ready source of such labor, enabling institutions to be more agile in their hiring practices, as compared with longer-term investments in people. Instructional budgets are one of the few places where institutions can control spending. But they are less willing to cut administrative budgets, which have expanded rapidly given additional obligations in areas such as research compliance and student services. Another notion associated with containing costs, even within various arms races, has been privatizing and outsourcing, as private sector management ideas have permeated even the public sector.

In the pursuit of additional revenues, institutions across types are also developing programs at their peripheries, including academic programs, especially when tuition revenue is essentially stagnant elsewhere. The ultimate idea is that the periphery, through generating resources, can protect the less agile, and thus likely less efficient, core of the institution. It can also be difficult to manage and challenge coherence within organizations (Collis, 2004). These academic programs, commonly offered at satellite campuses or online, tend to be more managed and reliant upon temporary faculty or core faculty on overload. They encourage viewing students as clients, representing another significant cultural departure in U.S. higher education away from traditional faculty influence. Even at "liberal arts" institutions, these academic programs are directed to students seeking convenience, often those working full-time, these nontraditional students being seen as an expanding market. Similarly, universities and colleges are emphasizing continuing education in areas in which they can generate revenue, as with business school executive education. But all of these activities occur in an increasingly crowded space, with for-profit and virtual universities having various advantages, both in pricing and efficiency.

Research universities are equally assertive in supporting faculty involvement outside research ventures, often as individual entrepreneurs, having invested in people and infrastructure, both administrative and facilities. There are new bureaucracies in areas such as information technology, fund raising, research administration, diversity, and international affairs. Institutions have had to manage various ethical challenges associated with accepting certain research funding and in commercializing university research. Institutions across types have invested in external affairs, especially fund raising, and continue to tend to government relations at the state and federal level. Fund raising, particularly for an endowment, enables institutional strategies such as discounting tuition and recruiting faculty—and is a variable in institutional prestige rankings.

Reforms in higher education over the past two decades have primarily focused on improving management, usually increasing the influence of administrators, while reducing that of faculty. Institutions have not dismantled traditional structures of faculty governance, but have increasingly supplanted them with new arrangements that allow managers greater discretion related to academic programs (Birnbaum, 2004). Strategic planning and administrative flexibility are increasingly esteemed, with market criteria and revenue generation, not only educational standards, deemed relevant. In such environments, once collegial relationships can become procedural, looking not at outcomes or even fairness, but instead at process. There is also a diminution in the influence of—and thus the institutional investment in—programs less directly connected with the commercial sphere, as with many areas in the arts and sciences.

Additionally, the boundaries of universities and colleges across types are expanding and blurring. The Internet has become the primary means of both internal and external communication, with students, faculty, and administrators assuming that institutions will invest in the latest technology and that universities and colleges will be Internet service providers. There are similar expectations associated with instructional technology and management information systems, with the latter tending to lag. Students and others are also expecting campuses to be "green," and security is of greater concern, including homeland security. Institutions are increasingly recognizing the realities of globalization, with competition from abroad becoming more apparent, although the United States continues to hold a decided advantage. Study abroad programs are expanding in popularity, as are cross-national collaborations between universities, as with joint degree programs and research partnerships.

Finally, institutions are ever more diverse. There are greater proportions of traditionally underrepresented students on campuses, including racial and ethnic minorities and nontraditional students. Both to advance their longstanding values and for strategic reasons, institutions are increasingly aggressive in their recruitment of minority students, faculty, and administrators. Values continue to matter in higher education, driving behaviors and approaches. But as institutions have become more entrepreneurial, these are no longer the only relevant consideration.[1]

* * *

I explore how those managing these increasingly entrepreneurial universities and colleges are having to adapt to various commercial realities in addressing the legal issues that inevitably arise in higher education. Drawing primarily on secondary sources to examine the contemporary state of the law, I indicate where doctrines and standards have evolved in response to the changing environment, identify where legal difficulties may be more likely to arise, and suggest where change may be merited. I consider these legal issues directly in the context of contemporary challenges in higher education management, particularly those associated across institution types with increased intersections with external markets. I address actual cases sparingly in the text, as it is the legal principle that these cases represent that will be of interest to readers, rather than the process of reaching it that judicial opinions explore. I cite over 550 sources in the book, most written for lawyers, endeavoring to present legal issues in a manner accessible to those without training in the area.

Additionally, in enabling administrators, faculty members, and interested others to better recognize legal issues when they arise, I hope to improve their abilities and confidence as consumers of legal services. My intention is to provide the general background necessary to ask thoughtful questions of counsel and engage in sophisticated discussions about possible responses to legal-related problems. Another goal of the book is to encourage readers to develop approaches specific to their own situations that are responsive to relevant strategic environments and legal contexts. Recognizing the commercial realities that increasingly shape American higher education and accounting for directions that legislatures and courts have defined and continue to define is necessary to be successful in managing institutions, particularly given the additional complexity and uncertainty associated with the emergent entrepreneurial university and college.

I organize the discussion that follows into five chapters. Each is spanned by a hypothetical case applying the concepts explored to a fictitious university or college that is representative of a broad type—a community college, less selective small private college, regional comprehensive university, elite liberal arts college, and public research university. Each chapter concludes with a simulation, primarily for use in teaching or training. I do not employ footnotes in the narrative (except once in this introduction), citing sources in the text. In concluding the book, I note six broad areas suggestive of the intersection among entrepreneurial institutions, effective management, and legal principles.

In Chapter 1, I address process issues in higher education, featuring increased expectations in the area, especially with the enhanced expectations of students and parents, who are both promised and charged more. The entrepreneurial university or college is a more contested space with more aggressive assertion of rights, but only for those in more privileged positions. In contrast, temporary faculty members tend to have few protections. For instance, academic freedom may technically apply to them, but these rights tend to mean little as a practical matter. Also, as situations across institutions become more particularized and less communal, and boundaries expand outward and complexity increases throughout, due process is more difficult to determine and assigning responsibility less certain, such as in determining liability and indemnifying employees. The result is that risk management often becomes the default emphasis. Another challenge is that as norms evolve with the emergence of the entrepreneurial university and college, the common law—the body of judicial precedents that guide present decisions—becomes less predictable. For instance, academic programs offered in peripheral settings may have little in common with those offered in more traditional environments—and the legal principles developed to order these.

Shifting from public purposes justifications to those grounded in individual benefit, enhanced efficiency, and strategic advantage also diminishes the basis for the deference courts and legislatures have traditionally afforded higher education in making decisions on academic matters. A loss of autonomy, including in increased accountability demands, may be the price of commercialization across higher education, as aspirations for prestige and efforts to secure resources can tend to outshine attention to realizing formal missions. But the basic principle continues to apply that institutions tend to insulate themselves when they follow their own reasonable rules. Also, governmental immunity can sometimes shield state universities and colleges, but there are often exceptions that make it inapplicable.

The emergence of the entrepreneurial university and college has had less effect on enforcing antidiscrimination measures in higher education, as I discuss in Chapter 2. As with Title VII, which addresses racial discrimination, or the Americans with

Disabilities Act (ADA), these tend to apply within commercial settings as well as to higher education, including at its periphery. With institutions increasingly image conscious, managing impressions more carefully within relevant markets in recruiting students and others, reputational risk associated with discrimination is a heightened concern. There is also an increased emphasis on allegations of direct discrimination in failing to accommodate religious prerogatives, but definitions and standards have become clearer in sexual harassment and disabilities law than was the situation a decade ago. Discrimination cases continue to be difficult to prove in academe, given the particularized nature of decisions in areas such as tenure, and the traditional academic deference afforded to universities and colleges continues in such situations. Courts have been responsive to diversity as an educational value, recognizing it as a sufficiently compelling governmental interest in justifying affirmative action in admission to elite institutions, provided programs are as narrowly constructed as possible.

In Chapter 3, I explore employment issues in higher education, referencing both the contractors and consultants (within which I include graduate students) that are increasingly prominent in providing instruction, as well as faculty in regular appointments, emphasizing the traditions such as academic deference and academic freedom that continue to be crucial to them. Particularly with the increased emphasis on funded research, research university faculty members among the "haves" enjoy greater leverage than ever before, often negotiating individualized packages. I ask whether, in effect, given that interests so diverge between the "haves" and others, it is still accurate to refer to "the faculty." For contingent faculty, collective bargaining may offer a means to enhance the position of adjunct faculty and graduate assistants, but there are practical barriers to realizing it. Contracts become more important in environments accentuating efficiency and deemphasizing collegiality, but with custom and practice in transition within higher education, they provide less clarity in interpreting agreements. For example, standards for tenure tend to change midstream for assistant professors at regional universities that are attempting to reach "the next level" through enhanced research activity.

Nevertheless, employees in higher education tend to have rights, as with institutional human resource rules that encourage progressive discipline before dismissal. As importantly, there remains a culture across universities and colleges that presents difficulties in dismissing ineffective faculty and others. But institutions increasingly assert themselves relative to employees, as in reducing the number of faculty in tenure significant lines, operating from the premise that institutional academic freedom rights outweigh such interests among individual faculty, or acting to reduce reputational risk associated with misbehavior by faculty and others. Universities and colleges also continue to have the right, as merited, to dismiss tenured faculty for cause and in program reductions based on financial exigency. Finally, affirmative action may well apply to employment in higher education as it does in admissions, although the concept has yet to be directly tested before the U.S. Supreme Court.

With students, discussed in Chapter 4, the historical parental relationship with the institution has evolved into a contractual one, with higher education no longer regarded as a privilege, but instead deemed a purchased good. Contractual theories define the rest of the entrepreneurial university or college, so it has seemed reasonable to extend the logic to students. Such arrangements afford students leverage, which enables them to enforce both direct and implied obligations, and they can take advantage of institutions being increasingly in competition with one another. For instance, strategies by universities and colleges intended to advance their aspirations through attracting accomplished students also suggest various promises to the students recruited. Additionally, in emphasizing the "special relationship" between students and institutions, courts have exhibited a greater willingness to impose liability for foreseeable harm, moving from *in loco parentis* and the later "bystander" era, in which universities and colleges had a duty only when they assumed a responsibility. Even with greater potential liability associated with protecting safety—and areas of possible exposure only growing broader and more diffuse, as with study abroad and internships—situations must still be foreseeable such that it is reasonable to assign a duty to institutions and deem them the cause of the injury. Hazing and suicide involve areas in which institutions can successfully challenge foreseeability and causation. Also, assumption of risk and contributory negligence remain available to institutions as defenses.

There is continued deference to decisions on academic matters, with institutions only having to follow their own rules, not acting in an arbitrary, capricious, or discriminatory manner. For example, courts tend to accept institutional justifications for denying students accommodations under the ADA, provided there is evidence of a deliberative process. There are also broad exceptions available to administrators under rules regulating the release of student records, as for foreign students or when health and welfare are implicated. Concerned with safety and reputation, institutions have taken to systematically identifying, monitoring, and referring students who are thought to constitute a threat. Additionally, although affirmative action is permissible, there are no due process rights available to applicants for admission. Students tend to have more due process rights in behavioral matters, as opposed to academic ones, whether constitutional at public universities or colleges or contractual at all institutions. But the question of what process is due remains inherently case specific, depending at a state institution on the liberty and property interests involved. Finally, free expression continues to be protected at entrepreneurial universities and colleges, especially in a public forum at state institutions, with prior restraints and content-based actions disfavored, but reasonable time, place, and manner allowed.

Chapter 5 addresses regulation in higher education, beginning with various compliance and integrity concerns that have justified institutions adding administrative infrastructure. These have only been heightened with concerns about terrorism, with universities and colleges subject to various bioterrorism and expert controls and the USA PATRIOT Act. Also, tightened immigration has had a strategic impact, making affordable graduate student and postdoctoral fellow labor to operate laboratories and full pay international students harder to come by. There are emerging issues with undocumented students, to whom states can deny in-state tuition and scholarships, but not access to universities and colleges.

Federal policy increasingly emphasizes accountability and consumer protection, with similar logic underlying rules on research integrity. With research universities so interested in commercializing research, including through faculty startup firms supported by institutions, conflicts of interest have become more pronounced and tax-exempt status has been called into question. Intellectual property has become more privatized, with fair use exceptions tightening and the public domain shrinking, as well as institutions being more inclined to enforce claimed rights, as with faculty work-made-for-hire related to online teaching. Private regulation of higher education is primarily concentrated in athletics, with National Collegiate Athletic Association (NCAA) rules governing recruitment and eligibility. There is also federal involvement through enforcement of Title IX. The significant revenues and expenditures connected with the highest profile athletic programs only complicate these issues.

I hope that you, as the reader, find the discussion below to be informative in considering legal issues and commercial realities in developing approaches to managing the entrepreneurial university.

Note

1. Several sources address academic and collegiate strategies toward advancing prestige (Bok, 2002; Brewer, Gates, and Goodman, 2002; Clotfelter, 1996; Ehrenberg, 2002; Geiger, 2004; Keller, 2004; Kirp, 2003; Newman, Couturier, and Scurry, 2004; Slaughter and Leslie, 2004; Slaughter and Rhoades, 2004; Toma, 2003; Winston, 2000; Zemsky, Wegner, and Massy, 2005). These books, articles, and chapters also consider institutional emphases on developing funded research and establishing activities at their peripheries. Other citations relate more directly to mission inflation (Massy and Zemsky, 1994; Morphew, 2002; Morphew and Huisman, 2002; Zemsky, 2004). Finally, several authors focus on critiquing the entrepreneurial university, as with the shift away from permanent faculty (Bousquet, 2008; Burgan, 2006; Giroux, 2007; Kronman, 2007; Lewis, 2006; Newfield, 2008; Rhodes, 2005).

1

PROCESS

Process is essential in managing the entrepreneurial university. Decisions made in an arbitrary or capricious manner, or following institutional rules that are underdeveloped or unreasonable, are likely to be rejected by the courts, resulting in the exposure of universities and colleges to liability. Expectations related to process have only heightened over the past few decades. But meeting such responsibilities has become more challenging for institutions as they expand in all directions, becoming ever more diffuse and complex. As situations in entrepreneurial universities and colleges thus become more particularized and less communal, institutions require more robust and nuanced approaches.

The discussion on process below begins with the sources of the law—constitutional, statutory, the common law, institutional rules, and custom and usage. The latter, in particular, has become more difficult to determine, as norms in higher education increasingly integrate commercial realities into traditional academic values. Although universities and colleges retain considerable autonomy, their increasing commercialization has caused—and it really should—the erosion of the deference that courts have long afforded academe in making values-based decisions on academic questions. Meanwhile, attempts to assert due process rights have expanded, but with the ongoing challenge of no real formula available to determine how much notice and how much hearing are appropriate in a given situation.

Whether courts hold university or college administrators and faculty personally liable for negligence continues to depend upon them acting within their authority. But even authority has become more difficult to define as the boundaries of institutions have expanded outward as they undertake a variety of more entrepreneurial activities at their peripheries. The same is true in determining the essential matter of who is the client in applying the attorney-client privilege. The chapter closes with an outline of the steps in litigation, providing a reference for the reader.

These matters of process apply in the various situations considered in the chapters that follow, beginning with discrimination. They are also relevant in cases involving employment, students, and regulation. The discussion that follows underscores developing fair procedures and following them in a neutral manner as the essential aspect in preventive legal strategies. What will also become clearer is that process is complicated by the situational nature of problems that arise.

Sources

The law derives from several sources: constitutional, statutory, and judicial. The rules a university or college itself adopts also have legal force, as do general practices and understandings within an industry or institution. How the U.S. Constitution is interpreted by a conservative U.S. Supreme Court, increases in applicable regulations, and the decline in deference to institutional decision making by courts are all relevant to managing increasingly entrepreneurial universities and colleges.

The federal constitution provides foundational rights, as do the constitutions of the various states. In higher education, the First and Fourteenth Amendments of the U.S. Constitution are most often relevant. Constitutional principles only protect against the state infringing upon basic rights—they do not apply directly to private institutions. The First Amendment guarantees freedom of expression, assembly, press, and religion. The right to due process within the Fourteenth Amendment requires that the government, if taking the property or seriously damaging the reputation of a person, provide the requisite notice and hearing. Equal protection demands that the state not discriminate in its treatment of citizens based upon immutable characteristics, such as gender, race, or religion—the government must treat different groups in a similar fashion. In working with students, constitutional provisions such as the Fourth Amendment (no unlawful search and seizure) and the Fifth Amendment (an individual cannot be compelled to provide testimony against him- or herself) can apply.

These rights are not absolute, however. The state may make an exception if it has a sufficiently strong justification. For instance, speech that is unpopular is protected, but not that deemed to lack any value. Similarly, affirmative action programs are an exception to the principle of equal protection, provided they are deemed necessary and constructed as narrowly as possible. Furthermore, constitutional rights are paramount—all provisions from other sources, such as a state, that conflict with the U.S. Constitution are invalid. The U.S. Supreme Court, ultimately, makes such determinations. With its present conservative majority, neoliberal notions at the foundation of the entrepreneurial university—ideas that privilege individual gain over the public good—are likely to find support. Finally, the constitutions of the states contain provisions parallel to those in the U.S. Constitution, sometimes providing individuals with even stronger protection, as with the right of privacy formally articulated in 10 state constitutions, as opposed to being read into the federal constitution in certain contexts by the courts.

Another source of the law is federal and state legislation. Federal statutes include antidiscrimination laws, the Copyright Act, and the Internal Revenue Code. Workers' compensation laws, commercial codes, and legislation creating public universities are representative state statutes. Legislation also creates administrative agencies, such as the U.S. Equal Employment Opportunity Commission (EEOC) and the National Labor Relations Board (NLRB), that implement statutes in given areas, promulgating binding rules and adjudicating certain disputes. (There are state agencies, such as public service commissions and civil service commissions, that serve a similar function, and universities and colleges must also abide by certain local ordinances, such as zoning.) Regulation of higher education has increased over the past few decades. The need to comply with these mandates has been one justification for impressive increases in the number of administrators employed by universities and colleges.

Although constitutional provisions apply only to public universities and colleges, various constitutional principles embodied in statutes apply to private institutions. For instance, federal antidiscrimination statutes, such as Title VII or the Americans with Disabilities Act (ADA), incorporate equal protection rights aligned with the Fourteenth Amendment. Private institutions that receive federal funds, which all but a few do, must comply with such statutes. But only when a private university or college assumes a function delegated to it by the state or usually performed by the state will it be deemed to be a "state actor"—and thus subject to the provisions of the U.S. Constitution. Under the Free Exercise Clause of the First Amendment, institutions expressly religious in nature are protected from government interference, but can receive public support for nonreligious ends, such as conducting scientific research, without offending the Establishment Clause, which prohibits the government from supporting religion. Additionally, private institutions will voluntarily adopt various constitutional principles, such as free expression, into their internal rules, with individuals able to enforce these through contract theories.

A common law comprised of holdings in various matters by state and federal courts comprises another source of the law. The common law is grounded in the concept of precedent. In deciding cases, judges are guided by previous decisions on similar issues, introducing some degree of predictability into what courts will conclude. In framing arguments for courts, lawyers on both sides reference precedent that supports the result they seek. They also distinguish cases that apply relevant law, but in ways favoring their opponent. Doing so, they can argue that the case before the court is sufficiently different from the facts in the case that provides the precedent—and is thus inapplicable. Much of the law in areas such as contracts and torts is the product of the common law. Courts also interpret the meaning of constitutional provisions, legislative statutes, administrative regulations, and municipal ordinances. Although prior judicial decisions from other jurisdictions can be instructive to courts, precedents have a binding effect only in the jurisdiction where the case was heard. But a court, in reality, can deem any precedent inapplicable, as no fact situation in a case is identical to one in a previous case.

The rules that institutions derive themselves are also relevant in determining disputes. For instance, an employment contract with a faculty member implicitly incorporates the rules of the institution, such as those mandating due process in the event of a dismissal, and can be determinative in the event of a dispute. The sources of such rules can be governing boards, administrative units, or faculty committees charged with oversight in certain areas. Determinations by adjudicatory bodies, such as grievance committees or student judiciaries, also have some precedential value. Written or implied arrangements between institutions and others can additionally be determinative, particularly when articulated clearly. Written contracts are more certain, but informal agreements also have force, if understood, as can established but unwritten practices and understandings within an institution or across higher education. Such custom and usage define expectations, so they can be applicable in interpreting disputes, such as those involving contracts.

But as relationships evolve within institutions as they become more commercialized, custom and usage grounded in more traditional values may become less applicable. For instance, at aspiring research universities, expectations of faculty members increasingly incorporate conducting research. But the research culture at these institutions can be less developed than its ambitions, with those seeking tenure and promotion finding standards unclear. Faculty members up for tenure may also be subject to voting by senior colleagues who have not been active in research and thus have a poor understanding of appropriate benchmarks.

Over the past five years, since the arrival of Elihu Smails as president, Bushwood Community College has expanded in size and scope. The college now enrolls 23,000 students in academic and vocational programs, as well as offering nondegree training courses. In addition to its original location in Davie, it has developed campuses in Plantation and Sunrise. For the past decade, it has partnered with Boca Raton University, which is about 30 miles away, to offer selected BRU courses on its Davie campus. Several BCC students have taken advantage of the arrangement to complete their bachelors degree.

Smails's signature initiative is to establish bachelors programs at BCC. He argues that students in the area are limited by distance from being able to complete all but the few four-year degrees BRU offers there. He has attempted to convince the state higher education coordinating board to allow Bushwood to offer bachelors degrees in fashion merchandising, hospitality management, and nursing administration—areas in which BCC already has strong programs, BRU has none, and for which there is strong student interest. Given opposition from Boca Raton University and Tamiami University, another public university located 20 miles in the other direction from BCC, the state has been unwilling to approve Bushwood's petition.

Bushwood is governed by a board drawn from the local community, which is as frustrated as Smails about the state throwing cold water on the ambitions of the college. The board envisions BCC becoming a state university someday relatively soon, following the same path as did BRU and TU and other newer universities in the state. With Smails encouraging them, they have imagined an institution, perhaps called Bushwood State University, with masters' (and even doctoral) degrees, Division I athletics, student residences, and various other trappings of a university. Smails and members of the board, meeting informally, have begun to consider strategies to get around what they see as the state's unreasonable position.

Although unprecedented nationally, the conversation keeps coming back to privatizing Bushwood. Smails knows that the board is quite politically conservative and keeps steering the discussion to government oppression. Through the small foundation—under $2 million in endowment—that he and his predecessor have built, Smails has hired a prominent local law firm, O'Hooligan and O'Hooligan, to quietly consider what would be involved in taking a public community college private. He has also asked his institutional research and finance and administration heads to run the numbers. Smails wrote his doctoral dissertation at TU on the business model for for-profit higher education, so he understands possibilities for charging higher tuition and providing students with popular majors, better services, and enhanced convenience. He thinks the business aspects of the privatization scheme might just work, believing there is a local market for a higher-tuition, higher-service provider.

Maggie O'Hooligan is similarly unwilling to reject the privatization idea as too steep a legal climb. She does not envision any federal constitutional issues. There is no right to public higher education under the U.S. Constitution. If existing students are grandparented into paying public tuition, as planned, there is not even a due process argument (which would be a stretch anyway), as they would not be losing something. As a private institution, Bushwood would still be exempt from federal taxation and subject to antidiscrimination laws, such as Title VII of the 1964 Civil Rights Act, because it would continue to accept federal funding through financial aid programs.

There also does not appear to be a problem with precedent—a court having ruled that a public university cannot choose to turn private. There have been cases of private universities and colleges becoming public institutions. Custom and practice in the higher education industry may also favor Bushwood's position. Elite public universities, such as the University of Michigan, have certainly discussed privatizing, as endowments and funded research have expanded and tuition and fees have increased—and annual state appropriations continue to decline in relative terms, dipping to a small fraction of the overall budget.

Bushwood would have to renegotiate its contacts with its unions, but the new situation would not necessarily disadvantage the employees, assuming the college could fix issues such as having to transition out of the state pension program to a private one. (The board views this as an advantage, not trusting the government as investors.) The faculty appears to be supportive of moving toward being a four-year college, expecting the lower teaching loads associated with

(*continued*)

that sector. BCC would also maintain various institutional rules, so as to not enable current employees to oppose privatization—and there would be some who would do so for reasons of principle—by arguing that the college is taking something from them.

The most significant challenge is likely with state statutes. Public universities and colleges in the state are established by act of the legislature, vesting authority in a local board. O'Hooligan interprets this as the board having the latitude to simply abandon the state charter and replace it with a corporate one, similar to other private universities and colleges. If there is going to be litigation, it might well be with the state arguing that a public community college cannot simply declare itself to be private, given the greater good served by public higher education. The state may go further and contend that it has made an investment in Bushwood over the years; for example, by financing construction. BCC can counter that the more entrepreneurial and commercialized nature of universities and colleges tends to weaken public good arguments—higher education is framed more commonly as not only about individual gain, but also a return on investment for the state. Smails has even considered "buying" Bushwood from the state, compensating it for its investments, adjusting for depreciation. Perhaps it is possible to take Bushwood private, he continues to think, assuming the local market is there.

Deference and Process

Courts have traditionally deferred to decisions on academic questions made by universities and colleges. The idea is that courts presume administrators and faculty members to be better positioned to make determinations on such matters, given the unique nature of the academic milieu. Academic decisions tend to be made within a collegial environment, based on norms, as in areas like granting tenure that are unfamiliar to outsiders. Courts make certain that universities and colleges have developed reasonable rules and apply them properly, without being discriminatory or arbitrary and capricious. They are more comfortable addressing behavioral issues because these do not necessarily involve the same specialized expertise as grading or tenure. They are also more likely to expect institutions to extend greater process in behavioral situations than in academic contexts.

A challenge is that seemingly behavioral disciplinary matters can be connected with academic concerns, as with plagiarism having both behavioral and academic aspects (Dutile, 2003). There is also the situation in *Board of Curators of the University of Missouri v. Horowitz* (1978), decided by the U.S. Supreme Court, in which a medical student challenged her dismissal for both poor academic performance and personal hygiene problems. Dutile (2003) argues that the academic-disciplinary distinction is not sensible, as the subjectivity inherent in academic decisions should prompt the same formal due process that typically attaches to disciplinary matters.

Deference has weakened over time, with expanded access to the judicial system, needing to balance institutional autonomy with state accountability, and higher education becoming more entrepreneurial in nature. Only relatively recently have individual litigants had realistic channels to challenge institutional authority in court. Before the 1960s, actions against institutions by faculty, administrators, and students were likely to have been dismissed. Federal regulation, as with the enforcement of the antidiscrimination statutes that followed the 1964 Civil Rights Act, now provides individual litigants with processes, standards, and remedies in challenging decisions by institutions in areas such as employment and admissions. The application of federal and state labor law to higher education, as with the introduction of collective bargaining, has also opened new avenues to challenge actions by universities and colleges. Additionally, there is more regulation specific to higher education, as in funded research and financial aid; federal courts have inserted themselves into state higher education policy in desegregation efforts; and states increased their coordination of public higher education in the 1960s, with the emergence of the "multiversity" and rapid expansion of enrollments.

Deference aligns with the traditional autonomy afforded higher education institutions in the United States, with universities and colleges expected to govern and regulate themselves. Even at public institutions, there remains wide discretion, certainly as compared with other units of state government. Higher education continues to be responsible for its own accreditation, both through regional associations and groups specific to disciplines. Additionally, funding tends to come from states through university systems and not directly from the state legislature, and in large blocks as opposed to detailed line items. Institutions are thus somewhat insulated from political pressure in determining how they spend funds appropriated. And for faculty members and senior administrators, the ethos is not one of a civil servant, but instead specific to higher education and a given institution.

But for public universities that have always been accountable to the states that provide a portion of their annual funding, there has been an increase in formal means to ensure performance over the past decade. The rationale for annual appropriations from the legislature has shifted from only advancing the public good, with states now seeking assurance that they will receive a return on investment. Similarly, students and parents are demanding more accountability, given increases in tuition and tightening employment opportunities following graduation—and institutions are assuming additional responsibilities, whether in student support or information technology. Additionally, more data are available, as with benchmarking and rankings, which enable the reporting that accompanies (and often seems to be the extent of) accountability.

Although universities and colleges continue to rely on academic values in making decisions, they do not do so exclusively as they commercialize, opening the door to courts being more skeptical about decisions on academic matters. Deference is grounded in trusting collegial decisions being made in accord with academic values. But as institutions have become more diverse and complex, consensus within them is more difficult to achieve and external influences have become more pronounced. For instance, admissions decisions at selective institutions are subject not only to the academic record of the applicant—a values-based judgment—but also nonacademic influences, such as the fund raising record and potential of parents and the desire to balance the composition of the class. Similarly, curricular and evaluation decisions made in market-sensitive academic programs at the periphery of an institution may not be governed solely by academic values.

Accordingly, courts have assumed a more active role in resolving the disputes inevitable within higher education. Flanders (2007) notes that courts are unlikely to defer to institutions in the dismissal of students for academic reasons (discussed more fully in Chapter 4) in situations in which there are behavioral issues intertwined with questions about due process, large stakes involved (as with dismissal from a professional school), or concerns about selective application or enforcement of policies. There remains considerable independence, particularly when institutions act in good faith and protect individual rights. But society has become more litigious, with the qualitative judgments connected with academic life present a ready target. And institutions are increasingly less able to plausibly claim that they acted solely apart from their entrepreneurial interests and various commercial realities. As universities and colleges must also increasingly balance values with demands, in addition to potential plaintiffs having more options and states demanding more accountability, some diminution in the traditional deference they have enjoyed is inevitable.

Additionally, as judicial deference to academic decisions has declined, due process rights within universities and colleges have formalized and are likely enhanced. A generic definition of due process is fairness in making decisions, which involves providing adequate notice and a sufficient opportunity to be heard. Stevens (1999) frames due process in higher education as "systematic" decision making in matters constitutional and administrative, as well as in criminal law. (In addition to procedural due process related to the fairness of a procedure, there is also substantive due process, which addresses rights not expressly addressed in the U.S. Constitution, as with reading a right to privacy into federal law.) Institutions are no longer simply assumed to act in the best interests of students—the central idea of *in loco parentis*—with the same being the situation in their relationship with employees. Due process in higher education has evolved into not infringing on the constitutional rights of employees and students, providing notice sufficient to prepare an adequate defense, and a hearing proportionate with the interest at stake. Considerable discretion remains for institutions, but courts will intercede if they violate standards (Stevens, 1999).

The Fourteenth Amendment to the U.S. Constitution establishes a right to due process when the state deprives someone of property or liberty (or life, as in a criminal prosecution). Property rights are akin to individuals owning land. If the state intends to take such property, it owes significant rights to process. The classic example in higher education is the due process that accompanies dismissing a tenured faculty member promised indefinite employment with just a few exceptions. Liberty interests involve the diminution through state action of the reputation of an individual—and the notice and hearing required in such circumstances. For instance, a student dismissed from medical school may have a difficult time being admitted elsewhere. Such constitutional principles apply only to the state, as with a public university or college. But private institutions—as well as public ones—incorporate due process principles into various institutional rules, thus entering into a contract with individuals that requires the institution to meet fairness standards. A lawsuit challenging due process at a public institution may proceed on constitutional and contractual grounds alike.

The basic—and open—question in due process is how much notice and how much hearing is due. The standard response is that these must be commensurate with the interest at stake. But there is no formula to determine the amount of due process an institution owes in a given circumstance. Universities and colleges establish procedures to attend to due process, but cannot anticipate and address all of the various circumstances that might arise (Stevens, 1999). Due process is thus more of a concept than a formal approach—it is the logic that there must be appropriate process and avoidance of arbitrary and capricious determinations. It incorporates ideas and values such as neutrality, predictability, and dignity that come with the opportunity to be heard before an unbiased decision maker (Stevens, 1999). There is a meaningful preventive component to due process, as fairness in making decisions can both be more satisfying to those subject to them and can protect the institution in the event of a later challenge to an action.

Bushwood, like other community colleges, is rather agile in developing and discontinuing various academic programs, as merited. The college is particularly responsive to the local market, commonly allowing demand to determine not only the location and schedule of a course, but also its content, approach, and instructor. For instance, in developing a new course for the program in fashion merchandising, the college interacted with local businesses as it made various curricular decisions—what material to include in the syllabus, how to actually teach the content, and what type of person to employ as teacher. BCC expects its faculty members, if in applied areas, to have meaningful connections with the local business or nonprofit community. Administrators are also involved in developing courses, concentrating more on market issues, and determine whether courses that do not attract interest should be discontinued.

The new fashion merchandising course has not gone well. The instructor, Danielle Noonan, is new to Bushwood, having been hired in the fall from the well-regarded textiles program at Spaulding Tech, where she had just earned her Ph.D. Given the competitive academic employment market, Bushwood is

(continued)

finding that it can attract candidates like Noonan, even though it continues to emphasize substantive expertise in an area over credentials. Despite teaching five courses each semester, Noonan prepared an impressive course—too impressive, as it turned out. The students enrolled were overwhelmed by the workload and failed to see the relevance of much of what she was teaching. When Noonan proved unsympathetic when they approached her, they quickly let the department chair, Lou Loomis, know about the problem. Loomis reviewed the syllabus and found it to be decidedly more focused on theory than practice—well beyond BCC norms and inappropriate for the audience, in his view. When Noonan refused to adapt her approach, Loomis pulled her from the course, teaching the remainder himself.

Noonan had signed the standard BCC annual contract for probationary faculty, with the provision that it would be renewed based on her continued satisfactory performance. There is no tenure at Bushwood. But at the end of a six-year probationary period, during which faculty members are on a series of one-year contracts, they can apply for what is termed a continuing appointment—a three-year renewable contract. The college determines continuing appointments based upon receiving positive evaluations during the probationary period, with such relevant measures as demonstrating effectiveness in teaching, productive participation in departmental responsibilities, and continuing involvement in professional development activities.

But Loomis had determined that Noonan would never reach that point at Bushwood—the student complaints being the last straw. He was frustrated with Noonan's approach during her first six months on the job. For instance, she resisted joining him—only relenting when he insisted—on visits to the local business community, and was unable to relate to people when with them. Following the applicable procedure, he informed the faculty union head that he would not be renewing her.

As expected, she challenged her nonrenewal within the regular BCC grievance process. When she did not prevail, she retained private counsel and moved her challenge to court. In its motion for summary judgment, which would end the case simply on the initial pleadings filed, Bushwood argued that the contract was clear that the institution only owed Noonan employment through the end of the academic year. As such, it met its obligations, the college argued, meriting the dismissal of the case. They also contended that absent a reasonable assertion of a procedural defect in the grievance process, the court should defer to its "academic judgment in determining the suitability of a faculty member for instructional work at the college."

In challenging the decision, Noonan asserted that she had an implied right under her contract to structure the course according to her own academic sensibilities, as shaped by the norms of the broader disciplinary community in fashion merchandising. She did not challenge that she received appropriate notice to prepare to confront the dismissal decision, but that the hearing itself was flawed because the panel refused to consider her implied contract argument, focusing solely on process. Noonan contended that the court should not defer to the academic judgment of Bushwood because it did not make the nonrenewal decision on academic grounds, but instead was only interested in "what would be popular with students and generate interest in the market." Her argument was, in essence, that BCC was operating not unlike just another business. As such, its decisions merited no more deference than those of any company—and the court should hear evidence on the basis of the dismissal.

Noonan conceded that she had no property or liberty interest in her faculty position—the state, acting through Bushwood, was not "taking" anything from her because it paid her though the end of the contract term—and understood that her prospects for recovery might be limited. She was mainly interested in getting into court—past the summary judgment hearing. She thought that Bushwood might be willing to enter into a settlement to avoid exposure, in open court, of what she viewed as its overwhelming interest in the marketability and convenience of its courses and the institution's lack of concern for academic rigor. She knew that Smails, the Bushwood president, is concerned about reputational risk, especially given his ambitions for BCC to become a four-year college. If she could portray the college as making academic decisions not based on traditional values, but as just another business, a settlement might just happen.

Authority and Boundaries

Those involved with managing or operating universities and colleges avoid personal liability for various failings when they act within their authority. The ultimate authority at any institution is vested in its governing board. Governing boards of public universities and colleges obtain their authority from state statute (or directly from constitutions, in some states), with charters, as with a corporation, organizing private universities and colleges (Hutchens, 2009). The tradition in the United States is to grant public institutions the degree of autonomy possible while maintaining some state oversight (McLendon, 2003).

Boards have responsibilities analogous to those of corporate boards of directors, responsible for policy decisions but not daily operations. They are also similar to corporate boards in tending to mostly include businesspeople—a group inclined to be supportive of universities and colleges assuming a more entrepreneurial orientation. Although boards are often the entity against which plaintiffs bring lawsuits, board members are shielded from liability provided they avoid three problems:

mismanagement (gross negligence beyond mere mistakes in judgment); nonmanagement (inattentiveness to acquiring needed information); and self-dealing (failure to disclose conflicts of interest).

Institutions, including private proprietary ones, are also regulated by federal statute, as is the case with laws intended to curb fraud in financial aid (Hirsch, 2005) or confront diploma mills (Cooley and Cooley, 2009). There is increasing attention to disclosure, as with the federal requirement for funded research and the logic of the 2002 Sarbanes-Oxley law mandating accounting reforms applicable to public companies and institutions, but not expressly higher education institutions. There is also state regulation in the area and the federal Internal Revenue Service has strict rules discouraging trustees or officials from exploiting tax-exempt organizations for personal gain (Dreier and Michaelson, 2006). As universities and colleges become more aggressive in managing their endowments, there are greater opportunities for conflicts to arise involving the trustees who commonly advise on investment strategy, as with having an interest in a firm in which the institution invests (Dreier and Michaelson, 2006).

Boards delegate authority to manage institutions to administrators, naming a president or chancellor. That person is, in turn, responsible for retaining others to assist in operating the institution. The key devices in defining the authority of various administrators and others are position descriptions and various operational procedures. When acting within their authority, these individuals are indemnified against personal liability, as well as properly being represented by institutional counsel, as opposed to having to hire a private attorney. The key concept is whether actions or omissions are within the scope of employment, with determinations made on a case-by-case basis. For example, liability associated with an auto accident while driving a state car in the course of conducting state business would be within the scope, but injuries associated with an altercation in a bar over the weekend would not (Long, 2002). Individuals represented by institutional counsel must abide by decisions to settle a case, even if they disagree with them.

Authority can be express or implied, either granted directly or inferred as being reasonably necessary for actually exercising express authority. Implied authority is sometimes needed, as not every situation can be anticipated and addressed specifically in a job description. Those who exceed their authority can escape personal liability for the consequences of their actions in various situations. For instance, the board can subsequently ratify the unauthorized act of an employee or authority can be imputed to protect someone who acted in reasonable reliance on the unauthorized act of another. Institutions can also choose to indemnify employees, when merited, even if they are found to have acted wrongly.

A related concept is governmental and charitable immunity. Just as subjects could not sue the sovereign, citizens may not bring actions against the state (or an arm of the state, such as a public university), unless the state has waived its exemption or otherwise expressly consented (Snow and Thro, 2001). The parallel for private institutions is the idea of charitable immunity. Both doctrines have become more restrictive over time, with more types of actions allowed, but remain potentially useful as a means to dismiss cases. The federal government has waived its immunity, with some limits, in tort and contract actions—and, more relevant to higher education, states have expressly done the same in certain areas (Snow and Thro, 2001). Some actions, as for declaratory or injunctive relief (meaning not monetary damages, but asking a court to require or prohibit some behavior), require naming an individual officer as defendant, as opposed to the state. An institution would likely indemnify that person, of course. And officials can be sued for damages as individuals when using a state position to act illegally (Hartley, 2001; Snow and Thro, 2001).

In addition, the Eleventh Amendment asserts that a state, again including public universities, cannot be sued in federal courts, unless it has waived immunity or has otherwise abrogated its constitutional rights. An example of a waiver is litigation by the federal government in equal protection actions against states under the Fourteenth Amendment, as in a desegregation case (Hartley, 2001; Thro, 2007). Finally, immunity does not always extend to local governments. As community colleges are often governed by locally elected boards and raise revenue through local tax districts, their officials may not be deemed "alter egos" of the state and thus eligible for immunity. An interesting question is whether immunity protection, as it exists, will continue to apply at public institutions that receive an ever-smaller fraction of their funding from the state.

Another set of issues related to liability involves the expanding edges of entrepreneurial institutions. As institutions expand from their cores in many directions toward their more agile peripheries, the boundaries of universities and colleges have become less clear. For instance, universities and colleges have developed police forces over the past few decades, raising questions such as their jurisdiction extending beyond the property of the institution. Some states recognize the boundary to include property used by an organization recognized by the institution, while others are more restrictive, requiring an area to be under the control of a university or college. Other states afford broader jurisdiction, extending it to a zone surrounding a campus or framing it not geographically but instead as to protect students and employees wherever they may be, recognizing that the boundary between campus and community is more permeable. Agreements between campus and municipal forces are also common, as are having university or college police deputized by the local sheriff, especially at private institutions that lack the statutory right to commission their own officers (these police become "state actors" and subject to constitutional provisions) (Jacobson, 2006).

Boundaries can also be uncertain when institutions, as they increasingly do, retain outside consultants and contractors to do work that was once done in-house. In situations such as privatized bookstores or dining services, universities and colleges have likely shifted liability in most situations to their partner corporation. Or when an institution forms a captive organization—a separate legal entity under its control, such as when an institution self-insures through forming its own insurance company—it will not be insulated from liability. Another example is an affiliated organization, such as an alumni association or research foundation, likely being deemed sufficiently connected with institutions for liability purposes, given institutions tend to retain the power to appoint trustees, conduct joint programs, and share facilities. (With an affiliated corporation, an institution would have an ownership stake, thus prompting liability.)

But when universities and colleges form partnerships with external organizations, boundaries are less clear—and exposure to liability more of a question. For instance, a university or college that contracts with an outside vendor to arrange logistics for a study abroad program, with the institution offering the curriculum and granting academic credit, could claim that it is not liable for the results of a mishap. But a plaintiff is likely to do all that he or she can to connect the problem to the institution, as the prospect of recovering a judgment from an institution is probably greater than from a vendor. There can also be the challenge in study abroad that faculty handbooks and employment discrimination law may not apply in overseas contexts (Dowling, 2006; Roberts, 2007). Finally, there can also be issues of partnerships introducing unfamiliar terminology and different customs and practices into an institution, prompting confusion and uncertainty about responsibilities (Blakeslee and Gallitano, 2007).

Particularly over the past five years, Bushwood has sought strategic advantage through international efforts. Upon arriving at the college as president, Smails named Carl Spackler as vice president for international affairs. It was a controversial move at the time, as few other community colleges in the state made such a bold investment in globalization. As had Bushwood, several had actively enrolled international students, developing recruitment networks. But Smails and Spackler envisioned two-way flows, with faculty and student exchanges and, especially, study abroad programs. They saw the latter as a potentially lucrative revenue source, attracting students from other institutions to "sexy" Bushwood programs in appealing locales. They had a ready source of instructors, offering BCC faculty the opportunity to teach aboard as part of their regular load, with their living expenses covered.

They also contracted with a firm, Pickering-Beeper Partners, which specializes in curriculum development, marketing and recruitment, and in-country logistics planning and support—so all Bushwood would have to do is arrange to teach the courses and process transcripts. The company offers programs in 10 countries and works with 22 institutions nationally. Pickering-Beeper has been successful in selling Bushwood programs, finding a niche in the market for students seeking a more applied study abroad experience. For instance, Bushwood has concentrated on offering programs such as fashion merchandising in Milan, hospitality management in St. Barts, and critical thinking and study skills in Zermatt. BCC now has more study abroad students, most of them from other institutions, than all but the two largest universities in the state.

Smails has also launched an honors program, seeking to enroll accomplished local students who would transfer to prestigious universities, thus enhancing the profile of the college. As with study aboard, the effort also proved successful, providing an option for academically talented students to continue to live at home—usually first generation students from working class backgrounds. An individualized study abroad experience is part of the honors program, included in the full scholarship (with living stipend) that the students receive. After spending their first summer in one of the regular BCC programs, the students could work with an honors advisor to develop an individualized experience—perhaps an internship in Tokyo or a volunteer opportunity in Morocco.

There have been occasional problems. It appears that Pickering-Beeper has overextended itself and has been skimping on the accommodations, transportation, and other services it is providing for Bushwood. Over the past summer, there were safety concerns at hotels, buses and vans in dangerously poor repair, and significant understaffing (with a few P-B staff simply walking away in the middle of programs). Even though the contract with Pickering-Beeper holds them responsible, Spackler knows that it is Bushwood's name on the programs and its reputation on the line—and that the college will likely need to step in and make right any situation that goes wrong. He now needs to decide whether to renew the contract with Pickering-Beeper, considering whether the "devil" he knows may be better than a vendor he does not.

But the most serious mishap that occurred abroad last winter was attributable to a BCC faculty member, Tony D'Annunzio, entering into a romantic relationship with a Zermatt student, who subsequently had to be treated for depression. The student's parents are suing both D'Annunzio and Bushwood. The institution could perhaps avoid liability, as D'Annunzio was clearly acting outside his authority to direct the Zermatt program. But it recently chose instead to indemnify D'Annunzio from liability, in the interest of settling the entire action and avoiding negative publicity. (It also suspended him without pay for one month, and is no longer allowing him to go abroad with students.)

But the issue that keeps Spackler up at night is the one in which there is no program director or private vendor on site. He fears that the individualized experiences abroad for the honors students create an unworkable situation, raising the reasonable expectation among students and parents that Bushwood will assume responsibility for remedying any problem that arises overseas. For instance, if there is an earthquake in Chile or political violence in Morocco, most of the parents of honors students have no means to address the situation, with limited financial resources and cultural capital. It will be up to Bushwood to rescue them—or risk its reputation or liability if something does go wrong. The challenge here is that BCC also has limited resources and Spackler has only a few staff. An elite private university might be able to stretch across a "boundaryless" campus, but a public community college cannot reasonably do so.

Attorneys and Litigation

Litigation is a process involving several steps, the first of which is to retain counsel. A lawsuit begins with a complaint by a plaintiff and answer by the defendant, the latter attempting, as much as possible, to avoid the lawsuit based on a lack of jurisdiction. If the plaintiff scales applicable jurisdictional hurdles, the case moves to discovery and mediation, in which both sides are compelled to produce relevant evidence and attempt to resolve the matter before trial. At the conclusion of the trial, the court dispenses a remedy, either monetary damages or an injunction compelling or preventing a certain behavior (Harrison, 2002).

Attorneys and Clients

Larger private institutions, as well as some public ones, tend to have in-house lawyers who perform general legal work, sending more specialized or complex work to private law firms. Other state universities and colleges receive legal services through attorneys at the state level, whether at the state system or via the state attorney general. Smaller institutions often retain a law firm that specializes in higher education law to represent them. Peri (2008) argues that in-house counsel provide institutions with financial and strategic advantages, being more cost effective and better able to advise presidents and other leaders.

The responsibilities of university counsel are varied: they participate by serving on committees and councils to provide guidance in steering administrative decisions clear of potential legal problems (advisor-counselor); explain legal requirements and procedures to often disagreeing members of the university or college community (educator-mediator); manage the legal affairs office and coordinate the activities of outside counsel retained by the institution (manager-administrator); represent the university or college in a variety of adjudicatory venues, such as regulatory agencies, and before the media on legal matters involving the university (litigator-spokesperson); draft and review legal documents (drafter-reviewer); and provide a buffer between the institution and outsiders by receiving documents that others may not know how the handle (insulator-dispatcher) (Daane, 1985; Peri, 2008). Counsel serve in more of an advisory role, as opposed to one focused on making policy decisions. They tend to be the conscience of the institution, providing skepticism, as appropriate. As pressures to drift from traditional academic values mount as institutions become more entrepreneurial, counsel can give voice to various concerns within the senior administration.

In their multiple roles and regardless of where they are situated, institutions can expect counsel to be loyal. Information revealed to a lawyer is privileged (attorney-client privilege)—he or she cannot reveal it. Nor can the release of material an attorney produces in the context of his or her work be compelled (the work product doctrine). (The only exception is when a client intends to commit a crime and dissemination is required to prevent it.) The relevant questions to be asked in determining privilege are whether the information at issue is a communication, and whether it was between those entitled to invoke the privilege, intended to be confidential, and made in the context of legal assistance. Privilege can be waived, either intentionally or inadvertently, and lawyers tend to take precautions such as labeling privileged documents as such. Communication through e-mail is subject to these same privileges and requires similar precautions (Burgoyne, McNabb, and Robinson, 1998).

But sometimes it is not always clear in higher education who is the client, which complicates the attorney-client relationship, including the assertion of privilege. Counsel regularly work with those across the university or college community—state system staff, board members, senior administration, other administrators, the faculty, and affiliated groups. When there is a conflict between or among those the counsel serves, he or she can only represent one side, choosing the interest closest to the locus of control at the institution. For instance, in a dispute between a faculty member and his or her dean, the attorney would serve the dean and inform the faculty member accordingly, who would need to retain independent counsel. In short, when the interests of the institution come into conflict with those of an employee, counsel must remain loyal to the university or college. Such conflicts are relatively straightforward to resolve. But the increasingly entrepreneurial nature of universities and colleges exacerbates other ethical challenges. Commercial pressures may cause institutions to be more likely to compel counsel to take indefensible positions in negotiation or litigation, or disregard, circumvent, or misuse his or her advice when it conflicts with institutional ambitions.

Finally, risk management has increased in emphasis in higher education, with counsel regularly consulted and otherwise participating. It consists of reviewing risks and evaluating those identified with a view to eliminating or mitigating them, planning for the management of the residual risk, and communicating that strategy and monitoring its implementation. Risk management extends to facilities, as with health and safety considerations, but also to relationships with employees and students (Hall and Ferguson, 2000). Stuart (2009) provides the illustration of developing risk management policies in order to prevent violent rampages on campuses, suggesting the need for attorneys to integrate their efforts into the overall academic culture, but also to recognize the commercial realities of contemporary higher education. She reminds them to recognize that faculty members and others often view risk management with suspicion—as just another example of the commoditization of the university.

Complaint and Answer

A plaintiff initiates a lawsuit by filing a complaint against the defendant. The complaint describes the facts of the situation at issue; outlines the legal theories (such as a contract or a constitutional right) on which the courts can decide the matter; and proposes a set of remedies to be imposed upon the defendant by the court. The plaintiff not only must file the complaint with the relevant court, but also must serve the complaint upon the defendant in the action. The complaint may be served upon individuals working within universities or colleges, who then refer it to counsel employed or retained by the institution.

The person being served is advised to not discuss the complaint with the plaintiff or anyone else (even close colleagues), instead notifying his or her supervisor and arranging to consult with a lawyer. Discussing the case could lead to the loss of attorney-client privilege (Tribbensee, 2002b). Once again, administrators and faculty members are protected from personal liability and represented by institutional counsel when they act within their authority. But if they have not done so, they can be sued as individuals and may be exposed as such.

Once the defendant has been served with a complaint, the defendant then has a specified number of days to respond through what is termed an answer. The answer addresses each of the contentions made in the complaint. In the answer, the defendant may also file a counterclaim, bringing an action against the plaintiff under the same set of facts. Defendants usually also file a motion to dismiss, which may involve respective counsel arguing before the judge or may be decided by him or her simply based on the written pleadings. In the motion, the defendant concedes that even if the facts the plaintiff alleges are true, the plaintiff has not stated a valid claim so as to enable relief. The idea is that there is no legal theory alleged that could entitle the plaintiff to relief.

For instance, a due process claim under the Fourteenth Amendment against a private institution would be dismissed unless the plaintiff could reasonably allege that the university or college is, in fact, operating as a surrogate of the state and thus subject to the U.S. Constitution. A parallel due process cause of action grounded in contract would be allowed to continue, if the plaintiff alleges sufficient facts, such that a contact granting these rights exists. Plaintiffs, accordingly, tend to allege all plausible theories under which a court might grant them relief. Motions to dismiss, meanwhile, provide a ready means for defendants, especially those perceived to have "deep pockets," such as universities, to dispose of frivolous lawsuits. Courts can allow failed plaintiffs to refile a claim to allege different causes or actions.

An answer will also focus on jurisdiction. A basic strategy employed by lawyers is to attempt to resolve matters on procedural grounds, such as the court being unable to hear the action the plaintiff attempts to bring before it. The defendant may challenge the jurisdiction of the court over the subject matter of the lawsuit (subject matter jurisdiction) or over the individuals who are involved (personal jurisdiction).

Federal courts have jurisdiction over federal questions—federal constitutional or statutory issues—as well as between citizens of different states (diversity jurisdiction). State courts can hear matters from another state, assuming no provision exists for exclusive federal jurisdiction over a matter (as in controversies between two states). When appropriate, a defendant in a state court action can petition the court to remove appropriate cases to federal court. Federal courts may hear questions of state law along with federal cases before them if both cases "derive from a common nucleus of operative fact"—the two actions arise out of the same facts—and are normally the type of issues heard together. A federal court may nevertheless decline to hear a state law claim it if is a novel or complex question of state law or if the state claim substantially predominates over the federal claim.

In personal jurisdiction, the idea is that courts have jurisdiction only over defendants who reside in the jurisdiction, commit torts or conduct business there, or consent to be sued there. For example, personal jurisdiction would likely attach to a visiting faculty member from another state working at a university or college or to out-of-state students attending classes there. "Long-arm" statutes determine whether courts have personal jurisdiction over nonresidents based on whether the defendant has "minimum contacts" with the state. The increasingly entrepreneurial nature of universities and colleges may cause personal jurisdiction questions to become more frequent. For instance, academic programs at the peripheries of institutions that are intended to attract working students through being offered in convenient settings, such as online or at satellite locations, are more likely to cross state lines.

Even if jurisdictional issues do not prevent access to court, several other situations may cause a court not to hear a case. A plaintiff is deemed to lack standing to initiate a lawsuit if he or she is not the actual aggrieved party—one cannot sue someone on behalf of another. (But class actions are allowed, with a large group of litigants having common characteristics banding together under the representation of a single counsel to attempt to redress a situation typical among them.) Another barrier to access is mootness, which is when the passage of time or a change in events causes a matter to no longer be a controversy. For instance, a student graduating renders moot a complaint he or she might have about a requirement for graduation.

Similarly, a statute of limitation places time limits on when a plaintiff may bring an action, with an open window of six years on contracts cases or three years for torts in many states. Statutes of limitation usually start from when a claim first accrues or when the potential plaintiff should have first noticed it, whichever circumstance is more reasonable, and pause (called "tolling") when deemed appropriate. Finally, a plaintiff must exhaust all internal administrative remedies before a court will hear a lawsuit, except when procedures appear to be stacked against the plaintiff so as to render the procedure a waste of time.

Discovery and Settlement

Any claims not subject to dismissal proceed along the route to trial into pretrial discovery, which begins with a scheduling order issued by the court. Although deadlines can change, they must be met at the risk of sanctions by the court. Discovery is the collection of relevant information by the various sides toward clarifying the facts and legal issues involved in an action. The notion in discovery is that information production should be broad and honest—and there are mechanisms to punish those who do not act in accordance with these principles.

The primary means to collect information during discovery are depositions, interrogatories, and document requests. Depositions are question-and-answer sessions between attorneys and those thought to have relevant information. Those deposed are either fact witnesses with direct knowledge of the particulars of the case, or outside expert witnesses retained by one side or the other to provide broader (but not necessarily neutral) context. Depositions are adversarial in nature, with opposing counsel having the right to directly examine the witness and raise objections to questions thought to lead to inadmissible evidence. They are transcribed by a court reporter for later reference, with the witness given the opportunity to correct mistakes. Interrogatories are written questions from counsel for one side in the litigation to various adversaries. Document requests, often attached to interrogatories, seek to reveal relevant files and similar materials, whether on paper or stored through electronic means.

For example, in a lawsuit that challenges alleged gender discrimination in a negative tenure decision, the plaintiff and defendant would likely request depositions (or compel them through a subpoena, if necessary) from various administrators involved in the process, members of various faulty tenure committees, and outside experts on tenure and gender discrimination. Interrogatories from the plaintiff would be directed toward locating relevant information in the case, such as any applicable institutional policies in the area and questions about the procedure actually followed, as would document requests for items such as letters from outside referees or dossiers of those who have recently received tenure. If an adversary is perceived to be nonresponsive during discovery, a litigant can file a motion with the court to compel a response.

Administrators can collect relevant documents in anticipation of discovery, even those that may prove disadvantageous, but are advised to not conduct their own investigations or respond to requests for information apart from the direction of counsel. Administrators may also ask questions of their counsel about the claim against the institution and the relevance of documents—and may provide potentially relevant information, such as whether the pending lawsuit is the latest instance in a pattern of behavior (Tibbensee, 2002b). When administrators and others are being deposed, they should respond truthfully, and only to questions that are not inappropriate, misleading, or vague (and thus likely the subject of an objection from his or her counsel). Witnesses should limit their responses to the actual question asked, not volunteering further information, and it is appropriate to answer by indicating a lack of memory about a situation (Griffin, 2002).

During discovery, as throughout the litigation, communication between counsel and clients, as in conversations about strategy, is privileged against being produced in discovery, as is any work produced by a lawyer in connection with the case. Attempts to claim privilege to prevent the production of information or documents as potential evidence are a significant aspect of discovery. During the process, courts hear motions *in limine* to resolve disputes about whether something is privileged or to otherwise argue that evidence would be unduly prejudicial for the jury to hear. Excluding or admitting damaging evidence can provide an advantage at trial for the respective litigants—and may even determine success in the action.

There is not capacity within any judicial system to hear all of the cases that move into discovery, so courts strongly encourage parties to settle their disputes short of going to trial. Entering into a voluntary settlement agreement is possible at any point in the litigation. The decree issued disposes of the action and any future claims, with monetary compensation commonly paid to the plaintiff often with a stipulation compelling the sides to keep the terms of the settlement confidential. Even if they believe themselves not to be in the wrong, universities and colleges sometimes have significant incentives to settle lawsuits, as with avoiding the time, expense, and publicity associated with litigation. Settlement decrees commonly include a provision that the agreement does not imply an admission of fault or liability—and even may script how the settlement will be presented to the public. There is also the question of who at the institution has the authority to actually settle the case (Tribbensee, 2002a).

In many jurisdictions, there are court-mandated mediation conferences and judges are inclined to be aggressive in pushing litigants toward settlement. Additionally, under certain contracts there are procedures for alternative dispute resolution. These avoid the court system altogether, providing for discovery at an accelerated pace and determination by an arbitrator or panel of arbitrators selected by the litigants. Finally, at the conclusion of discovery, defendants may file a motion for summary judgment, applying reasoning akin to the motion to dismiss, arguing that even considering the evidence in the most favorable way for the plaintiff, the defendant should prevail as a matter of law.

Trial and Remedies

In those cases that do not settle and in which a trial occurs, the court considers the evidence collected and arguments presented. Although a jury trial is a constitutional right in civil cases seeking monetary damages under the Seventh Amendment and is commonly available under state law, not all trials have juries. But in those that do, the trial begins with the selection of the jury.

Opening statement begin the trials, first by the plaintiff, with the plaintiff then presenting evidence and examining witnesses. Plaintiffs cannot ask leading questions, suggesting the answer as part of the question. In cross-examining, the defense may lead these same witnesses, focusing on identifying contradictions and inconsistencies. After cross-examination, the plaintiff has the opportunity to ask one more set of questions (redirect examination). Once the plaintiff rests, the defendant moves to dismiss the case, asking for a directed verdict—a request that the court usually denies. In then presenting its case, the defense repeats the process with its own witnesses—direct examination, cross-examination by the plaintiff, and redirect examination. During closing arguments, the defense continues to argue that the plaintiff did not prove its case by a preponderance of the evidence—the applicable burden of proof. A preponderance of evidence in this context is simply more than the other side has produced, unlike the more rigorous beyond a reasonable doubt standard in criminal cases.

Following closing arguments, the judge formally instructs the jury, commonly providing specific questions for the members of the jury to answer in their deliberations. The judge is responsible for applying the law, with the jury considering the facts—the judge instructs the jury on what legal standards the plaintiff must meet and the jury determines whether the relevant facts indicate whether that occurred. In civil cases, juries do not need to reach a unanimous decision. After the verdict, the court enters a judgment, thus either dismissing the case or fashioning a remedy.

A remedy can include monetary damages, which can be compensatory damages intended to replicate actual damage suffered by the plaintiff as a result of the actions of the defendant. Additional punitive damages, if applicable, go beyond "making whole" the plaintiff and are intended to punish the defendant. A different type of remedy, injunctive relief, is an order from the court compelling the defendant, either permanently or temporarily, to do something (mandatory injunction) or not to do something (prohibitory injunction). Given their urgency, judges will hear petitions for temporary injunctions as soon as possible, deciding them based on whether the plaintiff is likely to prevail on the merits of the action when eventually seeking a permanent injunction. Finally, attorney's fees are available in certain situations, such as lawsuits deemed to be of dubious merit, and are mandated by statute under certain civil rights laws. One who does not comply with the relief the court orders can be held in contempt and may be imprisoned or fined as punishment until coerced into compliance.

Following judgment, the losing party may file an appeal within the short time set by the court rules of the jurisdiction, subsequently losing the right. There are also procedural devices such as asking the trial court to issue a judgment n.o.v. (notwithstanding the verdict), a motion for a new trial, or a motion to set aside judgment—but these are unlikely to be granted. The appellant can only challenge the application of the law by the judge and cannot introduce additional facts. For instance, the appellant may rightly claim that the court did not follow relevant law in its rulings on excluding or admitting evidence. A positive decision by an appeals court entitles the appellant to have the trial court consider the action again, only with the judge correctly applying the contested legal principles. Under the concept of *res judicata*, those disappointed in a result may not simply relitigate the same case in a different court. The constitutional full faith and credit principle requires courts in one state to respect decisions rendered in another state.

Finally, decisions of the intermediate appellate courts situated directly above trial courts may be appealed to supreme courts, whether state or federal. Supreme courts have discretion over which cases they hear. The U.S. Supreme Court only decides, in principle, matters involving novel questions of constitutional law or issues on which various federal appellate courts have reached differing conclusions. An example of the latter is the court granting *certiorari* to consider affirmative action in selective admissions after inconsistent decisions among circuit courts had gathered. These cases sometimes attract considerable attention, with interested parties able to file amicus briefs as "friends of the court" to present arguments beyond what the litigants include (Alger and Krislov, 2004). In fact, advocacy groups are increasingly involved in higher education, whether challenging the perceived political bias of professors or attempting to influence admissions policy through so-called reverse discrimination litigation, as in the 2003 University of Michigan cases.

Al Czervik applied for honors program membership at Bushwood—and the attractive scholarship that accompanied it—but was not selected. He is convinced that the college chose what he perceives as "less qualified" students from underrepresented groups ahead of him. The admissions process is similar to any selective context, with a committee reviewing standardized test scores, high school grades, and extracurricular activities, as well as asking for an essay. BCC asked students to explain in the essay how they had overcome adversity and how it would motivate them to make the most of their honors experience. Under the decision of the U.S. Supreme Court in *Regents of the University of California v. Bakke* (1978), Bushwood could use race as a "plus factor" in its decision—it could not be determinative, but instead another favorable variable on an already stellar record for minority students.

Czervik brought a lawsuit in federal court against Bushwood, Lacy Underall, the director of the honors program, who was responsible for admitting students, as well as Smails, the Bushwood president. His attorneys suspect that he can sue Bushwood directly, especially since governmental immunity may not extend to community colleges given their local boards and funding, but he is also naming Underall and Smails as alter egos, if needed for Eleventh Amendment reasons. Even though there may be questions of whether Underall may have been too aggressive in admitting minority students under the *Bakke* standard, Bushwood will shield her and Smails from personal liability. They will also have the state attorney general's office defend them, along with the college, in the action, recognizing the advantages of a united defense. But if Underall had deviated from her authority in a more pronounced manner, Bushwood may have made a different decision, leaving her on her own.

In his complaint, Czervik, represented by a national public interest law group aligned with conservative causes, alleged discrimination under the Equal Protection clause of the Fourteenth Amendment and Title VII of the 1964 Civil Rights Act. He argued that Bushwood (and any affiliate organizations, such as its foundation) violated these in the preferential treatment it afforded minority

(*continued*)

applicants to the honors program, effectively operating an affirmative action program, exceeding what is allowable under *Bakke* (addressed in detail in the chapters that follow). In its answer, Bushwood effectively conceded that Czervik raised a reasonable inference of discrimination, thus not aggressively pursuing summary judgment. But it countered that the program was open to all applicants and it chose them through legitimate, nondiscriminatory means, focusing on their entire records and application materials, as mandated in *Bakke*. Bushwood continued that even assuming the honors program had affirmative action purposes, it was justified as a compelling state interest—the need to ensure diversity on campus, an argument supported by the U.S. Supreme Court in *Grutter v. Bollinger* (2003)—and the program was narrowly tailored, as required.

In the discovery period that followed, Czervik, as plaintiff, took the depositions, through his attorneys, of Smails and Underall, as well as three outside experts on affirmative action in higher education that they identified. Bushwood, as defendant, also provided expert witnesses of its choosing. Czervik requested all relevant documents related to the case, with Bushwood producing all except those connected with its attorneys, both O'Hooligan in the privatization matter and those related to establishing the honors program, claiming privilege. Both sets of documents included discussion of the strategic uses of the honors program and the need to have a diverse group of students involved. The judge assigned to the case, Ty Webb, who heard motions *in limine* on the matter, decided for the defendant, Bushwood.

At trial, Czervik presented his case, using his expert witnesses to introduce evidence that one-half of the 60 students admitted to the honors program over the past four years were from underrepresented groups—and that their "numbers" were well below those of both his and several other nonminority applicants. The experts also expressed the opinion that the practices were well beyond what *Bakke* allowed, with race becoming more than a "plus" in the process, but instead being determinative, in effect. The plaintiff was also able to get Underall to admit the extent to which she stretched to enroll underrepresented students in the program, sometimes looking past the low scores or grades of compelling minority applicants. On cross-examination, Bushwood was able to establish that Underall acted in the context of nearly one-half of the students at the college being racial or ethnic minorities. In then presenting its case, the defense focused on the fact that there were no express quotas and that race or ethnicity was only one factor among many.

Czervik was able, on cross-examination, to extract an admission from Smails that, in practice, it was very difficult and perhaps impossible to really not consider minority applicants separately. (The simulation that concludes Chapter 2 addresses this issue.) He also suggested, although not as strongly as if the privileged documents had been available, there was strategic advantage for Bushwood in having minority honors students because they were featured extensively in promotional materials. In the closing arguments, both sides reinforced their main arguments.

In deciding the case, Webb weighed the request by Czervik for damages equal to the value of the honors scholarship—as he already had two years of college at the conclusion of the case, an injunction related to the reconsideration of his application was moot. Were he to lose, Czervik was planning to appeal based on Webb's decision to exclude the evidence on diversity as strategy.

Tenure Application Process at Bushwood—A Simulation

The state higher education coordinating board recently elected to allow Bushwood Community College to award bachelors degrees in three fields: fashion merchandising, hospitality management, and nursing administration. The college will continue to offer associate degrees and provide various nondegree training—and anticipates continuing to systematically add bachelors programs. Whether having such diverse types of programs is sustainable within a single college remains an open question, but one the college is content to defer. The board also granted permission to the institution to change its name to Bushwood State College (BSC), packaging the decision with allowing neighboring four-year institutions to launch certain graduate programs that it had long proposed. The transition to the expanded mission has been relatively smooth, with the faculty union agreeing to continue under the existing contract. In exchange, the college reduced its teaching load from the former five courses per semester to four courses per semester for those teaching in bachelors programs, thus reflecting other institutions in the state offering the bachelors as their highest degree.

The contract is soon to expire. In recognition of the introduction of bachelors programs at Bushwood, the faculty union is interested in introducing tenure. The present arrangement issues three-year renewable contracts, called "continuing appointments" under the union contract, granted following a six-year probationary period, during which faculty members are on a series of one-year contracts. The institution determines continuing appointments based on annual evaluations from the appropriate department chair—there is no external review. Pursuant to the union contract, the review assesses three matters: demonstrated effectiveness in teaching, productive participation in departmental responsibilities, and continuing involvement in professional development activities. A four-year university that the state established a decade ago has a similar arrangement in lieu of tenure, except that it solicits letters from peer faculty from other institutions in support of an application. The norm is that tenure is available to faculty members at colleges and universities offering the bachelors degree. Smails, the BSC president, is not necessarily opposed to introducing tenure, but views it as incompatible with a unionized faculty and has argued that it is appropriate for only the most accomplished faculty members. Relatively few research university faculties nationally are unionized, but it is more common across public institutions with mainly a teaching concentration.

The president also appreciates the agility in launching and discontinuing academic programs enabled by using regular faculty on short-term assignments and employing nonunionized adjuncts. In the upcoming contract negotiation with the union, he plans to emphasize increasing the proportion of contingent faculty at Bushwood, expecting the unionized faculty to be more interested in issues such as their own salary and benefits. Smails is willing to trade tenure for as few regular faculty members as possible for preserving flexibility in the use of adjuncts, knowing that the approach is aligned with national trends toward shifting faculty staffing away from those with regular appointments. Additionally, there has been discussion among adjunct instructors of forming their own union, but the idea has gained little traction, as they have little leverage with the college. The interests of the group are not sufficiently similar to regular faculty to merit folding them into the faculty union (as considered in Chapter 3). The faculty union has expressed its support, but is more concerned with maximizing the situation of its own members than with the interests of faculty without regular appointments.

Smails has named a task force to attempt to resolve faculty appointment issues in anticipation of the upcoming contract negotiation with the faculty union. The task force has representatives from five groups: the faculty union, the academic deans and vice president for academic affairs, the student government, local business and nonprofit partners, and university counsel. Their recommendations are not binding in the negotiation, but are likely to be influential. Smails has charged the group in the following letter.

Office of the President

Bushwood State College

Dear Colleague:

Thank you for accepting appointment to the task force on faculty appointments at Bushwood State College. I look forward to meeting with the group upon the conclusion of your work together to hear your recommendations. These promise to assist greatly as we prepare to negotiate the next contract between the institution and its faculty union.

Please divide your work into three parts. The first is to determine the options related to faculty appointment schemes at BSC and to make an according recommendation. I am open to beginning tenure at Bushwood, but only with standards beyond those presently required to secure a three-year continuing appointment.

However, I encourage you to consider alternatives to tenure that achieve ends similar to it. The strategic plan does not anticipate the college adopting formal expectations that faculty members will regularly publish research, as at a research university. I recognize that even with a four course per semester teaching load, there is only so much scholarly work any faculty member can do and resources to support such work at Bushwood remain limited. Our recent initiative providing $2000 stipends to support annually 10 faculty-student partnerships in scholarly ventures is a small step in the right direction. But we do encourage our faculty members with teaching loads of four courses per semester to have active scholarly lives outside of the classroom, as at other bachelors granting institutions of what is now our type.

The second responsibility of the task force is to consider standards. There will likely need to be different approaches required for various clusters of faculty members at Bushwood. For instance, standards should reflect the different situations of faculty members involved exclusively or significantly in bachelors programs and thus teaching four courses per semester. Their situation is likely different than those working solely or primarily with our associate level students, both in academic and vocational programs, and teaching five courses each semester. Please recognize that present standards for securing continuing appointments—teaching effectiveness, departmental responsibilities, and professional development—alone are insufficient for faculty members involved in bachelors degree programs, given their reduced teaching load. Additionally, I encourage you to consider formalizing standards that express the importance to the college of faculty members involved with both bachelors and associate degree programs in relevant fields developing meaningful connections with the local business or nonprofit community.

The third charge to the group is to address processes related to the scheme you recommend. These will have to consider differences in the situations of probationary faculty members, those hired into the college in a senior position, and those senior faculty members currently on continuing appointments. (You do not have to address process issues for faculty hired directly into continuing appointments or tenured positions.) Please remember that the present union contract provides faculty members with the right to receive fair consideration of any application for an extended contract, with the grievance procedure available for those disappointed with their evaluation by the department chair. But there are not property or liberty interests associated with the contracts or process. In other words, the situation is not akin to a tenured professor being dismissed. Please note that it is not within your charge to consider changing the status of adjunct faculty members within the institution and that they are not covered by the due process rules embedded in the union contract for regular faculty.

(continued)

Finally, please align the overall scheme that you recommend for faculty teaching in bachelors programs—and the standards and processes related to it—with practice at public comprehensive institutions statewide and nationally. But I am also interested, as applicable, in Bushwood State College setting its own course, providing a model of innovative and effective practice. I also ask you to keep in mind the new strategic plan of the college, which anticipates developing additional bachelors programs. In closing, we cannot allow having different schemes, standards, and processes being applied to different groups of faculty to cause divisions within our college, so please do all that is possible in your work toward maintaining the strong and unified culture that we have developed at Bushwood over the years.

Once again, thank you for agreeing to work on this important effort and I look forward to meeting with you to discuss your recommendations.

Sincerely,

Elihu Smails, Ed.D.

President

The task force began its work by outlining various options. It arrived at three schemes for faculty members with regular involvement in bachelors programs. The first enables them to apply for tenure, either immediately for those now on continuing appointments or upon completing the current probationary period. The second maintains the continuing appointment approach as an alternative to tenure, extending it to a five-year contract and including a semester-long sabbatical within each contract term. Both options include an external review component and thus a consideration of scholarship. The third is the status quo—three-year continuing appointments based solely on internal evaluations, but with some additional requirements, such as recognizing engagement with the community, but not requiring any scholarly activity. It also decided that any of these options could be available to any faculty member, not considering those working only in associate degree programs, whether academic or vocational, differently from those involved in bachelors programs. It also recognized the need to offer the status quo option for faculty uninterested in changing their practices and orientation. Additionally, there are at present no faculty ranks—assistant professor, associate professor, and professor—at Bushwood. Each option could accommodate these—and there is no opposition within the administration or union leadership to introducing ranks.

The present discussion relates to standards and processes, with somewhat pronounced differences in opinion among the five main constituents. The simulation facilitator should divide the participants into roles within the five groups, assigning at least one person to each. If there are more than seven participants in the simulation, the facilitator should assign one to be academic vice president, one to be dean of professional studies, and one to be dean of vocational programs (and a fourth person, if available, to be dean of humanities and social sciences). The professional studies dean is responsible for the new bachelors programs in fashion merchandising, hospitality management, and nursing administration. There is a need for only one student representative. If possible, there should be both a representative of a local corporation and a director of a large nonprofit also connected with the college, but one participant could represent both. There can be multiple people serving in the university counsel role, as needed.

There should be at least two faculty union representatives, one sympathetic to the faculty more dubious about the expanded mission at the college and one support- ive of Bushwood moving toward being a comprehensive institution and initiating tenure. There can be as many faculty union representatives as needed, split evenly between the two perspectives, but no more than four should be active participants in the task force deliberations. Finally, the facilitator is chair of the task force, serving without a vote. He or she is the recently retired president of a nearby community col- lege who is viewed by all involved as neutral. The chair may also appoint a secretary, responsible for recording the recommendations of the task force.

Faculty Union. There are two main divides on the faculty. The first is between fac- ulty members teaching in bachelors programs—or in areas likely to become these— and those involved with associate degree programs, whether academic or vocational. The latter resent their colleagues being favored, as in having been assigned a reduced course load.

The second is between longer serving faculty in academic programs and newer hires in these. The former tend to be comfortable with the community college mission and many among them question the notion of adapting to an expanded one. They are concerned about being marginalized within the institution that they view themselves as having built, particularly the prospect of the college moving toward emphasizing scholarship, in which few have participated. They would have to remake themselves as faculty members to secure tenure, they fear. In contrast, many among the more recently appointed faculty members have doctoral training and accepted a teach- ing appointment at a community college as an available option in a poor academic employment market. They overwhelmingly embrace Bushwood becoming a compre- hensive institution. Provided they are measured by standards consistent with institu- tions like Bushwood, as with defining scholarly activity broadly to include work other than publications in refereed journals and presentations at scholarly conferences, the newer faculty members are comfortable with the prospect of requiring external peer evaluation of scholarly productivity. The more established faculty members are not.

The faculty union representatives on the task force are acutely aware of the need to balance these differing perspectives. Additionally, they know that many of their col- leagues are unenthusiastic about (but not necessarily adamant in opposition to) having work within the local community be considered in tenure or continuing appointment decisions for faculty members in relevant areas. They are also less inclined to favor having the tenure or continuing appointment process include the intermediate- and longer-term needs of a department—whether it already has enough faculty members in a certain area.

Finally, the faculty union leadership is interested in changing the application process to have the chair merely coordinate the preparation of the application and supporting materials with the candidate, passing it to a newly formed committee comprised of faculty members in the department for their determination. Doing so would be consistent with practices at the peer comprehensive institutions, but would represent a departure from the present approach of only having the chair involved in evaluation. In such an approach, the chair would then summarize the application and forward the recommendation of the faculty committee to the dean. The dean would make his or her own recommendation to an institution-wide faculty appointments committee, which would then make a recommendation to the academic vice president, with the president having the final vote. An application could be rejected at any step in the process.

Vice President for Academic Affairs and Academic Deans. The academic vice president arrived at Bushwood earlier in the year, recruited by Smails with the mandate to build bachelors programs at the college. He or she has experience at comprehensive institutions and is thus familiar with tenure and promotion standards and process in the sector. The dean of professional studies is similarly entirely supportive of the evolving mission of the college, although she has less of a direct understanding of what it means in practical terms, having spent an entire career in the community college sector. The vocational dean (like the dean of humanities and social sciences) has worked at Bushwood for 30 years and understands the inevitability of change at the college, but is sympathetic to those who are concerned about being marginalized within the institution. Each is concerned about recent difficulties in attracting and retaining needed faculty, losing them to industry or other institutions. They believe that tenure or a similar approach might prove useful.

Within the task force, the three (or four) are responsible for representing the interests of the president, meaning the inclusion of connections with the local community within the evaluation framework for faculty members in applied and vocational areas and the application of the highest possible standard for tenure. The latter entails incorporating standards that allow the denial of an application based upon having enough faculty members in a given area, as well as factoring in whether those applying have had a productive relationship with colleagues. They are also interested in continuing to have the department chairs predominantly influence the application process. But they recognize the possible need to compromise here, especially given norms at comprehensive institutions, although probably not to the extent the union favors.

Student Government. The representative from the student government knows that he or she is included on the task force for symbolic reasons and is reflective of students generally in not really being interested in faculty appointment issues. But that is unlikely to prevent the representative, who has political ambitions and is already active in Republican politics in the area, from expressing opinions, particularly those aligned with the local business community.

Local Business and Nonprofit Partners. The local business representative, the senior vice president of a regional hotel chain headquartered in the area and an active supporter of the new bachelors degree program in hospitality management, does not understand the need for tenure—or even the present continuing appointments. He or she believes the higher education institutions waste resources and would be more efficient and effective if run more like businesses—and there is no tenure in industry and long-term contracts are reserved for leaders. The nonprofit representative is more indifferent. He or she is the chief executive officer of the local Catholic hospital and is involved with the various health sciences programs at Bushwood. Smails has made it clear that the opinions of the local partners are important to him—and thus the college.

University Counsel. The university counsel is not inclined to offer an opinion on appropriate standards for tenure and promotion, but is instead interested in ensuring that the application process developed is clean. He or she is concerned with several issues, as with senior faculty voting on tenure applications involving even minimal scholarly activity when they are not acculturated to understand the norms related to such evaluations. Counsel is also struggling with the practicality of having different schemes, standards, and processes applied to different members of the regular faculty. For instance, vocational program faculty are likely to opt for the status quo, while newer faculty teaching in bachelors programs will probably seek tenure. He or she is further worried about the prospect of there being insufficient information available on matters such as scholarship and teaching for an external reviewer to draw reasonable conclusions. In addition, counsel is troubled by the prospect of faculty members (and perhaps even chairs, looking to avoid conflict and often having recently been promoted from the faculty) essentially approving all applications. Finally, counsel wonders, but is not inclined to state during a meeting, whether the present administrative review, with having the chair as the sole evaluator in the current annual review process, is open to due process problems. He or she has the same concern about (and same unwillingness to discuss) senior administrators being able to overturn a faculty committee recommendation, although such practice is common across higher education and applicants can bring legal challenges based on denial of due process.

* * *

The task force should meet, upon being called to order by the chair, for approximately 45 minutes, addressing each of the issues before it in a systematic way. The chair needs to keep the discussion moving if it stalls. At the conclusion of the meeting, the chair (or the secretary, if appointed) should summarize the recommendations of the task force—what are the scheme, standards, and processes agreed upon? In discussing the work of the task force following its meeting, the participants should consider whether its recommendations are practicable and provide proper due process for the applicants, as with a meaningful right to appeal.

In particular, the participants should consider several sets of qustions

- What could go wrong such that schemes, standards, and processes could be deemed in litigation to be unreasonable?
- What might prompt the college to not follow its own rules and be vulnerable in a lawsuit by a disappointed candidate?
- Does counsel make a good point about senior faculty voting on standards they do not really appreciate?
- Are there potential complications with soliciting external reviews?
- Might faculty (and chairs) simply grant most or all applications?
- Is there a greater or lesser likelihood of discrimination—and thus potential legal problems—with the former evaluation process or with the one the task force is recommending?
- Does the newer process support the strategic direction that Bushwood is pursuing under President Smails?
- Is it reflective of trends across American higher education toward institutions being more entrepreneurial and focused on external concerns?
- Does the entire discussion of faculty appointments at the college "sell out" adjunct faculty, who are excluded from both it and any meaningful protections apart from the term of their semester-long contracts—and is this "par for the course" in contemporary education?
- Should adjuncts have further rights—and what might these entail and at what cost in terms of the institution's agility?
- Is an increasingly stratified faculty inevitable, given trends in U.S. higher education?

Finally, please consider the following situation, either to conclude the simulation, or complete individually as a short "homework" assignment by each participant. Pursuant to the scheme, standards, and process that the task force recommends, a probationary faculty member in hospitality management has submitted an application. The chair worked with him or her to develop a portfolio of supporting materials, submitting these to three external reviewers, as required. A member of the faculty in the applicant's department decides to contact the reviewers to provide additional perspective, which is expressly prohibited under the applicable rules. Also, the applicant sees the letter from an external reviewer left on a photocopier and makes a copy for himself or herself. The faculty committee decides to reject the applicant, not based on the external reviews, which are positive, but on the perception within the department of the difficulty of working with this individual. The dean, provost, and president deny the application, following the recommendation of the committee. The applicant, after an unsuccessful internal appeal, initiates a lawsuit alleging denial of due process. Is he or she likely to prevail? If so, what remedy should the court grant? (The discussion of granting tenure in Chapter 3 may prove useful in considering the above situation.)

2

DISCRIMINATION

The commercialization of American higher education has little effect on the enforcement of statutes that provide considerable protection against discrimination on the basis of some immutable characteristic, such as race. Fearing the loss of reputation that can accompany a scandal involving discrimination, universities and colleges may be even more likely to avoid such behavior. The same is true in avoiding sexual harassment. In both areas, institutions tend to have established policies and processes—and have worked to raise sensitivity across campus.

But there continues to be discrimination, however, whether it is intentional or unintentional, and both *quid pro quo* and hostile environment sexual harassment. Direct discrimination on the basis of religion—and institutional responses to inappropriate behavior associated with the area—has drawn considerable attention from commentators over the past decade. Finally, as with sexual harassment, discrimination against those with disabilities attracted notice during the 1990s, particularly following the Clarence Thomas hearings and the passage of the Americans with Disabilities Act (ADA), both in 1990. After two decades of awareness, definitions and standards—and corresponding approaches—are reasonably well defined in both areas.

Federal Statutes

Under the U.S. Constitution, state constitutions, and federal and state legislation, universities and colleges as employers, both public and private, must base decisions in hiring and admissions on factors such as the qualifications of applicants and merit (or even seniority) of employees. Employment decisions influenced by the immutable characteristics of individuals can be discriminatory, unless there is a powerful reason to make the narrowest possible exception. For employees across universities and colleges, even in temporary positions, such as adjunct faculty, categories such as race, color, religion, national origin, sex, age, and disability are protected under various federal antidiscrimination statutes, such as Title VII of the Civil Rights Act of 1964. The Equal Protection Clause of the Fourteenth Amendment also applies at public institutions, protecting these rights.

The U.S. Congress has not chosen to amend Title VII to prohibit discrimination on the basis of sexual orientation (Bazluke and Nolan, 2006; Connell and Euben, 2004). Although with some confusion, it does protect, as interpreted by the U.S. Supreme

Court, against same-sex sexual harassment (Connell and Euben, 2004) and sex stereotyping (discrimination based on appearance, as opposed to sexual orientation). Bazluke and Nolan (2006) note that while courts are inclined to read the term "sex" as gender, scholars are likely to find significant distinctions between the two in arguing in favor of extending Title VII discrimination to include sexual identity as a basis for protections (being transgendered, for instance). Some state fair employment practices acts protect individuals in such categories (Bazluke and Nolan, 2006).

Courts afford discrimination cases involving the government (which includes public universities) the highest scrutiny, with the defendant needing to justify a compelling state interest to justify an action alleged to be discriminatory. For instance, affirmative action is an exception to the logic of equal protection—the state treating different groups similarly—sufficient in certain circumstances to meet the compelling interest standard. As higher education evolves, what is deemed compelling changes accordingly, as with a nondiverse public university or college having become unthinkable, both in aligning with values and protecting strategic position.

Not only do the antidiscrimination statutes, such as Title VII, extend the logic of equal protection to private actors, they also provide mechanisms for initiating and determining cases and can have less stringent standards than does the U.S. Constitution. In a discrimination case under one of the several federal antidiscrimination statutes, the U.S. Equal Employment Opportunity Commission (EEOC) is responsible for investigating complaints, employing subpoena power to collect evidence, as needed. These statutes protect against various types of discrimination:

- Title VII of the Civil Rights Act of 1964 covers race, color, religion, national origin, or sex (and later pregnancy, as considered above); Title IX of the Educational Amendments of 1972 also applies to sex discrimination, most prominently in participation opportunities for women in intercollegiate athletics; and Section 1981 of the 1991 Civil Rights Act prohibits discrimination based on race and ethnicity in contracts.
- The Equal Pay Act of 1963 (EPA) addresses gender discrimination related to unequal pay for equal work.
- Title I of the Americans with Disabilities Act of 1990 (ADA) requires the reasonable accommodation of those with a disability, with Sections 501 and 505 of the Rehabilitation Act of 1973 (for discrimination by the federal government based on disability) also relevant.
- The Genetic Information Nondiscrimination Act of 2008 (GINA).
- The Age Discrimination in Employment Act of 1967 (ADEA) protects people over age 40.

It is illegal under these statutes to retaliate against an individual for filing a complaint. As under ADEA, there is also the right to a jury trial and compensatory and punitive damages under Title VII and ADA under Sections 102 and 103 of the 1991

Civil Rights Act. There are also analogous state laws, which may be narrower or more expansive (Weitzner, 2006).

Plaintiffs begin actions under the antidiscrimination laws by raising a reasonable inference of discrimination, as with a suggestion that an employment decision may have been impermissibly influenced by gender. The defendant then must rebut the claim through evidence of a legitimate nondiscriminatory reason for the allegedly discriminatory action, perhaps that the decision was based on merit or the plaintiff has underperformed. The plaintiff then must prove, often through empirical evidence, that the nondiscriminatory reason is a pretext.

Especially in academe, given its subjective nature, discrimination cases are difficult to prove. For instance, demonstrating unequal treatment requires that a faculty member compare his or her situation to those similarly situated, suggesting a pattern of discrimination. But outside of contexts such as a faculty union at a community college or comprehensive institution, similarly situated individuals may be difficult to identify, making "apples to apples" comparisons nearly impossible. Employers can always distinguish a given situation from others based on factors such as type and time, as assessments across disciplines are difficult to make and performance standards often evolve. Because entrepreneurial universities and colleges are only more diffuse, with more activities at their peripheries, it is only more difficult for plaintiffs to draw needed comparisons.

Title VII

Actions intended to address discrimination on the basis of race, color, religion, national origin, or sex are of two types: disparate treatment and disparate impact.

Disparate Treatment. Disparate treatment is intentional discrimination based on one of these immutable characteristics. An example is a public university, concerned about avoiding an Establishment Clause problem, banning religious groups from being recognized as student organizations—thus directly discriminating against a protected group (albeit for a sincere reason). Another illustration is the allegation that male faculty members in an academic department expressly favored men over women in compensation, working conditions, giving awards, or granting tenure.

There is an exception to Title VII for disparate treatment occurring within the context of a bona fide occupational qualification (BFOQ), as with the discrimination on the basis of religion being permissible in retaining a chaplain at a private university or college with a particular religious orientation. For instance, a Catholic university or college can also discriminate on the basis of sex in hiring for positions requiring a priest. Such institutions might also be able to discriminate in requiring adherence to certain religious-based standards of personal conduct, such as those involving abortion rights. A BFOQ exception based on race or another protected class is possible, with appropriate justification, similar to the exception made to allow single-sex and single-race private higher education. The U.S. Supreme Court deemed single-sex public higher education illegal in United States v. Virginia (1996), which involved the Virginia Military Institute.

At a typical religiously affiliated institution, an employee in a nonministerial function, such as the campus director of public safety, would not fall under the BFOQ exception. But a university or college in which religion strongly permeates every aspect of institutional life would be able to justify a BFOQ exception across the institution. An institution that is secular in nature, but has a relationship with a religious order—perhaps only through its founding documents and minor connections involving governance—is unlikely to be able to take advantage of the exception in most areas. For instance, Emory University, though established by Methodists and including a few representatives of the local denomination on its board, operates in a secular environment. The situation is different at Catholic University or Brigham Young University, which have a pronounced religious character, as with a curriculum that concentrates, at least somewhat, on propagating a certain religion (Araujo, 2006; Guenther, 2006; Schimelfenig, Beckenhauer, and Yanikoski, 2006).

The situation is more evident at smaller institutions built around religion. At such universities and colleges, there may also be a reasonable interest in ensuring a critical mass of those of a certain religion, reinforcing or enhancing their mission through admissions and hiring (Araujo, 2006). In fact, a university or college emphasizing its specific religious character may be its most significant competitive advantage in an increasingly robust market for students or employees. The same is true of single-sex and single-race institutions. But there are limits, as illustrated by the decision of the U.S. Supreme Court in *Bob Jones University v. United States* (1983) refusing to extend tax exempt status typically granted religious institutions to one that was discriminating in its policies on what was deemed to be the basis of race.

Protecting against religious discrimination raises several other issues. One is the deference, akin to academic decision making across institutional contexts, that courts should give to decisions about religion made within a religious university or college (McLain, 2002). There is also the matter of what amount to "side businesses" at religious institutions, as with evening and weekend business programs attracting students primarily interested in convenience, as opposed to studying in a religious environment. Sometimes religion can be intertwined with national origin, as with anti-Semitism or bias against Muslims arising at universities and colleges. Weitzner (2006) offers the illustration of a private research university having a partnership with a Saudi hospital that discriminates against Jews. (The institution could frame the situation as membership in a religious group acceptable to the host being a BFOQ for the appointment.) As globalization is an emphasis across entrepreneurial universities and colleges, such situations are only more likely to arise. There can also be discrimination within a single religion, as with criticism that a member is insufficiently devout (Warner, 2006).

In disparate treatment cases, as the Jewish physician might bring when denied access to the Saudi hospital, a plaintiff must allege a prima facie case of discrimination, demonstrating that he or she is within a protected class, suffered an adverse employment action, was performing satisfactorily or was qualified for a position, and that the employers treated those similarly situated more favorably or that discrimination otherwise occurred (Weitzner, 2006). There must be actual consequences relating to matters such as compensation or working conditions, as well as a nexus between the adverse action or actions and religious discrimination (Weitzner, 2006). The employer must also be aware of the religious beliefs at issue. As in all Title VII cases, the defendant must proffer a legitimate nondiscriminatory reason for the action, which the plaintiff can then rebut as a pretext, as the actual reason was discrimination.

In addition, there is the question of what constitutes a religion. The U.S. Supreme Court has taken a broad view, with the sincerity of a person's beliefs being important, so long as they are religious in nature (Acero, 2006; Weitzner, 2006). But the line is not always clear between what is a religion, and thus protected, and what is a lifestyle, and thus not covered (Warner, 2005)—or whether discrimination against those who are atheist or agnostic is protected (Acevo, 2006). And there are challenges when reprehensible behavior, such as racism, is the basis of what someone may claim (perhaps appropriately, in a technical sense) as a religion.

Among disparate treatment situations under Title VII, there are cases of religious discrimination grounded in hostile environment, retaliation, and failure to accommodate (Weitzner, 2006). Hostile environment cases require pervasive and severe religious-based harassment that detrimentally affects an employee—and would have similarly affected a reasonable person of the same religion in that position. As with sexual harassment (discussed below), employers are liable when they knew or should have known about a situation (Weitzner, 2006). Kaminer (2000) extends the hostile environment argument to employees that subject others to the unwelcome insertion of religion into their work life. Retaliatory discharge can give rise to a successful Title VII action, if a plaintiff can connect his or her dismissal to protected activity, such as free expression (Hustoles and Griffin, 2000; Weber, 2000). However, as considered in the academic freedom section in Chapter 3, public employees can be disciplined for statements made pursuant to their official duties.

A failure to accommodate case might involve an employer not recognizing observances and practices associated with religion, such as holy days or dress and grooming requirements, or another protected group activity. The claim (or prima facie case) here is demonstrating a bona fide religious belief that conflicts with an employment requirement, informing the employer of that belief, and being disciplined or discharged for failing to comply with the requirement (Weitzner, 2006). There is no requirement that employees must compromise in their religious beliefs, as with meeting the employer halfway (Acero, 2006). Upon receiving appropriate notice, it is the employer that suggests the accommodation, not the employee. The employer is required to act in good faith, but has discretion, as in denying an accommodation for appropriate reasons (Acero, 2006).

Employers are obligated only to make those accommodations on the basis of religion (or another protected class) that are reasonable and do not involve undue hardship, as under the ADA (addressed in the next subsection). What is reasonable is determined on a case-by-case basis. For instance, institutions can accommodate most religious dress requirements or need for daily prayer time. The EEOC suggests approaches such as voluntary shift swaps, flexible schedules, changing of job assignments, or lateral transfers (Acero, 2006). If the employee does not view the accommodation as reasonable, the employer can argue that doing more would prove to be an undue hardship. Yunus (2006) contends that courts have interpreted liberally what degree of hardship constitutes being undue, making it difficult for plaintiffs to be successful in accommodations litigation. In fact, employees are unlikely to prevail unless the employer does nothing to accommodate them and can make no showing of undue hardship, Yunus argues—as a practical matter, any kind of accommodation is likely to be sufficient.

Often as problematic, especially at public institutions, as they are subject to the Establishment Clause, is employees inserting religion into their work life in ways unwelcome to colleagues (Weitzner, 2006). Certain religious practices of employees, such as religious statements in e-mail messages or inserting prayers into mandatory meetings, can conflict with legitimate practices or needs of an employer (or the beliefs of other employees). When employers assert their interest, there can be allegations of religious discrimination (Warner, 2006). Also tricky are religious-based objections to diversity initiatives, as with programs advancing tolerance toward gay and lesbian colleagues (Bodensteiner, 2005; Warner, 2006). Bernstein (2003) argues that antidiscrimination statutes can clash with protections under the First Amendment, such as requiring Catholic institutions to extend formal recognition to gay and lesbian groups under a local law, or imposing limits on speech within the workplace (Browne, 2001). Bodensteiner (2005) contends that such fears by conservative commentators are often overblown.

Additionally, the Establishment Clause prohibits government activities, including speech, endorsing or inhibiting religion, but not necessarily expression by employees acting in their individual capacity—someone speaking for himself or herself. But there are limits, as when such expression suggests to a reasonable observer that a government agency is becoming intertwined with religion (Woltz, 2006).

Finally, there can be a tension between the Establishment Clause and Free Exercise Clause at public institutions (Woltz, 2006). As interpreted by the U.S. Supreme Court in *Oregon v. Smith* (1990), free exercise does not provide an exemption from valid and neutral laws of general applicability. For instance, as in *Smith*, the state does not violate the Free Exercise Clause in prohibiting sacramental peyote use and later to denying unemployment benefits to persons discharged for such use. Although the right of people to believe what they wish is clear, the right to engage in actual religious conduct is not, provided limitations are not discriminatory (Woltz, 2006). In fact, free expression, also under the First Amendment, may provide employees at public institutions with greater protections than free exercise, according to Woltz, balancing employer interests, as with efficiency, with the right of employees to comment on matters of public concern.

Disparate Impact.   Disparate impact does not involve intent, like disparate treatment, but instead is an ostensibly neutral policy turning out to be discriminatory against a protected group. For instance, hiring employees such as police officers based solely on standardized test scores, while objective on the surface, might prove to be discriminatory if a protected underrepresented group regularly scores lower on the measure. There can be an exception, as when a criterion has a manifest relationship to job performance, such as a physical capacity standard for a worker in a position that involves heavy lifting, which might favor men. Disparate impact approaches began with the decision of the U.S. Supreme Court in *Griggs v. Duke Power Co.* (1971), which addressed standardized test scores and high school diploma requirements that disadvantaged minority applicants, requiring that they be reasonably related to the position involved and not a pretext for racial discrimination.

Courts have been inclined, as explored in Chapter 1, to defer to higher education institutions in matters involving academic issues. But if a university or college is alleged to have discriminated, even if in faculty employment or student admissions, both the EEOC and courts will assert themselves to remedy the situation. Doing so requires balancing deference, grounded in academic freedom, with attention to addressing discrimination under Title VII (Chase, 2007).

Establishing a disparate impact case, which plaintiffs can bring as a class action, requires statistical evidence of an approach being discriminatory. The "apples to apples" challenge is acute for research university or liberal arts college faculty, given the idiosyncratic nature of positions. It is commonly more possible to demonstrate a pattern of unintentional discrimination with larger, more generic groups of employees, as with all clerical workers at a university or college or even faculty at comprehensive institutions, at which their role is more limited to teaching. In comparable worth actions, as under the EPA, plaintiffs alleging salary or wage discrimination based on gender can often draw on analyses of voluminous empirical data in providing evidence of disparate impact.

A classic disparate impact situation in higher education involves gender disparities in compensation—typically paying similarly situated women less than men to perform the same job (Perez-Arrieta, 2005). Hutson (2006) contends that women and minority faculty are more likely to be employed at teaching institutions, hold positions of lower rank and status, and earn less pay. Accordingly, she argues, they are more likely to be assigned lower level, required courses, as opposed to upper level, elective seminars—and thus are more inclined to receive lower marks on teaching evaluations.

Such could constitute a potential ground for a disparate impact action, as these more negative assessments can impede career progress.

But such cases are complicated. For instance, men's and women's basketball coaches would seem to be doing comparable work, except when considering the expectation that a Division I men's program generates revenue for the athletic program. Such differences, if deemed apart from sex, are appropriate justifications. Salary differences may be defensible if resulting from differences in education and training, salary compression, retention packages, merit pay, or commissions or bonuses (Perez-Arrieta, 2005). Entrepreneurial universities and colleges are increasingly using compensation packages to attract and retain talent, further segmenting employees between stars and others, and thus complicating comparable worth matters.

Hart (2007) considers how difficult it is to be successful in such litigation, citing statistics that plaintiffs are only successful in a small percentage of cases. She argues that employers have become more sophisticated in the types of empirical evidence they employ and that courts are sympathetic to "business necessity" justifications for challenged policies. Hart also contends that disparate impact cases are often really disparate treatment cases in most instances, with the alleged discrimination being intentional. Duke Power, for instance, likely knew its "neutral" policies would result in keeping African Americans assigned to jobs as laborers. She suggests that the preferred approach to enhancing diversity may be to concentrate on encouraging institutional commitment to changing organizations from within. (In a twist on the *Griggs* situation, a city disregarding the results of a test determining promotions because they overwhelmingly favored a group of white fire fighters was held to be unconstitutional by the U.S. Supreme Court in *Ricci v. DiStefano* [2009].)

Whether employing a disparate treatment or disparate impact theory, remedies under Title VII are intended to return the victim to a neutral setting—one free of discrimination. But they can also include compensatory damages, such as back pay, as well as punitive ones. In a wrongful dismissal case, reinstatement is a common remedy, but a court would be unlikely to grant tenure in a successful discrimination case, instead instructing the defendant to repeat the process, having remedied the defects identified in it. In gender discrimination actions, Title IX has the advantages for plaintiffs of not including a cap on the amount of damages and often having a more favorable statute of limitation. Section 1981 similarly has more extensive remedies and a longer statute of limitation than Title VII in cases involving discrimination on the basis of race and ethnicity.

Finally, Pieronek (2005b) explores how Title IX, usually applied in higher education in athletics or sexual harassment, can be useful in academic contexts in addressing gender-based discrimination. She notes that successful Title IX litigation in athletics, considered at the end of Chapter 4, suggests possibilities to remedy similar disparities between women and men in the STEM fields (science, technology, engineering, and mathematics) in the contexts of admissions and employment.

Americans with Disabilities Act

The 1990 Americans with Disabilities Act, the Rehabilitation Act of 1973 (its predecessor), and applicable state fair employment practice acts prohibit discrimination on the basis of disability against a person who is otherwise qualified for a position or service, requiring that an institution make the necessary reasonable accommodations that can be achieved without undue hardship to it. Disability discrimination tends to be intentional, including deliberate indifference, but does not need to be grounded in animus or ill will (Gaal and Jones, 2003). The ADA has broad definitions of its key variables—otherwise qualified, reasonable accommodation, and undue hardship—with determinations necessarily made on a case-by-case basis. There is no affirmative obligation to hire or retain someone with a disability, only a prohibition against discrimination against those with disabilities who, with reasonable accommodations, can perform the essential functions of a position.

In employment, determining qualification depends on a position description that outlines the essential functions of the job—and whether there are reasonable adaptations available to enable someone with a disability to perform it. But accommodation may demand too much of an institution in certain situations, as with a profound hearing or vision impairment disqualifying someone from being employed as an emergency room physician. Even with a reasonable accommodation, a person must still be capable of performing the essentials of a given job, as evaluated according to usual standards. If not, he or she would not be otherwise qualified. The question is thus whether an employer can make modest adjustments to enable a person with a disability to perform in a position.

Employers do not need to extend accommodations deemed to impose an undue hardship on them. For instance, accommodations deemed reasonable at most universities and colleges might include adapting facilities, acquiring equipment, modifying examinations, providing readers, or modifying schedules. But a significant learning disability, even with generous accommodations, may simply be too much to overcome in certain situations. A university or college is not required to make accommodations that are excessive in the context of available resources. Installing a simple ramp into a building or using a ground floor office may be reasonable, while retrofitting a historic building (apart from a scheduled renovation) may not be.

The ADA defines a disabled person as one with a physical or mental impairment that substantially limits a major life activity—or a record or perception of such a disability (Gaal and Jones, 2003; Kaufman, 2005; Rose, 2004; Weber, 2000; Wilhelm, 2003). An illustration of discrimination associated with the latter is an applicant with past, but now managed, mental health issues being denied a position. Disabilities tend to be physical impairments, including certain diseases, with psychological challenges, such as bipolar disorder and obsessive-compulsive disorder, also appearing within the definition from the EEOC (Lee and Ruger, 2003). Given their physical effect, alcoholism and a contagious disease such as tuberculosis fit within the definition (Kaufman, 2005).

Disability does not excuse misconduct. Certain disorders such as compulsive gambling, kleptomania, and pyromania are accordingly excluded, as is substance abuse based upon the current use of illegal drugs (Kaufman, 2005). The same is true of learning and other disorders resulting from certain environmental, cultural, or economic disadvantages, such as poverty, as well as situations such as gender identity disorders, advanced age, or sexual behavior disorders. Common personality traits such as poor judgment or quick temper unconnected to mental or psychological disorder are also not covered (Kaufman, 2005; Rose, 2004). Temporary or insubstantial mental conditions are not included, as with occasional stress not covered (Kaufman, 2005)—and mental conditions controlled by medication may not be included (Bunting, 2004). The history or potential of a condition is insufficient—someone must be currently disabled (Hayward, 2000). Also, certain applicable state and local disabilities laws have different definitions of what constitutes a disability, as in California (Thomas, 2004). Once again, what qualifications are essential and what accommodations are reasonable are the main questions—and are always fact specific.

Once identified as disabled, the issue then becomes whether the person can perform appropriately in a position, provided an accommodation is not only possible, but also realistic under the applicable circumstances (Lee and Ruger, 2003; Wilhelm, 2003). Universities and colleges tend to be experienced and sophisticated in addressing accommodation requests from students (examined in detail in Chapter 4). Examples of reasonable accommodations include flexible course scheduling and modifying test formats, but not such substantial modifications that they dilute principles and methodology. Accommodations are not appropriate when they require a reduction in academic standards or expectations, involve behavior that causes disruption, or are disproportionally expensive (in relative terms) (Bunting, 2004).

In addressing requests by students for accommodations, institutions are not required to compromise the integrity of their academic programs and there is deference to reasoned academic decision making (Thomas, 2004). The same undue hardship logic applies to employees. Universities and colleges must follow their own applicable and appropriate processes in determining requests (Bunting, 2004). And accommodated employees still must meet standards of adequate performance and can be disciplined and dismissed under regular processes. Additionally, as considered in the section on hiring in Chapter 3, prospective employers may ask questions directed at ascertaining whether a candidate is capable of doing a particular job, but may not ask questions directly related to determining whether he or she has a disability. They may also not employ medical or psychological examinations to screen candidates.

Finally, as with other antidiscrimination cases under federal statutes, plaintiffs bring actions under the ADA and the Rehabilitation Act through the EEOC (Lee and Ruger, 2003). In *Board of Regents of the University of Alabama v. Garrett* (2001), the U.S. Supreme Court held that states are immune from lawsuits by individual plaintiffs for damages grounded in the ADA and Rehabilitation Act. Individuals may still seek injunctive relief under these statutes, and the federal government can still bring actions against states (Gaal and Jones, 2003; Weber, 2002).

Age Discrimination in Employment Act

The ADEA, also addressed later in this chapter in the context of wrongful termination, covers discrimination in employment against those 40 years of age or older, an area omitted under Title VII, covering also benefits and incentives related to retirement (also discussed at the end of the chapter). ADEA thus covers age discrimination in hiring, as well as in areas such as assignments, promotion, compensation, and dismissal. There are both disparate treatment and disparate impact cases, brought in ways similar to other discrimination cases involving the EEOC, and hostile work environment cases may be possible (Rosenberg and Skoning, 2006). As in other areas, disparate impact cases are difficult for plaintiffs to win, particularly after the decision in *Smith v. City of Jackson* (2005), which allows the theory, but imposes challenging evidentiary requirements.

Recovery in ADEA litigation is aided by provisions allowing jury trial, as well as liquidated damages equal to double back pay in cases of willful violations. Evidence in these cases usually involves employment evaluations, with usual good practices related to building personnel files and progressive discipline applicable. As with the ADA, states are immune from liability for monetary damages in age discrimination lawsuits under ADEA, as held by the U.S. Supreme Court in *Kimel v. Florida Board of Regents* (2000) (Weber, 2000).

The financial situation at private, nondenominational North Shore College has been fragile for several years. The board appointed Samantha Baker as president two years ago, in the hopes that she would repeat her success as the vice president for advancement at Hughes College. Baker has been a fund raiser for 20 years, recently earning a doctorate in higher education management through the executive program at Fort Dearborn University. North Shore has experienced declining enrollments over the past few years, falling below 1000 full-time students last year. It has raised its discount rate to almost 60 percent in an attempt to attract students, borrowing from the modest endowment of the college to finance the scholarships. NSC has also retained an admissions consulting firm, Bueller Partners, known for its aggressiveness in recruiting students. Baker expects that attrition will be high for a few years, as the firm is noted for filling classes with students who are not necessarily a good fit. But she knows that the college needs time to improve its financial position—or closure is a real possibility.

(continued)

Baker has also looked to reduce costs. The previous three presidents had kept certain liabilities and even expenses hidden from the board, so the budget was much worse than Baker had expected upon her arrival. Baker has not replaced retiring and departing faculty. The college has imposed 12 furlough days for all employees, constituting a 6 percent pay decrease, and has increased the contribution that faculty and administrators must make to their health benefits coverage. NSC has also implemented an early retirement program, strongly encouraging participation, but not mandating it so as to conform to applicable standards and avoid legal exposure on wrongful termination grounds. Baker intends to shift to less expensive options, such as adjunct faculty in lieu of replenishing the full-time faculty ranks, but if possible when the financial picture improves, she hopes to hire new assistant professors in areas with high enrollment and revenue potential.

She has also announced a program reduction plan, modeled on Coronado State University, discussed in Chapter 3, not simply wanting to make across-the-board cuts. Baker has identified three programs: religion, women's studies, and philosophy. Religion and philosophy have had dismal enrollments over the past several years—and two of four faculty members in each unit have recently retired or otherwise left the college. Cameron Frye, one of the remaining religion professors, has threatened a Title VII action if NSC singles out his department, contending discrimination on the basis of religion. Counsel advises Baker that the college is on solid ground here because their reason has nothing to do with actual religion, but is instead based in the legitimate nondiscriminatory reason of an academic department lacking viability.

Carolyn Mulford, the longtime chair of women's studies, has been a persistent critic of Baker and the presidents that preceded her. The women's studies program has had steady, although hardly impressive, enrollments. But it is widely perceived among the faculty to lack rigor, particularly by the standards of other such departments at smaller colleges nationally. There are other programs at North Shore with more modest enrollments, including two that have been formally censured by the college's faculty senate. Baker had hoped that Mulford would simply leave the college, but the professor has retained counsel, seemingly calling the president's bluff. Retaliation is not an appropriate ground for determining which programs are to be reduced, and Mulford is likely to argue that the college is doing just that.

Baker and NCC are also in dispute over refusing the request by faculty member Ted Farmer for an accommodation under the ADA. Farmer has long suffered from depression, recently receiving a diagnosis that he is unable to teach. He has requested indefinite paid leave to pursue treatment. Concerned about paying a professor who is unable to work when her budget is so stretched, Baker has offered him unpaid leave, with the promise that he can return to work when he is able. Farmer has approached the EEOC about his case, contending his disability qualifies, which is not disputed, and that his accommodation is reasonable. NSC is prepared to respond that his accommodation poses an undue hardship, particularly given the financial fragility of the college. The college has not declared financial exigency, Baker concluding that it would discourage prospective students and donors.

Finally, the college is entering its second year of an outsourcing agreement with a firm, Bender Services, which provides maintenance and food service work for the college. Part of the agreement was that existing employees would be able to transfer to the firm—and most did, accepting modest cuts in compensation and benefits. Subsequently, several of these employees have complained that the firm discriminates in favor of those who are overtly religious. Long Duk Dong, the president of the firm, is proud of his religious fundamentalist views, agreeing that the company operates in an expressly Christian environment. There are also allegations that the firm discriminates against women. Dong answers that he operates the firm according to biblical principles, speaking recently before the local Rotary Club about his interpretation that women should hold a subservient position to men in the workplace.

Counsel advises Baker that a Title VII lawsuit based on religious and gender discrimination may be successful, but that NSC is unlikely to be exposed because it is sufficiently separate from Bender Services. But there is reputational risk for the college resulting from a negative decision, along with the potential for protests on campus. Baker is thankful that such situations have not arisen in the context of other partnerships, as with one with a private corporation, Rooney Curriculum Solutions, which offers under the North Shore banner continuing education curricula prepared by Rooney. She knows the college might be implicated were discrimination to occur in that context, given the more direct connection.

Affirmative Action

Affirmative action is an exception to the constitutional principle of equal protection embodied in Title VII and the other antidiscrimination legislation, with poorly designed programs inviting litigation, whether by underrepresented groups or those claiming so-called reverse discrimination. Unlike in admissions, examined in Chapter 4, the U.S. Supreme Court has not specifically addressed affirmative action in employment within higher education. But cases in other areas uphold programs intended to remedy the present effects of past discrimination in hiring and promotion correcting imbalances in race or gender. Providing enough racial and ethnic diversity to have a multiplicity of viewpoints may also justify such efforts, given recent decisions by the U.S. Supreme Court (Eckes, 2005).

The constitutionality of affirmative action programs is evaluated somewhat differently for public and private universities and colleges. At public institutions, there is a more rigorous standard, given that the U.S. Constitution is applicable in addition to Title VII, which alone governs private universities and colleges. If the state, acting through a public university or college, targets certain groups in hiring or promotion, it must demonstrate a compelling governmental interest in having a program—the strict scrutiny test. Clear evidence of the present effects of its past discrimination may be such an interest, as might be advancing the values of workforce diversity. In order to avoid a successful challenge, an affirmative action program also must be tailored as narrowly as possible, while still achieving the desired end. In other words, if the government is going to act in a manner contrary to the Equal Protection clause, it must have an exceedingly strong justification for doing so, and operate in a manner that will damage the fewest possible people the least possible amount.

Whether the goal of promoting racial diversity in hiring within universities and colleges would meet the compelling interest standard and could be sufficiently narrowly tailored are open questions. The 2003 U.S. Supreme Court decision in *Grutter v. Bollinger*, which involved the University of Michigan, upheld the use of affirmative action in admissions, persuaded by the need for a diverse environment within higher education. The Court has not expressly prohibited such race conscious hiring under Title VII or the Equal Protection Clause, but Eckes (2005) argues that such viewpoint diversity arguments could extend to faculty hiring. There is also the decision in *Metro Broadcasting v. Federal Communications Commission* (1990), which upheld a program that sought to enhance viewpoint diversity by encouraging ownership of minority-owned television and radio stations. (The case was later overturned for applying the incorrect scrutiny standard.)

Additonally, sufficient evidence of manifest racial imbalance in traditionally segregated job categories has met the compelling justification standard (Eckes, 2005). For instance, applying Title VII, the U.S. Supreme Court upheld a private sector plan that reserved one-half of the slots in a training program for underrepresented groups, but not mandating placement of such individuals, in *United Steelworkers of America v. Weber* (1979). The Court also upheld affirmative action programs for governments setting aside a small percentage of contracts for minority employees in *Fullilove v. Klutznick* (1980). In *Johnson v. Transportation Agency* (1987), the Court allowed a scheme to remedy underrepresentation of women in various job categories, as it did not excessively harm men and was otherwise narrowly tailored. But the decision in *Regents of the University of California v. Bakke* (1978) held that reserving certain seats in an entering public medical school class was not sufficiently narrowly tailored. (I consider admissions cases such as *Grutter* and *Bakke* further in Chapter 4.) Also, in *Wygant v. Jackson Board of Education* (1986), the Court rejected the approach by a school district, grounded in preserving the presence of African American role models, which protected minority teachers with less seniority against layoffs.

Whether race-based affirmative action programs in employment meets the narrowly tailored standard is subject to factors such as the necessity for the relief, the efficacy of alternative remedies, whether there is a racial quota, the plan being framed as flexible goals, the duration of the program, and its impact on nonminority employees. Applying the standard, the U.S. Supreme Court, in *United States v. Paradise* (1987), upheld a court-ordered promotion plan in response to four decades of racial discrimination in the Alabama Department of Public Safety. But in *City of Richmond v. J. A. Crowson Co.* (1989), it rejected a requirement that 30 percent of subcontractors on government contracts be minority-owned businesses, on the grounds that the plan was not sufficiently narrowly tailored and there was an insufficient showing of its need. The Court rejected a similar policy in *Adarand v. Pena* (1995). Justifying a plan in the public sector thus requires not only concrete evidence of the present effects of past racial discrimination, but also the plan meeting the narrowly tailored test (Eckes, 2005). Once again, whether diversity-based rationales would be sufficient in higher education is an open question (Miller and Toma, forthcoming).

In the private sector, voluntary efforts to address a manifest racial imbalance in the labor market in a traditionally segregated field are permissible under the decision in *Weber v. Kaiser Aluminum Co.* (1979), provided they neither unnecessarily trammel the rights of white employees nor establish explicit quotas. Finally, gender-based affirmative action programs instituted by public employers are measured not under strict scrutiny, but under a lesser, intermediate standard requiring a program be substantially related to an important governmental objective. In *Mississippi University for Women v. Hogan* (1982), the U.S. Supreme Court indicated that importance is measured by the actual advantage given to women and degree of burden that the program places upon men.

It is three years later, and North Shore College is in a much better financial position. It closed the religion and philosophy departments, with a couple of faculty accepting a buyout to relinquish their tenure and three other faculty members, including Ryan, shifting to areas with more demand. One of these areas has involved the Rooney Curricular Solutions partnership, which has expanded from continuing education into coordinating degree programs at three local sites, with plans to launch a distance education program also under the NSC banner. With the emergence of extended campuses, the use of adjunct faculty has increased significantly at North Shore. But so have revenues from programs that can be quickly established—and just as rapidly closed if there is insufficient demand.

Traditional enrollments have stabilized at NSC, with the college transitioning from Bueller Partners, to hiring a new vice president for admissions and

(*continued*)

enrollment management and reaching its admissions targets last year. Retention has improved, but continues to be a struggle, and NSC has been able to lower its discount rate slightly. Baker has been successful in fund raising, building the annual fund and securing multiple seven-figure gifts. She has also invested heavily in building administrative capacity in advancement, admissions and enrollment management, and institutional research. The college did not renew its contract with Bender Services—and is now on its third outsourcing company for maintenance and food service. It remains active in seeking ways to reduce costs.

Not only have there been no further furloughs or retirement buyouts, but Baker is planning to hire toward replenishing a standing faculty that is 25 percent smaller than when she arrived. She realizes that it is a buyer's market for new faculty, in particular, given the dismal state of hiring over the past several years. Baker and Mulford, in working through the proposed closure of women's studies, which the president abandoned, found that they appreciated each other, with Mulford being named provost a few months ago. Mulford has long been frustrated that the North Shore faculty is entirely white, viewing this as not only a moral issue, but also a strategic disadvantage. Her argument is that a great liberal arts college, which is what NSC aspires to be, must have the multiplicity of viewpoints that only comes with diversity.

She has proposed targeting African Americans in the five searches planned, offering candidates what the market requires to attract them. When she presented her plan, essentially as a courtesy, to the faculty senate, they immediately began questioning her about salary compression issues, concerned that the new hires would make decidedly more than established professors at the college. Since then, the discussion has increased in intensity, with lawsuits threatened. Mulford is confident that the college can pursue such a plan, having discussed it with counsel. She views the plan addressing a manifest racial imbalance that neither trammels the rights of white employees nor establishes explicit quotas. As a private college, North Shore is not subject to the compelling state interest or narrowly tailored plan requirements, but Mulford believes that the college would meet these even if it were, given the present effects of past racial discrimination. (She is convinced that the NSC faculty did not become all white by accident, although she does not have concrete evidence to that effect.)

Mulford also does not see how the faculty members complaining of her hiring strategy would actually bring a lawsuit. Cases such as *Grutter* and *Bakke* arise from a plaintiff being denied admission, and actions such as those by the fire fighters who were passed over for promotions in *Ricci* or the teachers with more seniority facing layoffs in *Wygant* are inapplicable, as the current professors would not suffer any disadvantage from the hiring scheme (aside from perhaps there being fewer resources for future raises). Also, the U.S. Supreme Court has upheld programs to modestly adjust the racial and gender composition of the workforce, as Mulford is proposing—it is five professors out of a full-time faculty of 75. She is aware of the perception problem of paying newer faculty more than established ones, but such is life at the entrepreneurial institution, she argues, at which various professors and others can cut their own deals based on the leverage they possess.

Sexual Harassment

Misconduct involving sexual harassment may violate both Title VII and Title IX, as well as specific state laws that may provide even greater protection. Plaintiffs may also bring actions under a tort theory such as infliction of emotional distress, or based in contract, as for wrongful termination. Title VII defines sexual harassment as unwelcome sexual advances, requests for sexual favors, or other verbal or physical conduct of a sexual nature, in one of two forms: *quid pro quo* harassment and hostile work environment (Cole, 2003). Neither of these is gender-specific, as both men and women can be the target of the harassment (Lee, 2006).

Quid pro quo harassment involves submission to conduct explicitly or implicitly being made a condition of employment or determining decisions about it. For instance, asking an employee to have sex in exchange for a promotion is *quid pro quo* harassment. Such behavior affects not only its target, but also coworkers whose advancement may be limited or blocked. Voluntary participation can still involve sexual harassment, as differences in power often make it difficult to say "no." Accordingly, the standard is whether a woman or man in the place of the target would feel pressured. Sometimes consensual relations are between students and faculty, raising difficult questions. Some institutions have policies forbidding such relationships or requiring that faculty involved not have influence over the student, even if simply through colleagues (Carlson, 2001). Academic freedom does not protect faculty when they exploit students for private advantage, as supported by the American Association of University Professors (AAUP) in a 1995 policy document (Euben, 2006b; Lee and Ziegler, 2003). Gould (1999) contends that academic freedom has the potential to wrongly become, when interpreted with inappropriate broadness, a defense in sexual harassment cases.

The second type of sexual harassment is hostile work environment, in which behavior has the purpose or effect of substantially interfering with the performance of work through creating an intimidating or offensive environment. Such behaviors can involve demeaning or offensive cartoons displayed in the workplace or crude or unseemly language in class; repeatedly stating that a person is not equipped to succeed in a certain position or discipline on the basis of his or her gender; and unwelcome comments on appearance, leering or ogling, or the habitual use of patronizing or demeaning terms.

Similarly, repeatedly asking a coworker on dates after expressed or implied refusal—but not necessarily a single or isolated event—is considered severe or pervasive enough to constitute sexual harassment. Unwanted or inappropriate attention directed toward a student from a faculty member involves a similar situation, complicated by it occurring within the context of a regular academic relationship. Physical intimidation can be both sexual harassment and violate criminal laws, such as assault.

In order to constitute sexual harassment, under either *quid pro quo* or hostile environment theories, the behavior must be sufficiently severe and pervasive to affect the terms and conditions of employment (Bernard, 2003)—simple teasing or offhand comments are unlikely to amount to actionable harassment (Cole, 2003). Favoritism toward a "paramour" based on sex can constitute a hostile environment when it has a meaningful impact on others across the organization (and can involve quid pro quo problems) (U.S. Equal Employment Opportunity Commission [EEOC], 1990).

Once again, the issue in sexual harassment cases is not whether the conduct is consensual or voluntary, but whether it is unwelcome, as the U.S. Supreme Court decided in *Meritor Savings Bank v. Vinson* (1986), applying Title VII to sexual harassment (U.S. EEOC, 1990). Even if a target appears to be in a consensual relationship, there may be unwanted conduct. In determining whether conduct is unwelcome, which can sometimes prove challenging, courts examine it from the perspective of a reasonable person in circumstances similar to those of the subject of the harassment. For example, a woman offended or intimidated by sexist conduct should not be deemed unreasonable according to prevailing male standards, but instead judged according to a reasonable woman in a similar position. Such a standard can overcome the perceptions within certain organizations that sexual harassment is a harmless amusement, and those who complain are overreacting and lacking a sense of humor.

Also, as noted in the Title VII section above, same-sex harassment is actionable, as the U.S. Supreme Court held in *Oncale v. Sundowner Offshore Services, Inc.* (1998), a hostile work environment case. Same-sex harassment can extend to "desire cases," in which one employee is the sexual target of another, as well as to "hatred cases" involving a harasser disdaining the victim (Connell and Euben, 2004). Sexual stereotyping is also covered under the U.S. Supreme Court decision in *Price Waterhouse v. Hopkins* (1989), in which a woman was discriminated against for being perceived as being too masculine. But only a few courts—and not the U.S. Supreme Court and the U.S. Congress—have expressly extended protection for discrimination on the basis of sexual orientation (Connell and Euben, 2004). Alternative theories include claiming intentional torts, such as intentional infliction of emotional distress—which is unlikely to be successful—or relying, as available, on state and local antidiscrimination laws that cover sexual orientation (Connell and Euben, 2004).

Investigating complaints of sexual harassment promptly tends to minimize legal exposure, as employers are liable for what they knew or should have known and failing to take quick and responsible corrective action. Responding promptly also demonstrates institutional commitment, building credibility and increasing morale (Cole,

Hustoles, and McClain, 2006). Universities and colleges tend to have specific sexual harassment policies, work to increase awareness of challenges in the area, and encourage administrators to enforce rules. Some institutions incorporate sexual harassment complaints into existing grievance procedures, with some having different policies for students and employees. Approaches usually provide for the informal resolution of complaints. When such means are not possible or not successful, policies include protections for all involved, ensuring due process and against retaliation, as well as confidentiality, as appropriate. Policies should be tailored to the institutional environment, detailing factors such as those subject, prohibited conduct, various procedures, offices involved, and possible discipline.

The person or committee investigating a complaint should be impartial, familiar with institutional policies and culture, and attentive to due process concerns. Issues relevant to an investigation might include: identifying the behavior and where it occurred; ascertaining the response of the subject, the presence of any witnesses, whether the conduct was part of a pattern, and what could have been done to stop the behavior; and determining how the situation could be resolved. The investigator should document each issue fully, working as quickly as possible to document and resolve allegations. When faculty members are involved, investigators need to respect academic norms and rights associated with tenure. But there is also the risk of whitewashing problems when influential people are accused. In short, policies are insufficient unless the institution enforces them. (Cole et al. (2006) offer a handbook on how to conduct a sexual harassment investigation.)

When harassment is by a coworker, he or she may be liable under a traditional negligence analysis (Bernard, 2003). In the most acute cases of sexual harassment, liability can attach not only to the person involved, but also to supervisors and institutions. Supervisors can be subject to liability personally when they fail to investigate a plausible complaint or allow a known condition to persist. (And there is the potential conflict, noted in Chapter 1, associated with counsel defending both the institution and one of its employees, as their interests may come to differ [Dellaverson, 2003].) Institutions can similarly be liable when they neglect to resolve or prevent a severe and pervasive problem about which they knew or should have known. Basic agency principles, also discussed in Chapter 1, may further apply, with the employer responsible for the on-the-job actions of its employees. Under the decision of the U.S. Supreme Court in *Burlington Industries v. Ellerth* (1998), employers can be held vicariously liable for sexual harassment by a supervisor or superior when the behavior culminates in a so-called tangible employment action, such as dismissal or demotion (Bernard, 2003; U.S. EEOC, 1999). Finally, as in *Faragher v. City of Boca Raton* (1998), decided by the U.S. Supreme Court, liability attaches when an employer fails to disseminate its policy.

An employer has an affirmative defense against liability under two circumstances (U.S. EEOC, 1999). The first is if it exercised reasonable care to prevent or correct the problem, as with properly developing and enforcing a sexual harassment policy.

Sufficient responses include having a policy with effective complaint processes and necessary protection against retaliation, as well as prompt, thorough, and impartial investigations and immediate and appropriate corrective action (Bernard, 2003). The second is if the employee unreasonably disregarded the opportunity that the employer presented to avoid sexual harassment (Bernard, 2003; Connell and Euben, 2004). Grossman (2000) is concerned that the affirmative defenses, as applied by lower courts, can negate the liability of institutions for prior acts, thus providing them with a "free first bite" at harassment, depriving those harassed of compensation.

Judicical remedies include compensatory damages, with punitive damages in egregious cases. There are also internal sanctions or remedies at institutions that vary with severity of the behavior, as with formal warnings, promises to desist from future improper behavior, and public and private apologies—and even reassignment, suspension, or dismissal. Dismissal, including for tenured faculty, is similar to extreme situations in other areas in which there is a serious criminal violation, especially one with a nexus to the employment relationship, such as embezzlement. But it is important to remember that in addition to the threat of sanctions, preventing sexual harassment is a product of developing awareness and sensitivity at a university or college.

Finally, retaliation against someone complaining of sexual harassment is strongly disfavored, with the standard, as articulated by the U.S. Supreme Court in *Burlington Northern and Santa Fe Railway Co. v. White* (2006), whether one suffered an adverse employment decision or treatment likely to dissuade a reasonable worker from making or supporting a discrimination charge.

President Baker, who is married with two grown children, knew immediately that she had made a serious error. She had clearly mistaken the signals that English department chair Jake Ryan was sending, being rebuffed when inviting him up to her hotel room while the two were on a fund raising trip in Cincinnati. When Sloane Peterson, the university attorney, informed Baker that Ryan had complained in accordance with the North Shore sexual harassment policy, she instructed Peterson to follow the standard process in resolving the matter. Baker had heard about the situation in the 1980s in which the senior administration "whitewashed" a rather serious allegation of *quid pro quo* sexual harassment, eventually resulting in a large settlement against the college and the dismissal of two of those involved. The process unfolded quickly and Baker formally apologized to Ryan, who accepted. She also agreed to undergo counseling and allowed a letter to be added to her personnel file detailing the situation.

In confronting her mistake directly, Baker was confident that the situation would not damage her position at North Shore or otherwise. The board of trustees, several of whom she has appointed, credit her with saving the college, and she continues to be successful as a fund raiser. The board recently increased her compensation significantly in response to Baker receiving so many "feelers" from other colleges, adding several financial incentives tied to her continuing as president, as with a $500,000 annuity payable after she serves 10 years. Given the secular nature of the college, she also did not have the pressures that might have accompanied infidelity by the president of a religious institution. It helped that Ryan soon left the college for a position at a more prestigious college—and Baker knew that her ability to raise money would easily overcome any concerns were she to pursue another presidency.

But when confronted with another allegation of sexual harassment, Baker responded differently. Those around the NSC campus had come to joke about the "girls club" that ran the university. The president, provost, and three of four vice presidents—as well as all three deans and one-half of the board of trustees—are women. The fourth vice president, Richard Vernon, regularly found himself to be the subject of teasing and brunt of jokes from the other senior administrators. For example, a cartoon that Vernon viewed as sexist (and even borderline pornographic) was included in a recent presentation to the senior administration by the vice president for enrollment management, Andie Walsh; the others habitually called Vernon suggestive (and, in his mind, demeaning) names and commented on his appearance (which was, even he would say, rather dumpy); and they quipped that a man would never "have what it takes" to really have influence at North Shore.

After learning about the resolution of the situation involving Ryan—and believing that Baker was neither adequately punished or sufficiently contrite—Vernon decided that he could no longer take what he viewed as the abuse of such a hostile environment to men. At the meeting he requested with Baker and Peterson, with his personal counsel present, they responded to his allegations by belittling him, suggesting at one point that he "be a man and stop whining." Baker (perhaps still sensitive about the Ryan matter) refused to even investigate the charges through the regular North Shore College sexual harassment process. With internal remedies thus foreclosed, Vernon filed suit.

When Baker and Peterson assumed that the action would be disposed of quickly upon their motion for summary judgment, they were proved mistaken. Peterson knew that the standard in sexual harassment is whether behavior was unwelcome from the perspective of a reasonable person in circumstances similar to those of the subject of the harassment. She assumed that no reasonable man would be offended by what she saw as harmless, even collegial, behavior. But the judge was convinced that the behavior appeared to be sufficiently severe and pervasive to affect the terms and conditions of Vernon's employment. He denied NSC's motion for summary judgment and moving the lawsuit into discovery.

(continued)

Now Baker is concerned. Not only might North Shore be liable for failing to prevent behavior they knew or should have known about, but she also may be personally liable as a supervisor for failing to investigate a plausible complaint or allowing a known condition to persist. She also wonders, rightly, whether her entrepreneurial abilities will outweigh the embarrassment the two sexual harassment matters may cause the college—and whether she will be damaged goods relative to other institutions, thus losing much of her leverage with the NSC board. She has retained her own attorney, as has Walsh and even Peterson.

Highly Selective Admissions at North Shore College—A Simulation

Assume that North Shore College has become (miraculously) one of the most highly selective colleges nationally, not only competing favorably with the Ivy League and leading smaller institutions such as Swarthmore, Williams, and Grinnell, but now the "hottest" institution in the country. North Shore conducts its admission process through three-person teams making recommendations to the dean of admissions, with a faculty committee providing broad oversight.

Please begin the simulation by forming as many three-person admissions review teams as necessary. Have another person or form another team that will observe their work, assuming the role of the college president—as well as, if applicable given enough participants, the vice president for institutional advancement and secretary of the college, and the director of athletics. Also form one more "mystery" team—or assign an individual to assume the function. Their role is discussed in the Appendix—and those on the other teams should not peek. Each admissions review team is to consider the 44 students on the spreadsheet, selecting 18 of them (and expecting that about one-half will ultimately attend the institution). A previous process has eliminated other applicants, so these are the finalists, so to speak.

The college is strongly supportive of diversity, with about one-third of its present classes comprised of students from underrepresented groups. The college admits students on a need-blind basis, meaning all receive needed financial aid. But because the college does not have an impressive endowment, full-pay students are valuable, as are those from families with giving potential. You do not have any access to direct financial information, however. The college is deeply interested in maintaining its national ranking, which values variables such as test scores and grade point average, and even geographic diversity is somewhat important. Please pay attention to the averages at the bottom of the spread-sheet, attempting to not go below them, which approximate the averages for recent years. Also, maintaining the present racial and ethnic diversity among enrolled students is essential. Finally, North Shore is a national power in Division III (nonscholarship) athletics, with coaches expecting that recruited athletes will be admitted, as reasonable.

The review teams should take 45 minutes to make their selections. The president-vice president-athletic director team should meanwhile generate a list of "must have" applicants, keeping their ultimate responsibilities within the institution squarely in mind. In past years, they have limited their list to around seven applications. The "mystery" person or team should observe the deliberation of the various teams, not interacting with them directly. At the end of 45 minutes, each team should list the 18 students it selects on a whiteboard, with a column for each group. The facilitator should then summarize, listing all of the applications that received votes from each group, all but one group, all but two groups, and so on. Time permitting, the teams can work to reach consensus on a single 18-person group of recommended admits.

It is then time for the president-vice president-athletic director group to weigh in. They are willing to listen to argument from the various admissions teams about not admitting one of their must-have applicants, but they tend to be a difficult group to convince. After the discussion about the must-haves, the mystery group will have something to say.

Appendix

Do Not Read This Unless You Are Within the Mystery Group

The mystery group is a conservative public interest group advocating for the elimination of affirmative action in admissions. The group is interested in identifying an applicant denied admission, but who would have a sympathetic case in bringing a so-called reverse discrimination lawsuit. You should begin your discussion with the admissions teams by asking the straightforward question: Were you able to accomplish your work in sorting the students without, in effect, putting underrepresented students in a separate pool, and thus violating *Bakke*? You should also ask, following that discussion, whether there is affirmative action, essentially, for rich white students? While you observe the admissions teams in action, see if you can uncover evidence of separate pools or preferences for wealthy students.

*   *   *

Following the simulation, a possible written assignment for those involved would be to identify a rejected applicant, creating a fuller background story for him or her. Assuming that the college is public and all of the applicants are from in state, suggest how the disappointed student might bring a discrimination lawsuit against the college. Reference the applicable standards and indicate whether or not the plaintiff or plaintiffs are likely to meet them—and thus the likelihood of their success in the litigation. Finally, reflect on the process of attempting to build a class in the simulation.

Table 2.1 Applicant Profiles

NAME	HIGH SCHOOL	CITY, STATE	GENDER	RACE	GPA	RANK/TOTAL	SAT-V	SAT-M	SAT	LEGACY	GIFT	NOTES
Adams, Jane Q.	Boston Fine Arts HS	Quincy, MA	F	African-Am	3.8	11/180	550	550	1100	N	N	gifted violin player; severely impoverished background
Adams, Joan	Quincy Prep	Braintree, MA	F	White	3.6	45/106	800	660	1460	Y	$1,500,000	third generation; standard extracurriculars
Arthur, Chester	The Dalton School	New York, NY	M	White	4.0	11/147	780	780	1560	Y	$200,000	standard extracurriculars; father is successful investment banker
Buchanan, James	Lancaster Suburban HS	Lancaster, PA	M	White	4.0	3/376	800	740	1540	N	N	strong extracurriculars; upper middle class background
Bush, George W.	Choate Acad. (MA)	Midland, TX	M	White	3.1	43/67	550	530	1080	Y	$500,000	son of vice president of the United States
Bush, Georgia	Stamford Country Day	Stamford, CT	F	White	4.0	3/123	800	800	1600	Y	$100,000	strong extracurriculars; daughter of prominent Broadway actor-director-producer; giving potential
Carter, Jimmy	Plains Consol. HS	Plains, GA	M	Hispanic	4.0	1/138	650	600	1250	N	N	strong extracurriculars; middle class family; Spanish-speaking household
Cleveland, Gloria	Buffalo Country Day	Buffalo, NY	F	White	3.8	20/229	800	740	1540	N	N	upper middle class background; solid extracurriculars
Clinton, Bill	Hot Springs HS	Hot Springs, AR	M	White	3.5	18/190	800	650	1450	N	N	published novelist; amazing extracurriculars; several national and international awards
Coolidge, Coleen	The American School, Cairo	Plymouth Notch, VT	F	White	3.8	13/80	800	740	1540	Y	N	strong extracurriculars; possible walk (non-recruited) on tennis player; mother is ambassador to Egypt
Eisenhower, Dwighthia	Abiline HS	Abiline, KS	F	White	4.0	1/120	740	740	1480	N	N	governor of Kansas Girls State; lower middle class background
Fillmore, Millard	Cayuga HS	Cayuga, NY	M	White	4.0	2/190	780	780	1560	N	N	father is administrator at Syracuse; close friend of university president

Name	High School	City, State	Sex	Race	GPA	Rank						Notes
Ford, Geraldine	East Grand Rapids HS	East Grand Rapids, MI	F	African-Am	3.9	11/400	600	680	1280	Y	$125,000	mother is CEO of Steelcase; deceased father is law graduate; no advance placement classes
Garfield, J'amiah	University Prep	Shaker Heights, OH	F	African-Am	4.0	2/150	700	600	1300	N	N	class president; tennis and track participant; mother is senior partner in leading law firm
Grant, Ulyssa	Galena HS	Galena, IL	F	Hispanic	4.0	1/175	550	800	1350	N	N	national president, Future Farmers of America; strong letter from senator; no indication of Hispanic background until application
Harding, Warren	Western Military Acad.	Marion, OH	M	White	2.8	29/60	510	540	1050	Y	$50,000,000	grandson of largest donor to university; discipline problems
Harrison, Benjamin	Indianapolis Univ. Prep	Fishers, IN	M	White	4.0	1/150	780	780	1560	Y	$10,000	parents are both MBA graduates; mother in upper management at Lilly Corporation
Harrison, William Henry	Marion Central HS	Indianapolis, IN	M	African-Am	4.0	1/550	650	600	1250	N	N	student body president; attending summer talent identification program; free and reduced lunch; raised by grandmother
Hayes, Rutherford	Oberlin Prep	Delaware, OH	M	White	4.0	2/101	800	800	1600	N	N	class president; tennis and track participant; routine personal statement
Hoover, Herbert	Atherton HS	Atherton, CA	M	White	4.0	5/350	740	720	1460	N	N	mother is CFO at Google; solid extracurriculars; significant giving potential
Jackson, Andrew	The University School	Nashville, TN	M	White	3.3	111/155	700	600	1300	N	$3,000,000	recent gift from parents; father is CEO of largest health insurer in US
Jefferson, Thomas	Charlottesville Regional HS	Charlottesville, VA	M	White	4.0	3/444	800	800	1600	Y	$500	child of professors, UVA
Johnson, Andrew	Greenville Christian	Greenville, TN	M	White	3.3	80/111	680	580	1260	N	N	recruited baseball player

Table 2.1 Continued

NAME	HIGH SCHOOL	CITY, STATE	GENDER	RACE	GPA	RANK/TOTAL	SAT-V	SAT-M	SAT	LEGACY	GIFT	NOTES
Johnson, Lyndon	Austin Country Day	Austin, TX	F	Native Am	4.0	3/110	800	600	1400	Y	$10,000	father heads human resources at Dell; mother is professor at UT-Austin
Kennedy, John	Boston Cath. Central	Brookline, MA	M	White	3.8	11/139	800	700	1500	N	N	strong extracurriculars; overcome severe learning disability
Lincoln, Abby	Springfield West HS	Springfield, IL	F	White	3.8	10/444	700	700	1400	N	N	extraordinary extracurriculars; founded charity with $10 million in donations last year
Madison, Janet	Charlottesville Regional HS	Charlottes- ville, VA	F	White	3.6	55/444	660	680	1340	Y	$10,000,000	heir to Dolly Madison snack food fortune; significant future giving potential
McKinley, Willamina	Niles High School	Niles, OH	F	Asian- Am	4.0	1/305	700	800	1500	N	N	solid extracurriculars
Monroe, James	Westmoreland Consol. HS	Westmore- land VA	M	White	3.3	44/150	570	450	1020	N	N	recruited All-State football player; Eno other activities; minor trouble with the law
Nixon, Richard	Whittier HS	Whittier, CA	M	White	4.0	1/267	800	800	1600	N	N	strong extracurriculars; second-team athlete
Obama, Barackia	The Punahou School	Honolulu, HI	F	African- Am	4.0	3/150	650	650	1300	N	N	daughter of president of the University of Hawaii
Pierce, Franklina	Phillips Exeter Academy	Hills- borough, NH	F	White	3.5	45/90	740	700	1440	N	N	child of world famous actor; significant future giving potential
Polk, James	Charlotte Country Day	Charlotte, NC	M	White	4.0	4/180	780	760	1540	N	N	state champion debater; home schooled until junior year

Name	High School	City, State	Sex	Race	GPA	Rank	SAT	SAT	SAT			Notes
Reagan, Rhonda	Eureka HS	Eureka, IL	F	White	3.9	10/388	650	650	1300	N	N	recruited swimmer; Olympic caliber athlete
Roosevelt, Frances	Hyde Park Prep	Hyde Park, NY	F	Asian-Am	4.0	1/333	800	800	1600	N	N	some extracurriculars; upper middle class background
Roosevelt, Theodore	Manhattan HS for the Arts	New York, NY	M	White	4.0	19/444	660	660	1320	Y	$50,000	accomplished actor, director, musician; mother is prominent designer, father vice-chair at Goldman Sachs
Taft, William	Cincinnati Jesuit HS	Cincinnati, OH	M	White	4.0	3/205	760	740	1500	N	N	state champion in discus; class vice president; letter from archbishop
Taylor, Zacheviah	Orange Co. Regional HS	Orangeville, VA	F	African-Am	3.8	10/150	680	540	1220	Y	$5,000	grandmother was first African American student at university; three siblings attended
Truman, Harry	Southeastern HS	Kansas City, MO	M	African-Am	4.0	1/567	600	650	1250	N	N	class president; severe physical disability
Tyler, Joelle	Charles County HS	Charles City, VA	F	African-Am	4.0	3/222	800	550	1350	Y	$1,000	possible walk-on (non-recruited) softball player; strong extracurriculars
Van Buren, Martina	Kinderhook County HS	Kinderhook, NY	F	Hispanic	3.8	3/101	550	700	1250	N	N	child of migrant farmers; five high schools in three years
Washington, George	Arlington Central HS	Arlington, VA	M	White	4.0	5/680	670	670	1340	N	N	strong extracurriculars; drama, debate
Wilson, Wendy	Princeton Wilson HS	Princeton, NJ	F	Asian-Am	4.0	3/300	800	800	1600	Y	$3,000	mother is Ph.D. graduate and prominent academic; adopted at age 8 from Viet Nam
					3.8		710	684	1427			

3
EMPLOYMENT

The relationship between institutions and those employed is increasingly one of contractors and consultants, who have fewer contractual rights than do regular employees, especially than those faculty members who, having earned tenure, can only be dismissed for cause. While entrepreneurial universities and colleges have attempted to reduce costs by shifting instruction to graduate assistants and adjunct faculty, the most prominent institutions are aggressive in recruiting and retaining faculty (and even administrators) thought to bring prestige or resources. The means to interpret employment contracts, such as custom and practice within institutions and across higher education, provide less guidance in practice or dispute resolution, being products of an earlier, less commercialized time. The same is true of judicial precedent, state statutes, and institutional provisions.

Collective bargaining defines some contractual relationships in higher education, especially at less selective institutions in certain regions of the country. Given its foundations in industrial settings, it may be more applicable in higher education as universities and colleges become commercialized. As faculty interests increasingly diverge, with some in comfortable permanent positions and a growing class of temporary, poorly paid labor, an interesting question emerges: is "the faculty" a sufficient community of interest to bargain together? In hiring, the issues also tend to relate to process, as with avoiding improper interview questions, conducting background checks only in appropriate areas, considering what is permissible under antidiscrimination statutes and affirmative action standards, and addressing transparency concerns in high profile searches.

There are also best practices in the evaluation and disciplining of employees, although increasingly those working for institutions as consultants and contractors are not subject to evaluation, at least formative efforts. Given the need for the expert judgment of peers in the inherently subjective and qualitative process of granting tenure and promotion, courts remain reluctant to upset seemingly reasonable decisions arrived at through appropriate processes. Measures in tenure and promotion decisions are so inaccessible to outsiders that traditional deference to academic decision making in the area remains appropriate, even at the most commercialized universities and colleges.

Academic freedom rights to pursue controversial work continue, but for the increasing number of faculty members in nontenured positions, the realistic ability to assert them may not be an option because it is questionable that a "troublemaker" on a one-year contract will have it renewed. Even tenured faculty can be dismissed if there is sufficient cause or in the event of financial exigency. Given the significant property interests (at public institutions) and contractual obligations (across institution types) involved, institutions can only fire tenured faculty in extreme circumstances.

Employment Contracts

The employment relationship between employees and institutions is grounded in contract law. The contract commonly consists of an appointment letter addressing basics such as classification and compensation. It may also refer expressly to duties and responsibilities, but such information may be in a separate document. Letters also incorporate various relevant institutional rules. These might include provisions included in an employee handbook, as with those addressing renewal and dismissal or codifying ethical standards, as with those proffered by the American Association of University Professors (AAUP, 2005b; Hirschfeld, 2008a). It is an open question whether a handbook must be expressly referenced in an employment letter or whether its inclusion is implied. Other tricky issues are handling changes in handbooks and related documents; whether an institution can disclaim certain documents as not contractually binding in certain circumstances; and the effect of handbooks from institutions merged into other universities or colleges (AAUP, 2005b; Franke, 2008a).

Different provisions in handbooks and other relevant documents apply to various types of employees, and institutions differ in the degree of detail they choose to include in various rules (Franke, 2008a). It is increasingly difficult to know to whom a rule actually applies. As entrepreneurial universities and colleges shift instruction to graduate assistants and those on temporary appointments, move academic programs away from the traditional institutional core and direct faculty influence to less structured and more managed peripheries, and otherwise outsource to the extent they can, they can be creative in framing relationships with contractors and consultants to minimize their responsiblities.

There are also regular issues of different institutional policies overlapping—and even conflicting—with one another, as well as sloppiness in drafting policies, creating rules that may be too broad or too narrow. Developing peripheral programs only complicates standardization across institutions, creating a hub-and-spoke structure that encourages each program to develop its own approaches. New rules often "grandparent" in those covered by older ones. An example is a reduced level of benefits applying only to new employees, but established employees working under the former rules. Much in the contemporary university is similarly bimodal, with established faculty and administrators enjoying security and benefits that far exceed that of less well positioned people. Finally, difficulties arise when rules exist without having an "owner"— some entity to regularly enforce them—or when they are applied in an inconsistent manner, the latter often occurring when there are not adequate standards in policies to guide those making decisions (Franke, 2008a). Again, entrepreneurial behavior that causes institutions to become more diffuse only exacerbates such problems.

At religious universities and colleges, there may be contract provisions requiring the adherence to a set of denominational or institutional values. At public universities and colleges, statutes and regulations applicable to state employees, as with legislation addressing due process, are embedded into contracts. But, once again, not every institutional provision and state rule applies to every employee. For instance, there are different standards for those who can only be dismissed for proper cause, as with tenured faculty, and for those employed at will and who thus can be relieved for any reason. Some rights embedded in contracts may apply to contractors, as with certain temporary faculty having the academic freedom rights included within institutional rules. Whether as a practical matter they have the latitude to realize and enforce them is another question. Outside consultants are unlikely to have any such contractual rights beyond being paid for services. The bottom line is clear: as increasingly entrepreneurial institutions seek agility, they are moving toward these contractors and consultants to whom the law affords limited protection.

On the other side of the coin, entrepreneurial universities and colleges increasingly have complex matters arise in negotiating individual contracts for their most highly paid employees, such as presidents, certain coaches, or star researchers. These include buyout provisions and noncompete agreements; performance bonuses and deferred salaries; and compensation drawn from outside sources such as university foundations, apparel companies, or media outlets (Callison and Varady, 2008; Robben, 2008; Vullo, Lewkowicz, and Rosenbaum, 2008).

There are bound to be matters that an appointment letter and the various other documents incorporated into a contract do not consider. In a breach of contract lawsuit, these gaps are filled by outside evidence suggestive of what the parties to the contract intended, such as unwritten statements made during the hiring process (AAUP, 2005a). Another means is through reference to custom and practice, which are the common understandings and usual approaches within an institution—or even across higher education. But these unwritten standards cannot contradict express contract terms. For instance, if institutional rules limit faculty members to one day of compensated outside consulting per month, but individuals commonly do more than that, the formal rule is determinative in the event of a dispute. But if there is no formal consulting policy at the institution, then what faculty members commonly do is instructive.

When actions involving the interpretation of employment contracts reach the courts, common law precedent is also relevant. The common law, discussed in Chapter 1, is the collection of previous decisions on matters similar to the one at issue—and that, ideally, guide a court. The challenge is that judicial precedent, like state statutes, institutional provisions, and custom and practice is likely to have evolved from when universities and colleges were much less commercialized. Higher education has hardly abandoned traditional values as emphases have evolved, but there is increasingly less guidance to faculty and administrators in both performing responsibilities and resolving disputes.

But some contractual principles are timeless. A contract can be changed or waived, as with the mutual consent of the parties to it. A contract can also be voided, as when entered into based on fraud; significant misrepresentation of risks, duties, or obligations undertaken; or when there is the violation of a provision prohibiting certain conduct. Illustrations include a faculty member later found to have misstated his or her credentials during the hiring process; a building contractor that is so undercapitalized as to be unable to perform, despite representations to the contrary in securing the relationship with the institution; or an employee violating an express rule against amorous relationships with students.

Additionally, various federal provisions that institutions must incorporate into their rules afford employees protection. The Family and Medical Leave Act (FMLA) of 1993 requires public universities and colleges and private ones with more than 50 employees to provide up to 12 weeks of unpaid leave for eligible employees during any 12-month period, as for the birth or adoption of a child; care of a spouse, child, or parent with a serious health condition; or the same involving the employee himself or herself. Employees are eligible having worked 1250 hours (about 25 hours per week on average) during the previous year. Accordingly, as institutions shift to more temporary, part-time faculty, questions related to eligibility become more complicated. The same is true of permanent faculty released from teaching commitments through grant funding (Fliegel and Curley, 2006). If the need for leave is foreseeable, 30 days of notice by the employee is required; institutions must maintain health benefits, provided employees continue to make mandated contributions; and employees are entitled to the same position or an equivalent one upon their return, with an exception for those in executive positions (Euben and Thornton, 2002; VanDeusen, 2008). There is a similar issue with returning military reservists (Erwin, 2007).

The Pregnancy Discrimination Act of 1978, which amends Title VII of the 1964 Civil Rights Act, also provides protections. A routine pregnancy is not covered under the Americans with Disabilities Act (ADA), explored in detail in Chapter 2, as well as in Chapter 4, as it relates to students, but complications may be so severe as to create impairments that fall under the act, with universities required to make reasonable accommodations (Thornton, 2006). FMLA, ADA, and workers' compensation can thus overlap in some situations (Bunting, 2008; VanDeusen, 2006). There are also protections for discrimination based on family responsibilities (Williams and Pinto, 2007). Finally, entrepreneurial institutions have available the same options as do more progressive corporations in using policies such as pregnancy leave, spousal and partner hiring, and child care to attract and retain high demand faculty and administrators.

Particularly under President Ron Burgundy, over the past five years, Coronado State University (CSU) has made impressive progress, transforming over the past three decades from a new two-year campus into a 27,000-student university offering bachelors degrees in 50 fields, a variety of masters degrees, new doctorates through its school of education and a D.Psych. in psychology. The university has been aggressive in seeking new markets, adding three satellite locations, and it is moving into distance education. It has also petitioned the state higher education system to begin a law school, as well as add several additional bachelors, masters, and doctoral programs.

CSU has remade its campus, building housing for 2,500 students, a state-of-the-art fitness center, and a student center—and it has recently entered into a partnership with a private developer to construct a commercial district with apartments and condominiums. There has also been the construction of several new academic buildings, notably an impressive facility for the rapidly growing business school and its executive education programs. The university has moved to Division I in athletics, launching a football program and building a stadium with the aspiration of competing at the top level. Finally, it also received permission to develop a brand identity to distinguish it further from the other 22 state university system institutions. Burgundy, who entered his second decade as president last year, has been clear about his vision of transforming CSU into an institution akin to a state flagship.

In adding the D.Psych., CSU is interested both in enhancing its prestige and taking advantage of the low-cost undergraduate instruction that graduate assistants can provide. Graduate assistants with teaching assignments receive tuition and stipends, as well as subsidized health insurance. As is common across the United States, they do not receive pensions or other employee benefits, since they are deemed to be students and not workers. As a new doctoral program at an institution that is still making a name, CSU is less selective in admissions, with its students tending to have few other offers. Amidst significant recent budget reductions, the university has not filled the positions of several retiring and departing faculty. It has turned to adjunct faculty members, who are generally available in Coronado, with some even driving down from an adjacent metropolitan area—and is relying more heavily on its graduate assistants, whether in day programs at the main campus or at the satellite sites.

Brique Tamland, one of these graduate students, is representative. Returning to school after 15 years in commercial real estate, she initially was the teaching assistant for various psychology faculty members, mostly grading papers and holding office hours. She is now teaching two courses of her own each semester, one of them a 200-person introductory course. Tamland is also seeing newer doctoral students in her program begin teaching large sections in their first semester.

(continued)

Her progress toward her degree has been slow. After three years, she is still at least a year away from taking her comprehensive examinations, has not presented or published any research, and has put off the internship required of all students. Tamland attributes her situation to having to withdraw from at least one course per semester due to her teaching obligations. It has not helped that standards in the department are often unclear, as some newer faculty members are applying norms from their elite Ph.D. programs, while some older ones have little experience with graduate education. She also has come to appreciate that the D.Psych., while technically an applied degree, is really just a Ph.D. with a different name—and she knows that the younger faculty, in particular, have been agitating to get the degree "upgraded" to a Ph.D. for students coming after her.

But Tamland counts herself as fortunate to be able to work with Professor Champ Kind, whom CSU recently attracted from a more prominent university with a lucrative package. Core to Burgundy's vision for CSU is to enhance funded research. Kind has sufficient grants to buy out of at least two of his courses each year and the endowment that comes with his professorship enables him to purchase the most recent technology and travel as he pleases. When he teaches, much of the daily responsibility rests with his teaching assistants, most of whom he finds to be quite capable, relating well to the students and current on theory and research in the discipline.

Tamland does not have guaranteed funding from year-to-year, but is confident that CSU will continue to retain her because she is so inexpensive and solid as a teacher. But she is feeling exploited and her morale is low. Like other universities, CSU deems Tamland to be a graduate student, who happens to teach as part of her professional apprenticeship. She is wondering if improving her situation—even if just to have enough time to complete her program—may require legal action, perhaps as a class action with other graduate assistants. Her annual appointment letter is not specific about the degree of her involvement in teaching, only referencing that she is to engage in up to 20 hours of work weekly in exchange for her tuition and stipend. Additionally, there are no express institutional policies on graduate student teaching. Having graduate assistants so involved in instruction emerged suddenly at CSU—and its policies have not caught up to various realities. The university did not promise Tamland a given teaching load when it admitted her and first granted her funding. But she did not contemplate the present situation and is convinced that neither did CSU.

Does Tamland have reasonable grounds for a lawsuit? She has spoken with the dean of arts and sciences, the psychology department chair, the graduate school ombudsperson, and Professor Kind. They have been sympathetic, but unwilling or unable to reduce her teaching assignment. She has thus met her obligation to exhaust administrative remedies before pursuing an action in court. Given that her annual offer letter and the various institutional policies that constitute her contract are essentially silent on the matter, she can draw on outside evidence suggestive of intent. For instance, if conversations during recruiting suggested a situation concentrated more on studies than teaching, Tamland can draw on these—with written materials, as on a program website, being even more persuasive. She can also reference custom and practice in graduate education, particularly the lesser teaching obligations for teaching assistants at more established universities.

Tamland would have to consider what she wants from legal action, which might be an injunction against CSU reducing her obligations—or even, although unlikely, damages associated with her slowed progress. The university will certainly mount an aggressive defense, arguing that teaching, even a heavy load, is essential to Tamland's preparation and that it is reasonable for a doctoral student to multitask, balancing courses, research, and an assistantship.

Collective Bargaining

Collective bargaining governs agreements with unionized employees. Contract agreements result from structured negotiations between management and accredited representatives of labor. They cover employment conditions, which include compensation, and are governed by the National Labor Relations Act (NLRA) of 1935 (also known as the Wagner Act) at private institutions. Various state labor relations or public employee relations acts cover other situations (Sun and Parmuth, 2007). Negotiations are bilateral and adversarial in nature, but require some degree of openness and cooperation to be successful. More collegial attributes have traditionally characterized higher education, as with the practice of shared governance involving faculty. But there have always been disputes between faculty and administrators, some quite heated and protracted, similar to other industries.

With universities and colleges becoming more managed and shifting more toward contingent faculty appointment, collective bargaining may provide a more fitting framework, especially for those employees without the leverage of star faculty. For instance, contingent faculty, while being professionals, may be more akin to the factory workers for whom collective bargaining developed. Collective bargaining is most developed among employees with the least influence, as with clerical and trade workers, as well as faculty members at community colleges and comprehensive institutions. It is also much more common in areas of the country in which union activity is more pronounced.

Collective bargaining begins with the identification of a bargaining unit, defined a "community of interest" of people with similar situations and concerns. These people can petition the National Labor Relations Board (NLRB) or other relevant agency for a certification election, or can be recognized by a university or college voluntarily (Gaal, Kaplan, and Murphy, 2008). Gaal et al. (2008) caution against threats toward, interrogation of, promises to, and surveillance involving those involved in organizing. Once certified, the union negotiates exclusively for those in the bargaining unit. When collective bargaining applies to private institutions, the NLRA and the Labor–Management Relations Act of 1947 (also know as the Taft-Hartley Act) both govern it. Religious colleges and universities are subject when activities have become "secularized," but not when there is a risk of entanglement with purely religious activities (Gaal et al., 2008). Public institutions are subject to state labor law—and federal anti-discrimination laws apply across institutional contexts.

Managers within an organization do not have the right to organize. Courts have usually not viewed faculty as managers, although the 1980 decision in *NLRB v. Yeshiva University* makes an exception for small private college faculty so significantly involved in administration such that their interests coincided with those of management (Gaal et al., 2008). In a 2004 ruling involving Brown University, the NLRB deemed graduate student instructors to be students, not employees (reversing a 2000 ruling), and thus not eligible to bargain collectively. But there are public institutions, including those in the University of California and California State University systems, that recognize graduate instructor unions. And there are likely no legal barriers to adjunct faculty organizing (Gaal et al., 2008), although there may be practical ones, as they are commonly on semester-to-semester contracts and can often be readily replaced.

The AAUP is supportive of unions and is involved in organizing, grounding the need for doing so in the increasing corporatization of the university (AAUP, 1993; AAUP, 2006a). Perhaps the most interesting question is whether there really is a community of interest as faculties continue to bifurcate, such as at research universities, with an ever smaller group of "haves" making six-figure salaries and an increasing collection of "have-nots" operating at a level closer to subsistence in temporary positions. At institutions with collective bargaining, there are typically multiple unions, each representing a different class of employees, such as clerical workers and maintenance workers. At entrepreneurial universities and colleges, are all faculty members still a single group?

Once established, collective bargaining involves negotiation toward an agreement, or if one proves impossible, declaring an impasse between the parties. An agreement includes provisions indicating the rights of both management and employees, as well as addressing matters such as tenure and contractors, furloughs and layoffs, grievance and arbitration (Hustoles and DiGiovanni, 2005). Faculty union contracts are also likely to address matters such as academic freedom and program reduction and closure (Hustoles, 2006c; Santoro, 2006). Tactics used by labor to resolve an impasse include calling a strike or filing an unfair labor practices claim with the NLRB, with management able to impose a lockout or present to labor what is termed its "last, best offer."

Mediation or arbitration also provides options. Hustoles and DiGiovanni (2005) suggest what they term an interest-based approach to collective bargaining, with the sides engaged in more preliminary work, frank discussions, joint communication, and preventive strategies.

Finally, alternative dispute resolution is available in any contractual relationship, and is common in collective agreements. Voluntary arbitration, a common form of alternative dispute resolution embedded into contracts, involves automatically referring disputes to an impartial individual or panel selected by the parties to hear arguments and evidence and render a binding decision, thus moving the case outside of the judicial system (DiNardo, Sherrill, and Palmer, 2001).

Brian Fontana has worked for the past 30 years as a technical writer. For the past five years he has taught at least one course per semester—and sometimes as many as three—at Coronado State University, supplementing his income and enjoying the opportunity to work with so many interesting students. He mostly teaches at the CSU satellite campus in Del Mar, where the university has come to offer most of its courses in communications, now both at the bachelors and masters level. CSU has turned more to adjuncts in response to attrition in tenure-significant faculty and the need to reduce its instructional budget to fund increases in various nondiscretionary spending, such as health benefits. CSU is funding most of the construction projects that it is undertaking through private means, such as donations and bonds. But there is the perception on campus that the institution is investing in facilities, as well as graduate education and prominent faculty, while impoverishing its core academic programs.

Fontana is active in his program, working with both the professional managers assigned to market and operate it, as well as the core faculty members primarily responsible for curricular matters. He has noticed that he is taking on more administrative work over time, serving as a de facto academic advisor—and has even discussed with the head of the Del Mar campus the prospect of working with the program full-time as its coordinator. But Fontana is concerned about both compensation and security issues in doing so, especially given his union membership in his "day job." He dislikes the direction that CSU is headed, with what he sees as a "revolving door" of adjuncts, many of whom are retained and assigned just a few days before the beginning of classes each semester.

Although it has been difficult to secure contact information for the other adjuncts at CSU, Fontana has begun to reach out to them, primarily through a blog he launched to explore the notion of establishing a union for CSU contingent faculty. He has connected with the NLRB to see what doing so would entail, but has not taken formal action, such as steps toward an election to certify a union. Fontana believes that there is an appropriate community of

(continued)

interest among adjunct faculty, whether those teaching an occasional class, a class or two each semester in addition to their regular job, or those on full-time nonregular appointments. He also knows what he wants—and what he thinks his fellow adjuncts desire—from a collective agreement, such as enhanced compensation and security and having processes available when there are disputes.

Like the other adjuncts at CSU, Fontana has worked on what is likely to be deemed a semester-to-semester contract, with his appointment dependent upon such matters as the classes he is assigned having enough students. (Many full-time adjuncts at CSU have year-to-year contracts that are not dependent upon courses "making.") When Ed Harkin, the manager of the Del Mar programs, heard of Fontana's blog, he consulted with the dean of arts and sciences, Veronica Corningstone, in which the communications programs are located, resulting in the two deciding not to continue to employ Fontana after he concluded his current courses. They informed him two weeks before the end of the semester, which was when Fontina and Harkin normally arranged his teaching for the coming semester.

Fontana was devastated—and angry. He knew that he had no real recourse against not being renewed, as his contract (such as it was) covered only the past semester. He wondered if he had moved along sufficiently with the NLRB to have a claim that Harkin and Corningstone acted in retaliation for his activities toward organizing the faculty. In meeting with Fontana and the attorney he retained, Harkin and university counsel, overdoing it, argued that even had Fontana reached the threshold for NLRB protection, there was no community of interest among the adjuncts, given their diverse roles, such that there could be collective bargaining. Also, they contended Fontana was more a manager than an instructor and thus could not be part of a union, in a tortured reading of the *Yeshiva* decision. Fontana is convinced, however, that CSU has failed to recognize just how much it has come to rely upon adjunct faculty—and that would provide a compelling argument before the NLRB in response to CSU's contentions.

Hiring

Hochel and Wilson (2007) suggest the frustration and resentment that can result from making a poor hire in higher education, with costs in reputation and efficiency. As do others who write on the topic, they outline steps to follow in conducting the hiring process, beginning with forming the search committee, carefully defining the position and process for applicants to follow, and recruiting a diverse pool of candidates. They also discuss evaluating candidate files, identifying "short list" finalists, managing campus interviews, negotiating a contract, and welcoming the new hire to the institution (Marchese and Lawrence, 2006; Vicker and Royer, 2006).

A primary issue in hiring is what types of questions during interviews are nondiscriminatory and thus permissible. The basic rule is that questions are acceptable when related to whether an applicant meets the reasonable requirements of a position. Those seeking to identify information that could prompt discrimination are not (Hockel and Wilson, 2007; Marchese and Lawrence, 2006; Vicker and Royer, 2006). For instance, a prospective employer may ask an applicant whether he or she has commitments that may impede attending meetings, but cannot ask about specific arrangements for child care or whether the applicant is planning to have children. Questions about marital status and number and ages of children, while similarly seemingly benign, are ultimately improper. In the same way, prospective employers may ask if a candidate is prevented from lawfully becoming employed because of immigration status or about his or her fluency in English, but direct questions related to national origin or native language are forbidden. (Chapter 5 considers immigration in greater detail.) The rare exception to the general rule is when a certain status in an area such as citizenship or religion is a *bona fide* occupational qualification (BFOQ)—a necessity of the job. For example, a particular denominational affiliation may be relevant in certain positions at certain types of religious colleges or universities (see the discussion of Title VII in Chapter 2), or an employee may require clearance to work on a project involving the Department of Defense.

Various types of screening related to drug use, financial information, workers' compensation claims, military discharge, and criminal background are permissible. But those hiring need to exercise due care in complying with restrictions under federal and state laws (Finkin, 2008; Mathieu, 2008; Kaplin and Lee, 2006; Lee, 2006). Lee (2006) notes that screening is prompted by concerns about fraudulent credentials, as with degrees from diploma mills or misrepresenting credentials on resumes, and failing to disclose relevant criminal convictions. The AAUP recommends a proportionality principle, compromising the privacy of a candidate only as necessary to secure information that applicants are qualified to meet the particular obligations of specific positions (Finkin, 2008). An example would be appointments involving access to classified data that merit more extensive background checks. In extreme situations, there can be institutional liability for negligent hiring—the failure to discover relevant information connected to later harm caused by an employee (Lee, 2006). Finally, lawsuits by dismissed employees following discovery of their fraudulent credentials or failure to disclose are unlikely to be successful (Lee, 2006).

But even if an applicant believes a prospective employer has asked an improper interview question, he or she may be more interested in securing the position than asserting his or her rights, especially when openings are few. For those interested in mounting challenges, possibilities include filing a complaint with the U.S. Equal Employment Opportunity Commission (EEOC) or applicable state agency, bringing a lawsuit as an individual against the prospective employer, or joining a class action with other similarly aggrieved plaintiffs. A plaintiff must establish specific discrimination, which can prove difficult, in order to secure monetary damages or relief enjoining future wrongdoing. In the end, hiring processes marked by thoroughness, consistency, and transparency are less likely to be perceived as unfair and later deemed as such in a legal action.

Various antidiscrimination laws, discussed in Chapter 2, are applicable to hiring. These include federal legislation incorporating the logic of equal protection, as well as related state, local, and institutional rules. For instance, the Americans with Disabilities Act prohibits interview questions directed at the nature and severity of any physical or mental disability. There are also equal pay practices statutes (Doyle, 2005; Monopoli, 2008) and fair labor standards acts, as well as significant regulation of employee benefits. But such rules are applicable to ever fewer employees at universities and colleges, as positions shift away from full-time status, in which rules about overtime would apply or health and retirement benefits would accrue. Even when they do apply, there remain significant disparities in higher education between compensation for men and women doing the same work (Monopoli, 2008). At the local level, there is increasing protection against discrimination on the basis of sexual orientation or transgendered status (Keaney, 2007), as well as the extension of benefits to domestic partners, but there is no federal protection in these areas, as under Title VII.

Affirmative action, discussed more fully in Chapter 2, is also relevant in hiring, especially in searches for senior level positions. It requires efforts to identify talent among underrepresented groups, but stops short of only considering these candidates (Hochel and Wilson, 2007). In other words, everyone must compete against the entire pool, with race merely a "plus factor." Public institutions must have compelling reasons for implementing affirmative action programs, as with past discrimination accounting for present underrepresentation of certain groups, and policies must be as narrowly constructed as possible to accomplish intended ends (Alger, 2008).

In the *Grutter v. Bollinger* (2003) decision upholding affirmative action in selective admissions, the U.S. Supreme Court was influenced by amicus briefs from corporations underscoring the need for diversity in their workforces—and thus in higher education. Bulman-Pozen (2006) contends that the case is likely to migrate into employment law, particularly as applied in higher education to faculty and even senior administrators (Alger, 2008). There are also strategic reasons for implementing affirmative action. For example, an exclusively white senior administration, or predominantly male senior faculty, is no longer a viable option for an ambitious university or college. Accordingly, institutions are increasingly aggressive in their efforts to attract underrepresented groups, as Alger (2008) suggests in laying out several recruitment strategies, such as visiting professorships, target of opportunity hires, and pipeline programs (AAUP, 1983).

Finally, there are particular issues in searches for presidents at public institutions. There is a need to balance the chilling effect that disclosure may have on attracting the most desirable candidates into an applicant pool with the right of the media to report and the public to know the direction of taxpayer-supported institutions (Estes, 2000). Recognizing the challenge, state open records statutes typically have an exemption for candidates for employment, with universities and colleges generally releasing only the names of finalists scheduled to visit campus. (Florida, prominently, requires the release of all candidates' names, under its broad "sunshine" laws.) Courts have sometimes been less accommodating to confidentiality concerns than legislatures, opting for more openness, according to Estes (2000). In athletics, there is commonly significant interest in the search for a coach in football or men's basketball. Those leading searches, increasingly simply the athletic director and president, tend to act sufficiently rapidly so as to avoid open records requests. As in searches, athletics tends to have its own standards in employment issues, as with the common practice of having relatives serve as assistant coaches.

The athletics program at Coronado State University, recently having moved to Division I, had been uninspiring until this past year, when the men's basketball team won its conference tournament and earned an National College Athletic Association (NCAA) tournament slot. The Panthers, drawing a 15 seed, took the heavily favored Apatow State team, seeded second in the East region, to overtime before losing by six points.

In addition to capital expenses associated with constructing facilities, CSU has invested $5 million per year in its athletics program, recouping only a small fraction of that through ticket sales and corporate partnerships connected with men's basketball. As such, it is similar to most programs outside of the prominent conferences in Division I. Burgundy has aspirations to move CSU into one of these leagues, but realizes that doing so is many years—and many basketball wins—away. He argues that it is impossible to put a price tag on the publicity the institution generates through basketball—and the legitimacy it provides in making CSU more like a state flagship. In these ways, it is like the doctoral programs the university is launching.

Following the tournament, Kurtis University, a regional power, announced that it had hired CSU coach Frank Vitchard. Vitchard informed the CSU athletic director, Garth Holladay, the day before the press conference at Kurtis was to be held to introduce him. Even had there been time to prepare a counteroffer, Burgundy knew that it was unlikely that he could have kept Vitchard. Each year, the provost and deans faced a similar situation as more prominent universities raided their most promising and accomplished faculty. Burgundy and Holladay had known that Vitchard would attract interest and had prepared a list of possible successors. Within two days, they had arranged to hire Tino Armisen, who had led nearby Baxter University to a Division II national championship two years ago. The Armisen hire was well received in the media and by the relatively few (but perhaps increasing, with the tournament appearance) CSU alumni and others interested in the program.

(*continued*)

Burgundy and Holladay formed, in essence, a two-person search committee, advised by a search consultant specializing in men's basketball coaches, bypassing seemingly every CSU policy and process. For instance, CSU has explicit rules related to affirmative action in searches that align with the state university system and other applicable requirements. Burgundy chose to ask, if necessary, for "forgiveness, not permission"—something that had become a catch phrase for him—sensing that he needed to move fast in the hypercompetitive market for top coaches that only functions for a few weeks following the tournament each year. A careful and inclusive process, he reasoned, works well for a faculty search, but is impractical in hiring a Division I men's basketball coach.

Burgundy is also willing to argue, if needed, that the athletic association, like the foundations CSU has established for holding its endowments, making real estate investments, and facilitating funded research, is not subject to all state rules. Each area requires a foundation, as the institution must contend with realities that do not fit within the regulatory framework the state provides. In other words, universities operate in manners and contexts different from the state agencies, like corrections or public health, in reference to which the state develops rules. Successfully competing in Division I men's basketball, Burgundy contends, supported by practices at universities across the country, demands some agility, operating less like a bureaucracy and more like a business.

Burgundy is also not particularly concerned about the objection of faculty or others to the process—or that CSU is paying the coach more than any other employee on campus, including Burgundy himself. (He is comforted by the fact that the state flagship is paying its football coach four times what the president makes—and it had an 8-5 season last year.) Faculty have griped about spending on athletics, contending that the $2 million in student fees and $2.5 million direct transfer from the institution each year could be applied toward instruction. But they have not been willing to attempt to do something about it. Faculty governance at CSU is underdeveloped, and those representing the faculty in athletics tend to be supporters of the program and senior administration.

All but a few faculty members even noticed another example of the different rules applied in the context of athletics, as Armisen, the new coach, hired his son, Katow, as an assistant coach (again, with no real process). Katow will formally report to an associate athletic director, but clearly works for his father. Such arrangements are common within intercollegiate athletics, although unheard of elsewhere in the university. Professor Kind quipped that he was going to propose hiring his brother, Todd, to fill the open position in the psychology department.

Burgundy is also aware that in three years or so, he would be likely to be undergoing the same process again. Armisen would either win big and be recruited by a larger program or would not win and have to be replaced. Burgundy did not feel as though he had a choice but to compete in Division I, given his aspirations for the institution—and rather enjoyed aspects of overseeing a sports program. He worried that Armisen, who had only a limited sense of academic norms and values, would not be able to avoid a scandal. Burgundy agreed to provide him with the ability to recruit athletes of questionable academic abilities, so as to be able to compete successfully—and knew that there might be problems with behavior or complying with NCAA recruiting and academic performance rules.

Evaluation and Discipline

Performance evaluations are both formative and summative, suggesting areas of improvement, as well as establishing a record. That record is the basis of positive personnel actions, such as promotion—and negative ones, as with discipline or termination. Evaluations should be as objective and specific as is possible, involving only criteria relevant to a given position and always be applied consistently. Neither the criteria used nor their application should discriminate, with the evaluation concentrating only on the responsibilities of a given position and avoiding unrelated factors such as lifestyle or religion. But apart from considering responsibilities, employers may establish standards for dress and grooming, provided they apply them uniformly and the rules do not have a disproportionate impact on members of classes protected under the antidiscrimination laws.

Evaluation criteria should also incorporate the entire position, as with evaluating service along with research and teaching for research university faculty. Evaluations should also consider both present performance and past achievements—and be grounded in the traditions and realities of higher education overall, as well as those specific to a given institution type. The latter requires institutions to have the clarity of purpose that is increasingly compromised as universities and colleges obsess over "getting to the next level" in prestige. For instance, some institutions encourage faculty to engage more in activities such as research, even when the conditions to be successful are not established. There is also the challenge at research universities, in particular, of different faculty tending to have negotiated different arrangements, as with compensation, teaching load, research support, and travel budgets. Applying standard evaluation criteria to employees differently situated—or even uniquely so—can prove difficult and perhaps unrealistic.

Given their nature and purposes, it is best to write evaluations by following a standard format that indicates strengths and weaknesses, and include express recommendations for improvement. Additionally, evaluations should respect privacy concerns and include the opportunity for the employee to respond and even appeal, if necessary. (As noted in Chapter 1, courts will not consider matters until a plaintiff has exhausted reasonable internal administrative remedies.) Evaluation of tenured faculty, if applicable, is formative (providing suggestions for improvement) not summative (determining success or failure), absent a system for posttenure review (Cameron, Olswang, and Kamai, 2006). Even with posttenure review, a for-cause dismissal of a tenured faculty member requires an extreme situation that could not be remedied through extended formative means (Olswang, 2006). In anticipation of entering the tenure and promotion process, evaluation can be both formative and summative, as with the third-year reviews that gauge readiness and suggest needed remedial action.

Institutions can discipline employees, potentially leading to dismissal, as a result of negative evaluations or situations that arise between evaluation cycles. The standard approach is progressive discipline, in which supervisors attempt to remedy problems beginning with more modest steps, such as a warning, before moving into more formal and complex actions. For instance, in addressing the problem of an employee being habitually tardy, the supervisor may begin with a conversation, documenting it. If the behavior continues, a formal warning letter may put the employee on notice that he or she will be dismissed if the difficulty is not resolved within a certain period of time.

Situations involving employees with psychiatric disabilities, which may include an accommodation pursuant to the ADA, may require additional effort, as with a supervisor involving a specialist from human resources, especially when there is the suggestion of a safety threat (Barnett, 2008; Parrot, 2006). Domestic violence, when it enters the workplace (Porter, 2006), and workplace bullying are similar issues (Simon and Simon, 2006). Finally, when applicable, there are federal statutes that protect whistleblowers in the event of employer retaliation (Ecker, Gagliardo, and Becker, 2008; Franke, 2008b).

Short of meriting termination for serious misconduct, such as plagiarism, falsification of credentials, or sexual harassment, disciplining faculty, especially those with tenure, raises particular issues (Euben and Lee, 2006). For instance, continued inattentiveness to teaching, even after identifying problems and attempting to correct them, may require some discipline to "get the attention" of a faculty member (Franke, 2006). There are due process concerns, both constitutional, at public institutions, and contractual ones. Euben and Lee (2006) note that simply defining faculty misconduct can be challenging, but there are ethical standards within the profession, as well as behavioral norms, including those collected into codes of conduct developed by the AAUP, various disciplinary associations, and institutions (Hamilton, 2001). As in other areas, institutions are likely to withstand legal challenges when they apply reasonable rules fairly.

But the same progressive discipline that institutions tend to apply to all employees also applies to faculty, as adapted to the peculiarities of the position. Once again, progressive discipline involves penalties increasing in severity: a verbal warning, followed by a written one, then a suspension, and culminating in censure or reassignment to another unit. Faculty may be removed from certain teaching or program responsibilities or be directed to mandatory counseling—and there may be denial of salary increases, reductions in compensation, or demotion in rank (Franke, 2006).

Conflicts of interest involving faculty are a particular concern associated with discipline (discussed further in Chapter 5). With more faculty at entrepreneurial universities and colleges engaging in "outside" business ventures and other activities, possibilities for conflicts increase (Harrington, 2001). An illustration is a researcher having a financial interest in a corporation sponsoring his or her research—and perhaps even engaging in behavior that compromises research subjects, as in a clinical setting, in the interest of protecting a financial investment. Partnerships between and among faculty, institutions, and industry to commercialize research have become more prominent, particularly following the 1980 Bayh-Dole Act. The Act enables researchers, universities and colleges, and others to secure intellectual property rights that arise from federally funded research. Upon making a significant discovery, funded by federal money and while on "university time," faculty launch a "startup" company to commercialize it, with the institution taking an equity interest. How much time faculty members allocate to the new company—and thus away from their university duties—or the degree to which they involve graduate students can raise conflicts.

Harrington (2001) argues that commercializing research has the potential to skew the research agendas of faculty—and shift entire units or even institutions away from pure research and toward applied efforts. It not only creates situations in which objectivity can be compromised or the commitment of a faculty member to his or her university questioned, but also raises questions as basic as what norms apply to matters such as disseminating knowledge. For instance, approaches in academe can differ from corporate standards that are less inclined toward a broad release of findings (Harrington, 2001). Recognizing these concerns, universities and colleges have developed more robust conflict of interest policies, and the federal agencies such as the National Science Foundation (NSF) and National Institutes of Health (NIH), as well as disciplinary associations, have offered guidelines. The AAUP has also weighed in (AAUP, 1990). Disclosure, approvals, and review are potential tools in managing conflicts and avoiding the need for discipline—and these must align with applicable federal and state statutes. There are also more traditional conflicts of interest in areas such as those involving personal relationships and bringing personal political or religious activities onto campus (Harrington, 2001).

Federal courts are increasingly favoring employers that implement effective compliance programs, not only in research integrity, but also in areas such as sexual harassment and employment discrimination (Vinik, Babbitt, and Friebus, 2006). These programs include comprehensive policies and effective training, as well as appropriate procedures for registering, investigating, and appealing complaints. They can provide an employer with an affirmative defense to liability and elimination of punitive damages if something goes wrong, as well as minimizing the risk of individual liability attaching to negligent managers. But it is important to remember that investigations must be conducted in a competent manner, with care exercised in deciding whether to investigate, who should do so, and what the process should entail (Heller, 2008; Hirschfeld, 2008b).

There are also restrictions under federal law on the electronic and other surveillance of employees, as under the Electronic Communications Privacy Act of 1986. Some monitoring is likely permissible, as with office e-mail, but employees have reasonable expectations of privacy related to certain activities, particularly where there is not sufficient notice (Ambash and Avila, 2008; Green, 2005). Personal online activities, such as blogging, conducted during work hours can be cause for discipline, but the lines between personal and professional computer use are not always clear (AAUP, 2005a; Sprague, 2007). But public institution employees have free expression rights as citizens, although these are more limited for on-the-job speech that is contrary to the interests of universities and colleges, as discussed in the academic freedom section below (Niehoff, 2008). Additionally, institutional rules regulating activities such as consulting and other work outside of the university are permissible (Olswang, 2006).

As with due process, considered in Chapter 1, universities and colleges that develop reasonable standards and thorough processes in evaluation, discipline, and dismissal—and apply these in neither an arbitrary nor capricious manner—are unlikely to run into legal difficulties. But a question is how many employees are actually subject to formal evaluation as universities and colleges turn increasingly to contractors and consultants. It may be that their performance is assessed by whether they are renewed for another contract, but there is little of a formative nature involved in doing so.

Little in her training as a sociologist prepared Veronica Corningstone, the arts and sciences dean, for the personnel matters that seem to be consuming ever more of her time. When Burgundy recruited her from a Big Ten university, it was to realign the college to advance his vision of building Coronado State into a research university. Over the past five years, at least until the recent budget cuts effectively stalled faculty hiring, she has been fortunate in being able to replace one-quarter of her regular faculty, mostly with new assistant professors, but also with senior hires, such as Champ Kind in psychology. Several of the assistant professors have used CSU as a steppingstone, but others have stayed—and there is no shortage of replacements, given the tight faculty job market across arts and sciences disciplines. The newer faculty members, along with many longer serving faculty, are invested in establishing CSU as a research university. Corningstone has also been able to appoint supportive department chairs.

But there are several other faculty members who are resistant to the changes at CSU. They have built careers as teachers and resent being made to feel like, as one put it, "second class citizens" at an institution they consider themselves to have built. Arturo Mendez, a professor in sociology, is representative. He arrived at CSU when it was becoming a four-year institution, regularly teaching a four- or five-course load per semester load. He reads in his area, but has not been active as a scholar. He has seen his salary stagnate, with several younger faculty members moving ahead of him in compensation and teaching as few as two courses per semester. (Teaching load continues to be an issue at CSU, with a formal 3-3 load, with faculty involved in research assigned, in practice, a 2-2 one.) In response, he has grown disinterested in his work, failing to prepare interesting courses, being indifferent in his advising, and no longer providing comments to students on their papers.

His state-mandated posttenure review was not positive, with the review committee recommending that he participate in a faculty development program established at CSU to reinvigorate teaching and encourage scholarship. Mendez began the program, but soon became discouraged—remaking himself so late in his career was daunting (although some who took part found that the program reenergized them). He understands that his continued lack of progress may lead to his dismissal. But he also knows that simply gathering the needed documentation to dismiss a tenured professor for what amounts to indifference, as opposed to some sort of malfeasance, is a drawn out process. Even if he is dismissed, Mendez believes that he would have a strong case against CSU in arguing that indifferent teaching does not reach the level of misbehavior needed for a for-cause dismissal. He also trusts there will be a new dean at some point in the not-so-distant future—and that he or she may not be as aggressive as the current one.

Corningstone thought that posttenure review, which her predecessors did not emphasize, would provide a tool for moving her most nonproductive faculty along, but has found it to be of limited utility, given its complicated process and glacial pace. There is also the issue of productive teachers who are not active scholars (nor likely to be so), which she has yet to really tackle, recognizing that her only realistic option may be to work around them until they retire. At least with the increasing number of non-tenure-significant faculty—lecturers on one-year appointments and adjuncts hired on a semester-to-semester basis—she has some latitude to not renew those who are not advancing the cause.

The challenge with nonfaculty staff is different. Although they are at-will employees, able to be terminated without cause as a technical matter, there is the perception among them—and their supervisors—that they have what amounts

(*continued*)

to more permanent status. Few are ever dismissed, even during their six-month probationary period. The human resources office encourages progressive discipline for those identified for dismissal, recognizing its advantages in avoiding discriminatory behavior by managers. They are supportive of dismissing nonproductive or otherwise problematic employees, but want to follow a process that can sometimes take several months. There is also the perception among midlevel managers, supported by examples over the years, that even when they take necessary steps, senior administrators will not support them actually dismissing someone.

Accordingly, there has been no "right sizing" at CSU, as it would be called in the corporate world. In the sociology department, for instance, there is an abundance of secretaries, a legacy of the pre-desktop computer days, but too few administrative staff to assist with more substantive matters, such as managing budgets for research grants. Few support staff fear dismissal. Faculty and managers have come to tolerate a lack of productivity, believing that there is something akin to tenure for even the lowest level employees. Those who spend much of their workday on Facebook, talking with relatives on their mobile telephones, or even working on a side business, tend to do so with impunity. The right to dismiss at-will employees simply does not translate into the practice of doing so.

There is also an "old boys" problem at CSU. Administrators are on a defined benefits plan that during retirement pays out a percentage of the average of the last three years of salary. Accordingly, there is a longstanding practice at CSU of appointing those about to retire to a senior—and well-compensated—position. Burgundy and Corningstone would like to end the practice, but are concerned that the "old boys" have connections to important alumni and various trustees. As with the less productive senior faculty, they are also concerned about having the "old boys" delay or even sabotage various initiatives. Corningstone has attempted progressive discipline with a few particularly underperforming midlevel administrators in her college, but with limited success. Even those who believe there will be consequences simply adapt their behavior just enough to avoid real sanctions. Although she has the formal means to move people along, the culture of the institution continues to be at odds with doing so.

Finally, the senior faculty members, like Kind, that CSU has recruited to improve its research profile pose another set of challenges. She has little leverage with him, although he spends more time with his startup evaluation and testing firm than on his university work, mixing his research with his business—and thus involving his doctoral students in the latter. Given the funding he has attracted and promised to continue generating, he can always leave the university.

Granting Tenure

In granting tenure, institutions afford faculty members employment, as a contractual right, for an indefinite term, with dismissal only for cause (as discussed in a section below) (Olswang, 2006). These rights are embodied in governance documents, faculty handbooks, and appointment letters (Munsch and Verdi, 2006). Tenure has advantages for individuals, providing recognition and security, and tends to generate loyalty toward institutions. But it is sometimes criticized for limiting the agility of institutions and not necessarily preventing abuses (as during the McCarthy Era) (Michaelson, 2001; O'Neil, 2001). There is also the misperception that tenure is immutable. In reality, institutions can dismiss tenured faculty for appropriate reasons, such as termination for cause or upon a declaration of financial exigency (O'Neil and White, 2006). These reasons can even be related to expression, in extreme cases, as with the Ward Churchill case at the University of Colorado (O'Neil, 2008a).

Apart from the merits of the concept, there is the reality of increasingly more faculty in nontenured positions with nonrenewal a regular threat, as well as experiments at a few institutions with abandoning tenure and attempting to preserve faculty rights through other means (O'Neil, 2001; O'Neil and White, 2006). Additionally, O'Neil and White (2006) report the trend toward research university faculty increasingly being expected to generate their salaries and operate their laboratories through extramural funding. Medical schools have similarly reduced compensation for some faculty in reaction to severe budget reduction due to factors such as managed care, reduced federal reimbursement under Medicare, and less federal funding for basic research (Babbitt and Silverstein, 2006). The vague "economic security" guarantee included in the 1940 AAUP statement (updated in 1995) incorporated into many institutional tenure policies provides faculty with a weak defense against such reductions in compensation (O'Neil and White, 2006). Faculty members with salary supplements for administrative appointments, have no automatic right to retain the supplement when returning to the faculty (Babbitt and Silverstein, 2006). The same is true of rights to continued laboratory space or teaching assignments (Babbitt and Silverstein, 2006).

Tenure decisions are significant, with a negative determination disrupting or derailing a faculty career, and an ill-advised favorable one disrupting or limiting a department for years. Litigation is costly, both financially and emotionally, for individuals and institutions alike. Recognizing the inherently subjective nature of the decision, there continues to be deference by courts to the expertise of faculty and administrators when they arrive at a negative decision in a fair manner (Fox, 2006). Courts recognize the specialized knowledge needed to assess the scholarly output or teaching acumen of a faculty member working in a narrow area. But decisions made in arbitrary or capricious ways or those that are discriminatory in nature are subject to favorable decisions for plaintiffs.

Under AAUP guidelines incorporated into most institutions' own rules, faculty in tenure-significant lines have the right to petition for it toward the conclusion of a probationary period not to exceed seven years (AAUP, 2006b; Fox, 2006). The probationary period includes a series of annual appointments with no right to renewal. Failed candidates for tenure are not offered reappointment to a non-tenured position—it is an "up or out" proposition. There are also standard institutional rules associated with counting service at a prior institution and stopping the "tenure clock" for health or family reasons (Fox, 2006). Additionally, institutions have policies for whether probationary faculty can apply for tenure early.

The typical process entails a pyramid of reviewing committees, with recommendations made at one level able to be later reversed at a higher level. A dossier developed for each candidate includes statements of accomplishments, as well as, particularly at research universities, letters solicited from those in his or her discipline doing similar work in departments of similar regard. The first level of review is usually by the tenured faculty at the department level, moving then to a tenure and promotion committee at the institution level, perhaps with an intermediate step in between. It then reaches the provost and president, who present a recommendation to the governing board for final approval. Most institutions have an internal appeals process for negative decisions (Fox, 2006), which is included in collective bargaining agreements, with arbitration often available, in situations where there is a faculty union (Munsch and Verdi, 2006).

Multiple factors are relevant to a tenure decision. There are academic measures, which are inherently subjective, whether in scholarship, teaching, and service (professional, institutional, and community). Additionally, having collegial relations with other faculty members is a variable, albeit a more controversial one (Connell and Savage, 2001; Fox, 2006). The AAUP has issued a statement recognizing the importance of collegiality, but arguing that isolating it as a variable in the tenure decision is a potential danger to academic freedom (AAUP, 1999b; Dyer, 2001; Hustoles, 2006a). Collegiality is not sociability or likeability, but more professional in nature, as with fitting into the mission and longer-term goals of the unit and contributing to shared departmental academic and administrative tasks (Hustoles, 2006a). Connell and Savage (2001) offer the reminder that collegiality is inherently subjective and can be used as a pretext for discrimination. But even factors such as scholarship are not quantifiable, with "apples to apples" comparisons essentially impossible.

A negative decision based upon retaliation for asserting a right protected by academic freedom would not be appropriate, although one based on consistently poor teaching or insufficient or unexceptional research output would be. Provided expectations were appropriate and unambiguous, a denial would also likely be upheld for failure to meet expectations for generating funding within a department—a particular challenge at institutions with ever-higher aspirations. Nonacademic concerns are also relevant, such as a department already having enough faculty members in a certain specialty, or a bleak budget climate at the institution level (Springer and Gage, 2006).

There are also the issues of the kinds of information a tenure committee can rely on, as with that beyond what is required of the process or submitted by the candidate; what are the appropriate comparators, whether other institutions or the boundaries of a discipline; and how much information about the ongoing process should a committee share with a candidate (Springer and Gage, 2006).

While tenure processes are rather consistent across universities and colleges, what is required to reach tenure differs greatly, not only between and among institutions of different types, but also from one academic unit to another on a campus (Hustoles, 2006a; Fox, 2006). For instance, those earning tenure at a leading research university are likely to have published regularly in leading outlets and received supportive letters from senior colleagues at peer institutions, while there are lesser expectations at less prominent universities. At universities and colleges with higher teaching loads and fewer expectations of research productivity, tenure decisions are primarily based on teaching. In addition, different academic fields have different emphases, as with some disciplines at research universities valuing publishing a book and others focused on journal articles—and those in the sciences, in particular, stressing research funding. There may also be different concentrations across units on service, as between an education school and a physics department at a research university (Fox, 2006).

But little about the standards for tenure can be quantified—mandating a set number of publications, for instance—with institutions rightly preferring to maintain flexibility. Quality matters, not simply quantity—and assessing teaching and collegiality is inherently qualitative. For instance, a truly path-breaking article or chapter can be worth more than multiple lesser publications—and perhaps even enough, in itself, to merit tenure. Accordingly, courts are reluctant to upset seemingly reasonable decisions arrived at via standard and appropriate processes, and that are absent evidence of discrimination. They recognize the particularized context and criteria involved, as well as the stakes for the institution. The basic rule is that a legitimate reason for denying tenure will suffice, even if there are criteria that support granting it and regardless of whether the faculty member belongs to a group protected by the antidiscrimination laws. Once again, universities and colleges do not need to apply the same factors to different candidates for tenure, and various departments within an institution can have different standards for granting tenure.

Plaintiffs ground a challenge to a failure to grant tenure in contract or discrimination. Contract actions involve institutions being found either to have not followed their own stated process or standards or having made an arbitrary or capricious decision. A reasonable argument by a plaintiff, grounded in due process would be that the standards indicated to a faculty member during his or her probationary period were not the ones applied in the tenure decision. Another would be a faculty member who claimed a lack of support and resources—perhaps excessive teaching and service obligations—making it virtually impossible to achieve an acceptable level of performance, particularly in research in institutional settings at which that is a consideration. In more of an equal protection argument, a plaintiff might contend that the unfavorable decision resulted in the institution applying different standards to similarly situated faculty, perhaps with politics rather than merit being the basis for the decision. Evidence in support of such allegations is weighed against what the institution contends are appropriate considerations and resulting decisions. Practices that can help avoid such potential challenges include improving the recruitment and mentoring of faculty, clarifying reasonable criteria and regular formal evaluations, and addressing organizational culture problems. Documentation is also important for institutions as a preventive strategy.

Discrimination lawsuits involve disparate impact or disparate treatment arguments, discussed in Chapter 2. These require providing sufficient evidence that the institution treated the individual differently, even if unintentionally, on the basis of some protected immutable characteristics, such as race or gender (Munsch and Verdi, 2006). In determining a discrimination claim, the EEOC has access to relevant information, such as the material reviewed by the committee and records of other faculty subject to a tenure decision so as to allow a comparison. Included here are letters solicited from outside experts, even if confidential, as such interests are outweighed by the need for these data in order to mount a case. (State freedom of information act rules may also compel the release of confidential information.) Institutions defend these lawsuits through evidence that they rejected tenure based on a legitimate nondiscriminatory reason.

Furthermore, due process, considered in Chapter 1, is limited for nontenured faculty, given the lack of property interests involved—these accrue once tenure is granted. (There may be applicable institutional due process rules, as well as state personnel laws at public universities and colleges.) In the end, there is no right to tenure, only the expectation of a fair process, one that is not arbitrary or capricious, with standards that are not vague and policies that are applied equitably (Hustoles, 2006a).

When plaintiffs are successful in challenging a rejection, courts will usually order a university or college to undertake a new tenure review, correcting the error or errors. They may also issue preliminary relief, as with an injunction against termination before a grievance hearing is resolved. There may also be compensatory damages (as for lost wages) or punitive ones (perhaps including attorneys' fees). Only in the most extreme circumstances will a court actually award tenure. And they may overlook minor procedural shortcomings and uphold negative decisions, again given the deference afforded academic decisions in the area.

Wesella Mantooth arrived six years ago as a new assistant professor of communications at a moment of transition at CSU. Her department chair, Bill Lawson, assigned her a four course per semester teaching load, reduced in her second year to three, when the institution formally changed its policies in the area. With enrollments expanding, Lawson encouraged Mantooth to teach summer courses. In her second year, she had seven "preps" (different courses to prepare).

She also taught regularly on the Del Mar satellite campus (enjoying her interactions with Fontana). There are no doctoral students in communications, but there have been 30 masters students per year following the launch of a program four years ago. Students can opt to complete a thesis, with Mantooth agreeing to supervise 12 thesis students during the first two-year cycle. She has never had a graduate student research assistant, but has lately made use of undergraduates through a new CSU program, finding their contributions to be of only marginal use.

Mantooth came to Coronado prepared to conduct research. Studying in a leading graduate program, she was appropriately acculturated—knowing not only how to publish, but that she needed to publish in order to advance in her career. She spent nights and weekends during her first two years working on breaking her dissertation into articles, three of which she eventually published in journals of middling status. But with a heavy teaching load, she simply did not have time to move her research agenda forward. There was also the challenge of not having senior colleagues to mentor her. They were only interested in whether she was covering her classes (and, with the arrival of the master's program, contributing to advising theses), not her development as a researcher. There were other new assistant professors with whom to discuss ideas, but several departed after a year or two.

When her third-year review went poorly, Mantooth was stunned. (She said to a friend from graduate school, "I am at Coronado State, for goodness sake, but these people think it is Yale.") In a meeting (followed by a letter), Veronica Corningstone, the arts and science dean, joined by Lawson, who mostly remained quiet, indicated that Mantooth was unlikely to earn tenure under the standards now applicable at CSU. The dean advised that probationary faculty should be publishing at least annually, mostly in leading journals. (There are four leading journals in Mantooth's area of communications, each publishing about 20 articles annually, meaning there are far more interested authors than available pages.) She also announced that if Mantooth made it to submitting her tenure dossier in three years, the college would solicit letters from faculty members at research universities nationally.

Mantooth redoubled her efforts in research, attempting to reduce other obligations, as with abandoning summer teaching (to the chagrin of her chair and colleagues) and attempting to minimize her thesis advising responsibilities. As she approached the point of applying for tenure, she had published (or had accepted for publication) a lengthy literature review, two book chapters drawing on her dissertation work, and three articles in lesser journals. As she did not have new data and had pretty much exhausted her dissertation research, she felt as though she did what was possible. She was involved with several interesting

(continued)

research projects, looked forward to concentrating on and publishing from them over the next few years. She was also looking forward to starting a family, having delayed that until getting through tenure.

As part of the tenure process, Lawson asked Mantooth to submit five names of people in her field who could comment on the quality of her work. She presented the names of professors she had met through her national association, having attending its conference since graduate school (and only that meeting, given limits in travel funding). Her list included people working at institutions similar to CSU, Mantooth thinking that they would be more likely to be able to realistically assess her situation. Lawson, who had never published and had only occasionally attended national conferences (and did not really even keep current with the literature in his area), consulted with Corningstone, who instructed him to "find people at places I have heard of." Lawson located a list of the 20 top programs in communications and kept asking faculty in them to review Mantooth's file until he found five that would do so. He and Mantooth then agreed on six people, three from her list and three from his.

The letters from faculty at institutions similar to CSU were positive. They suggested, even though not expressly asked, that Mantooth would earn tenure in their department. One of the letters from a professor at a leading program took into account Mantooth's situation and argued that, under the circumstances, she had done well. Two others, applying the standards of a leading research university, as requested by CSU in its letter to them, argued that Mantooth had fallen short.

Having collected the external reviews, the tenured faculty in the communications department voted 8-0 in favor of Mantooth being granted tenure, with the university-wide tenure and promotion committee also advancing her application. When she received the file before it went to the provost and the president, Corningstone was livid, calling in Lawson and explaining that she thought she had been clear about the standards for tenure in the college. She refused to move the application forward, arguing that Mantooth's scholarship was deficient under college and institutional standards. Corningstone added an argument that Mantooth had not adequately participated in departmental activities, having heard that she had scaled back her summer teaching and thesis advising work since her third-year review. The provost and president accepted Corningstone's recommendation and denied Mantooth's tenure application.

Not surprisingly, Mantooth has filed suit. No plausible allegations of specific discrimination or a pattern of discrimination are available. She is thus arguing, in essence, that CSU made an arbitrary and capricious decision in applying the standards of institutions so different in character as to be inapplicable to her. Mantooth needs to prevail on the argument that she did not have the support and resources available to make tenure at CSU possible. She is also challenging the collegiality argument, suggesting that it is pretextual.

CSU is confident that its decision will withstand scrutiny. It followed to the letter its process, assessed in earlier court cases to be solid, and is relying on the traditional deference that courts extend to academic expertise in such situations. As the university argues in its pleadings, there is no right to tenure, only to a fair process. It also relies upon Corningstone explaining the standards during her third year review that she later applied to Mantooth.

Academic Freedom and Other Expression

Academic freedom is a somewhat nebulous right claimed by both institutions and faculty members within them. The bases of academic freedom are in the traditional German concepts of *lehrfreiheit* (teaching freedom), *lernfreiheit* (learning freedom), and *freiheit der wessenschaft* (academic self-government) (O'Neil and White, 2006; Spurgeon, 2007). Supported by the concept of academic freedom, faculty members have an extraordinary degree of autonomy, governing much of their professional lives through peer review, tending to determine themselves what constitutes ethical and productive behavior (Hamilton, 2001). But student academic freedom rights are relatively undeveloped in the United States, although there is a 1967 AAUP statement supporting their free expression rights (Euben, 2006a; Springer, 2008). Public universities and colleges justify their autonomy relative to the state through the extension of the academic freedom concept to institutions.

The rationale for academic freedom, both professional privilege and institutional autonomy, is to encourage the robust exchange of ideas within a community of scholars—and the resulting societal benefits. The conceptual foundations of academic freedom are deference to scholarly work and academic decisions as codified in various AAUP statements (professional academic freedom), and legal protections from unwarranted restrictions from courts and legislatures (constitutional academic freedom) (Metzger, 1988; Spurgeon, 2007).

Professional academic freedom protects individual faculty from institutional penalty for pursuing their chosen research, teaching and evaluating students in the ways they see fit, speaking on matters of public concern, and expressing views on institutional matters (Byrne, 2001). Under the 1940 AAUP statement (as interpreted in 1970), incorporated into institutional rules, whether expressly or by custom and practice, instructors and researchers have the contractual right to address even the most controversial work, without fear of negative employment consequences (AAUP, 2006b; O'Neil and White, 2006). A primary purpose of tenure is to support academic freedom, as expressed in the 1915 AAUP Declaration of Principles. (The present

AAUP statement, contained in the 2006 *Redbook*, is titled: *Recommended Institutional Regulations on Academic Freedom and Tenure*.)

Constitutional academic freedom discourages institutions from implementing policies such as loyalty oaths (Olswang, 2006). In the 1940s and 1950s, several court decisions applied First Amendment principles to determine that institutions could not terminate faculty for membership in political organizations, require disclaimer oaths, and engage in "fishing expeditions" to seek information related to professional associations (Cope, 2007). But academic freedom, whether based in professional deference or constitutional protections, does not protect disruptive speech or unethical conduct, classroom speech unrelated to the subject of the course, and behavior such as sexual harassment (Olswang, 2006). For instance, a biology professor at a public university probably does not have the right to teach "intelligent design," given the religious nature of the theory and the requirements of the Establishment Clause (Ravitch, 2008; Springer, 2008). Courts tend to defer to institutions on academic questions such as what constitutes biology (Hiers, 2002).

Appointment type is immaterial to the academic freedom of individuals, with probationary faculty members having the same technical rights as tenured faculty do (DeGeorge, 2001). Protections extend, in theory, to those in nontenure-significant appointments. The idea is to protect instructors and researchers against reprisals from their employers, as pressured from outside, when their work may conflict with institutional interests or public sensibilities. However, academic freedom expectations are adjusted at expressly religious universities and colleges when there is the need for deference to doctrinal authority.

Although emphasizing the importance of free inquiry in a democratic society, the U.S. Supreme Court has not held that academic freedom is an express constitutional principle. (It is protected by state statute or regulation in some jurisdictions [Euben, 2006a].) Todd (2007) refers to academic freedom as a law of "concurrences and footnotes," with the clearest statements by courts having little precedential values (Rendleman, 2002). For instance, in *Keyishian v. Board of Regents of the University of the State of New York* (1967), the U.S. Supreme Court only suggests that courts may act to protect public institutions from the state when its actions have a chilling effect on First Amendment rights (Todd, 2007). DeMitchell (2002) argues that the Court has not articulated a clear standard of what academic freedom protects—its substance, boundaries, and locus (Euben, 2006a). This includes regularly failing to expressly distinguish between the academic freedom rights of institutions and those of individuals (Hiers, 2002).

These academic freedom interests of individuals and institutions can conflict (DeMitchell, 2002). When they do, concerns about institutional autonomy tend to outweigh the academic freedom rights attributed to individual professors (Hiers, 2002). But both individuals and institutions assert the right to determine who should teach, what they may teach, how they should teach it, and who should be admitted to study it, as Justice Frankfurter articulated the scope of academic freedom in concurrence in the U.S. Supreme Court decision in *Sweezy v. New Hampshire* (1957) (Hiers, 2002). (The majority decision of the U.S. Supreme Court in *Regents of the University of Michigan v. Ewing* [1985] reinforced the latter two principles.) For example, both professors and departments claim the right to oversee instructional activities such as grading (Dyer, 2002; Euben, 2006a).

But on matters such as course content, teaching method, and faculty evaluation, university or college interests are likely to take precedence (Langhauser, 2006). Research tends to have the strongest academic freedom protection, but even it is not absolute—there may be more compelling institutional interests. Universities and colleges also preserve the right to prevent against abusive speech or harassing behavior by faculty in the classroom (Fossey and Roberts, 2002), or inappropriate religious expression in that setting at public universities and colleges (Langhauser, 2006). Under the U.S. Supreme Court decisions in *Connick v. Myers* (1983) and *Pickering v. Board of Education* (1968), individuals employed by public universities have the right to discuss matters of public concern (but not merely individual personal matters). But universities and colleges can assert interests here, if such expression is intolerable given institutional purposes and needs and thus outweighs the interests of the employee (Niehoff, 2008).

Furthermore, the U.S. Supreme Court held in *Garcetti v. Ceballos* (2006) that public employers are not limited by the First Amendment in disciplining employees for statements made pursuant to their official duties. Niehoff (2008) argues that lower courts have been inclined to treat faculty members like these employees, although Justice Souter wrote in dissent expressing concern about the impact of *Garcetti* on academic freedom (Spurgeon, 2007). At religious institutions, the AAUP has recognized the right to limit the academic freedom of individuals, including in expression, to preserve religious missions (Gordon, 2003).

DeMitchell (2002) concludes that academic freedom resides not with faculty but with institutions, but that professors still have rights when their interests align with those of their employers. The AAUP tends to champion the academic freedom rights of individual faculty, but concludes that institutions also have rights when academic questions (as opposed to managerial ones) are at issue (Euben, 2006a). Outside of academic freedom, there are also protections for professors, as applicable, through constitutional law (at public institutions), contracts, and academic custom and practice (Euben, 2006a).

The real issue in academic freedom may not be where rights exist, but if individuals, particularly those lacking tenure, are positioned to assert those that do apply. For instance, a temporary faculty member may have the right to pursue controversial questions in his or her teaching or writing or speak his or her mind about public concerns or institutional priorities. But there is no requirement that administrators who view these actions as contrary to institutional interests reappoint that person (Byrne, 2001). Furthermore, tenured faculty can be indifferent in their support of their temporary colleagues, even when dismissal decisions are on inappropriate academic grounds.

Tenured colleagues can tend to perceive temporary faculty as removed from the peer review that occurs in hiring and promoting regular faculty, and thus not fully meriting protection (Byrne, 2001; DeGeorge, 2001). The AAUP, most recently in a 2009 statement, argued strenuously that institutions should be adding tenure-significant appointments, but trends are in the opposite direction.

There is also the question in the entrepreneurial university of whether graduate students, who are assuming more of the overall teaching load at research universities, have the rather limited academic freedom rights of students or are deemed faculty and afforded greater rights. Institutions have attempted to frame graduate students as students, thus avoiding obligations such as employee benefits, in the same ways that they have deemed athletes in sports such as football at larger universities as students and not workers, so as to bypass issues such as financial compensation or applying workers' compensation laws. In a 2000 statement, the AAUP outlined the freedoms that graduate students should have to teach and learn, as well as in governance.

Another suggested deficiency of academic freedom in practice is the argument that conservative faculty and students are discriminated against in academe for their viewpoints and religious beliefs, with their supporters threatening legislative action that would provide a perceived counterbalance (Cameron, Meyers, and Olswang, 2005; Pendleton, 2008; Springer, 2008). It is an open question whether such "academic bills of rights" to balance perceived bias from the political and cultural left are correctly framed as academic freedom (Euben, 2006b)—or whether government should even become involved here. It also may be that heightened political sensibilities at institutions and devices such as speech codes have diminished academic freedom (O'Neil and White, 2006; Rendleman, 2002). The situation may be just the opposite. Byrne (2004) contends that courts have been increasingly likely to intrude on academic decision making in response to allegations that universities and colleges have been intolerant when they value "political correctness" over individual liberties and discipline faculty and students for offensive speech. He views the decision in *Grutter* as perhaps indicating a return to the traditions of constitutional academic freedom, in affirming deference to the academic determination that a diverse institutional environment is essential.

There is the further question of whether demands for increased accountability by states and the more competitive environment in higher education have increased pressure on administrators in ways that may work against institutional autonomy and the academic freedom of individual faculty members. States have always had legitimate interests over academic matters such as what is taught at public universities—and the market increasingly has the same influence over academic programs when they are offered in certain institutional settings. But as Cope (2007) argues, in the first decade of the 2000s, governments have sought increasingly to curb expression and regulate academic knowledge. There are the examples of limits on federally funded stem-cell research and actions that discourage disseminating certain results of climate change studies, as well as corporate sponsorship of academic research doing the same (O'Neil, 2008b).

Finally, defamation issues can arise in higher education. Defamatory statements, either libel (recorded) or slander (spoken), are, by definition, false, disseminated, injurious, and attributable. They are sometimes privileged, absolutely within a legislative or judicial context and in a qualified manner between two people within an organization. For instance, allegedly defamatory communication contained in performance evaluations at a university or college is privileged if written by the appropriate institutional official, relevant to employment issues reviewed, and conveyed only to those with a legitimate interest in it. Letters of reference can also be the subject of defamation claims. Public figures who allege defamation, such as the president of a prominent university, must prove the defendant made the statement with actual malice. For others, the standard is negligence. Recovery may include compensatory and punitive damages, as well as injunctive relief to deter similar future conduct.

The state legislature recently passed legislation instituting what it is calling an academic bill of rights. The intent behind the bill was to protect the free expression rights of politically and religiously conservative students and faculty members, who perceive themselves to be disadvantaged at universities and colleges that they argue are dominated by those on the left. The statute, modeled on standard language circulating across the country, requires that public universities and colleges in the state, including CSU, integrate several new principles into their governance documents. Perhaps the legislation will be declared unconstitutional as overly broad or vague, as several of its doctrines could yield countless possible results or be so unclear as to be unenforceable, if read literally. Also, the legislation may be more symbolic than anything, as it lacks a realistic enforcement mechanism and even penalties for violations. Nevertheless, it will become part of CSU policies on academic freedom.

As do the other institutions in the state, CSU views the legislation as contrary to its institutional academic freedom rights—an inappropriate government intrusion into institutional autonomy and professional privilege. Its provisions directly address factors such as whom to hire, what to teach, and how to teach—three of Frankfurter's four essential freedoms (the other being admissions, which the statute does not address). As such, institutional and individual academic freedom becomes simply a principle, as a statute that is essentially symbolic can become its equal. The statute does not upset basic academic freedom rights as in the case of a professor pursuing his or her chosen research, speaking on matters of public concern, or expressing views on institutional matters. But it does limit the traditional right of those at universities and colleges to determine teaching approaches and evaluation methods.

(continued)

One element of the legislation requires that faculty hired or tenured in the humanities, social sciences, and fine arts represent a "plurality of methodologies and perspectives." Veronica Corningstone, the arts and sciences dean, is concerned about several upcoming faculty searches. For instance, in sociology, one of the political conservatives on the faculty is demanding that the next several hires "balance out" what he views as the overall liberal political leanings of the faculty. He has proposed hiring, as he terms it, one conservative and one moderate for every liberal already on the faculty. How status as a liberal, moderate, or conservative might be verified, or even identified, is an open question. In economics, the faculty has, only semiseriously, entered into a discussion of whether they need to represent the tens of different schools of economic thinking in their future hiring—and have passed around a list in a half-serious attempt to define what these all are.

Another provision mandates that students are to be graded solely on their "reasoned answers and appropriate knowledge" related to the subject being studied, not on the basis of political or religious beliefs. Additionally, lectures and readings in humanities and social science courses should include dissenting sources and viewpoints, offering a "diversity of approaches to unsettled questions." Scotty Rogen, an undergraduate accounting major, challenged his grade in introductory biology, as he answered several multiple-choice questions by attempting to address creationism—and thus incorrectly, as the professor saw it. He also petitioned the college to change the syllabus in the ecology course he was to take next semester because it did not pay equal attention to arguments denying global warming. At a recent arts and sciences faculty senate meeting, colleagues spun out several similar scenarios. For instance, how could a professor select a set of books in an English class and still offer a plurality that would please every prospective student?

Equally troubling to the faculty is the doctrine that faculty must not "indoctrinate" students with particular political or religious views—or nonreligious ones. A few of the faculties in arts and sciences have asked Corningstone for clarification on whether "indoctrinate" means that they must take all political or religious content out of the courses, so as not to offend a sensitive student. For instance, for some students, evolution is not a scientific issue, but is instead a political one. Would a biology professor need to offer the opposing view to evolution in order to not be indoctrinating his or her students? Corningstone has no idea of how to respond, her initial attempt of suggesting to the faculty that they should do what they normally would, given the legislation does not have sanctions attached, falling flat. In raising concerns, the faculty views the bill of rights as a matter of principle, not as a practical problem.

Furthermore, a provision of the bill mandates that speakers visiting campus should be selected based on principles of pluralism, with no tolerance for obstructing a given speech. Jess Moondragon, the university attorney, is concerned about possible First Amendment violations if CSU attempts to enforce the rule, as "no tolerance" likely goes beyond reasonable time, place, and manner restrictions imposed on speech by the institution (discussed in Chapter 4). The final element of the legislation requires that academic institutions and professional societies maintain a "posture of organizational neutrality with respect to the substantive disagreements that divide researchers on questions within, or outside, their fields of inquiry." There is the potential difficulty of someone such as a Holocaust denier, published in that isolated community, claiming protection under the act for activities on campus, perhaps as a visiting lecturer or as a student seeking to establish a recognized student organization.

Wrongful Dismissal

Other employees, including temporary faculty and probationary faculty on the tenure track, are more limited in their ability to challenge their dismissal than are tenured faculty members. The former, employed "at will," can be dismissed at anytime or, if applicable, at the end of any contract term (Hustoles, 2006a). Universities and colleges tend to have processes for "at will" dismissals, especially for administrators, who do not always have an appointment for a set term. These commonly involve progressive discipline (discussed above) and otherwise "building a file." Doing so aligns with the general culture of higher education and helps to ensure that there is not discrimination connected with a dismissal. The latter, faculty holding tenure, can only be dismissed for cause or in the event of financial exigency.

At-Will Employees and Temporary Faculty

The right to be dismissed only for cause or in exigency must be created. With tenure, these rights are express. Other employees can argue wrongful dismissal based on enforceable contractual expectations having been created through various means, such as spoken and written assurances or promises made by supervisors. For instance, seemingly innocuous but sufficiently ambiguous letters sent to employees to improve morale may create the unintended, but reasonable and perhaps enforcable, perception of assurances of something beyond at-will employment. There may also be arguments grounded in written contracts, formal policies at an institution, or its customs and practices suggestive of for-cause dismissal. Formal documents expressly acknowledging the at-will status of relevant employees are useful to institutions as counterevidence, as is a clear statement that completing a probationary period at the beginning of employment does not create for-cause rights. In other words, it is within the power of institutions to preserve their at-will rights (Franke, 2008a).

In addition to contract theories, there are arguments challenging the at-will rule grounded in tort, although these tend to be much more difficult cases to establish. For instance, plaintiffs allege in constructive discharge actions that the institution forced their resignation through abusive or retaliatory behavior directed toward them—working conditions were made so unpleasant that a reasonable person would feel compelled to resign. Similarly, actions for negligent or intentional infliction of emotional distress involve outrageous or extreme behavior directed toward an employee that results in severe personal problems. In cases claiming negligent performance of a contractual obligation, the institution is said to fail to meet a duty of ordinary care in performing a contractual obligation toward an employee. An example is an employer conducting an annual employment evaluation in a negligent fashion. A plaintiff may also argue that an employer was negligent in hiring him or her, misrepresenting the institution and its capacities and not ensuring that the employee was competent and qualified for the position filled. Finally, defamation actions are possible, alleging that the reasons stated for the discharge are false. Once again, these tort theories are typically a significant stretch for plaintiffs, with contract actions having much greater likelihood of success.

Additionally, at-will employees are protected when they are terminated for refusing to engage in illegal acts, insist on performing a duty required by statute, or when they are whistleblowers. Finally, certain state laws, such as workers' compensation, may be connected with at-will dismissals. Human resources staff can advise about standard approaches to handling the termination of an employee, whether at-will or otherwise. It can prove helpful in a later challenge if a record of due diligence, good faith, and fair dealing has been established. If there is cause for dismissal, as with the failure to meet specified performance standards or the commission or omission of specified acts, such evidence enables the institution to make an argument that the termination was proper even if the employee was not at-will. The same is true for actions grounded in institutional necessity.

Tenured Faculty

Institutions grant tenured faculty members interests in a position such that they can only be dismissed, upon receiving appropriate due process, for cause or in the event of financial exigency. Both are recognized in the 1940 AAUP Statement of Principles on Academic Freedom and Tenure, which is only definitive when an institution and the AAUP are involved in a union contract or if an institution expressly adopts it as policy. Otherwise, it is merely advisory. Other faculty members have no such rights, with institutions only owing them compensation for the term of their contract, whether this is semester-to-semester or for a longer term. There are de facto tenure situations, which are unusual, in which an institution mistakenly creates a reasonable expectation of continued employment so as to constitute a property interest.

Courts are traditionally reluctant to substitute their judgment for administrative decisions made within established and reasonable rules or according to the terms of contracts at universities and colleges. Dismissals cannot be retaliatory, of course, as with for pursuing unpopular intellectual interests. There is no standard definition of adequate cause for the dismissal of a tenured faculty member, with the AAUP deferring to individual institutions and the courts relying upon the professional judgment of academic administrators and faculty committees. Definitions by institutions should be as clear as possible, given the stakes involved and as a preventive strategy. But they need not anticipate or delineate all possible types of conduct. Also, interpretations are grounded in the customs and practices both of the institution and across U.S. higher education.

For tenured professors, due process requirements are heightened, given the property and liberty interests at issues, as discussed in Chapter 1 (Babbitt, 2006; Dyer, 2003). But there are no due process rights particular to them (Hustoles, 2006b; Olswang et al, 2003). These interests accrue when there is a reasonable claim of entitlement to a position (property) and when a dismissal has the potential to seriously damage the reputation of the faculty member and cause a stigma with an impact on future employment (liberty). Appropriate due process likely requires notice of the cause for dismissal, sufficient information to defend against the charges and identify any error that may have occurred, a meaningful opportunity to be heard before an impartial decision maker, the process to occur within a reasonable amount of time, and the ability to draw on the advice of counsel (Hustoles, 2006b; Olswang, 2006). At public institutions, there may also be state due process requirements.

Due process is always case-by-case in nature. Given that program reduction and elimination tend to be more clinical than personal, there may be fewer rights afforded than in a for-cause situation, albeit perhaps still considerable ones. Also, as little stigma attaches to faculty dismissed as a result of downsizing or closure, liberty interests are less relevant than when there is institutional necessity. In lawsuits resulting from program changes, institutions tend to fare well when they have established policies and follow them carefully, as well as when they employ appropriate metrics, such as enrollments and costs per unit. At applicable institutions, such provisions may be included in collective bargaining contracts. When there are not such policies, courts refer to custom and practice across higher education, commonly referring to AAUP guidelines, which tend to be constraining to universities and colleges (management) and more favorable to faculty (labor) (Olswang et al., 2003).

The classic misconduct that amounts to adequate cause is some combination of incompetence, insubordination, immorality, neglect of duty, and incapacity (Hustoles, 2006a; Olswang, 2006). Defining incompetence, insubordination, and immorality is difficult, and substantiating these through evidence is also quite challenging. Neglect of duty is more procedural—someone was either regularly present or not—as is sometimes incapacity, but even expectations related to these can be unclear. Removing tenured faculty members is thus inherently difficult. But without arduous standards for dismissal, tenure would be a hollow right.

Incompetence requires a manifest inability or unwillingness to contribute to the dissemination or advancement of knowledge through effective teaching or research. For instance, incompetence in teaching would involve a faculty member failing to keep current in his or her discipline, delivering irrelevant lectures, or failing to make course requirements clear to students. In supporting an incompetence decision, institutions are likely to reference having attempted reasonable remedial measures. But sometimes the inadequacy or indifference is so egregious that rehabilitation through professional development is improbable or impractical. With students having heightened expectations as tuition increases and understanding that they have other options in a competitive higher education market, entrepreneurial institutions may deem themselves less able to tolerate incompetence.

Insubordination is the manifest failure to follow reasonable requests of administrators. Institutions are likely to tolerate more of certain faculty members, as with those with the highest external profiles, while being less patient with those in adjunct or contract appointments. The same may even extend to *immorality*, also known as moral turpitude, as with a professor who makes improper sexual advances toward a student. It may also involve dishonesty, such as research fraud or misrepresentation of credentials, or conviction of a felony. *Neglect of duty* is the failure to meet obligations, such as attendance at classes. But what about when it is caused by the entrepreneurial activities of a faculty member associated with a technology transfer partnership with the institution? The formal definition of *incapacity* is being physically or mentally unable to perform the duties of the faculty position (Hustoles, 2006a). Once again, these violations must be extreme, given the protection that tenure affords.

Dismissal for serious criminal misconduct, especially when it occurs on the job, is rather straightforward. Off-duty, off-campus violations merit dismissal when there is a nexus to the employment relationship, as with significant adverse publicity or the inability of the employee to continue to do his or her job in an effective manner (Hustoles, 2008). Carefully prepared separation agreements can limit institutional liability (Murphy and Kaesebier, 2008), as can effective settlement documents (Fleischer, 2006). Apart from misconduct, with the nonappointment to tenure of faculty in probationary (tenure-track) appointments, or full-time term appointments (as with a lecturer), the AAUP standards recommend that notice be given sufficiently early that the person can search for another position (AAUP, 1995b). There are also AAUP statements on procedural standards, such as third year reviews and due process recommendations, in renewing and dismissing faculty (AAUP, 1989; AAUP 1990). But institutions can readily act, if they choose, to dismiss nontenured faculty, particular those on annual contracts.

Similarly, when institutions dismiss tenured faculty as a result of financial exigency, they must demonstrate that a bona fide emergency exists (Babbitt, 2006). The crisis must be imminent, such that it threatens the viability or even survival of an institution, and of a nature that it cannot be adequately alleviated by means other than a reduction in tenured faculty. As with dismissals for cause, the burden of proof is on the employer, as with demonstrating operating deficits that cannot realistically be solved in any other way. The cause of deficits can be either active, as with overly aggressive hiring, or due to factors such as declines in enrollment or reductions in appropriations. Also, financial exigency—and resulting program reduction or elimination—can be confined to a given academic unit, not extending across the university or college (Klein, 2009). For instance, a university or college might have solid finances overall, but its dental school might be deeply in the red.

The process by which an institution determined that financial exigency exists and the decision it made subsequently in targeting programs and individuals is also at issue (Babbitt, 2006). As with for-cause dismissals, courts tend to defer to the judgment of institutions that can demonstrate they acted in a systematic and fair manner, following their own reasonable policies, and not making arbitrary or capricious determinations (Dyer, 2003; Olswang et al., 2003). Financial exigency cannot serve as a pretext for dismissing faculty for other reasons or be used to subvert academic freedom. Nor can dismissal decisions be discriminatory in nature.

There is no "last hired, first fired" requirement in financial exigency dismissals. Institutions must neither base decisions solely on seniority nor dismiss all nontenured faculty members before terminating any tenured faculty. The standard is the need for reductions to certain programs in the context of the overall university or college. Which faculty members are affected is relevant, but not determinative. But institutions put themselves in the best position to successfully defend legal challenges when they consider and reasonably reject every alternative to dismissing tenured faculty. For instance, before dismissing tenured faculty, did an institution reduce discretionary spending, as with implementing furloughs, discontinuing administrative positions, reducing annual or tenure-track faculty appointments, and even deny tenure to current applicants—and did the university or college draw fully on sources such as federal stimulus funds (Klein, 2009)? Options such as furloughs and layoffs are preferable to dismissals, reducing programs is better than eliminating them, and declaring financial exigency across an institution is less drastic than merging with another institution or closing a university or college (Klein, 2009; Olswang et al., 2003). Entrepreneurial institutions also are conscious that their continued spending on capital projects, including in arms races in constructing or renovating facilities, may call into question whether they actually have the bona fide exigency needed to reduce tenured faculty. In other words, if declaring exigency means they need to halt all such activity, potentially to their severe strategic disadvantage, institutions may view options differently (Klein, 2009).

As with reducing and eliminating programs in the context of financial exigency, tenured faculty may also be affected by merger or affiliation with another university or college—or the outright closure of an institution. The question arises of whether an acquiring institution assumes the obligations of the failing one. Recognizing the difficulty of not wanting to discourage necessary mergers or affiliations, the AAUP has not taken a position on the issue (Olswang et al., 2003). One relevant consideration is whether the failing institution retains its status as a corporate entity, thus arguably preserving the tenured status of its faculty. Additionally, students have rights, based in implied contract, in program reduction and elimination situations, with institutions needing to address matters such as disruption in their academic programs, usually by securing alternatives.

Finally, under the 1986 Amendments to the Age Discrimination in Employment Act of 1967 (ADEA), institutions may no longer compel the mandatory retirement of employees at a certain age (Olswang, 2006; Rosenberg and Skoning, 2006; Sciscoe, 2006). It is permissible to offer incentive packages for early retirement, whether under a broader program or negotiated individually, through a continuing effort or one responding to a particular situation, or via a one-time buyout or phased retirement. Programs must not discriminate "because of age," as mandated in ADEA, and decisions by employees must be strictly voluntary and well informed (Sciscoe, 2006). There are specific rules applicable to tenured faculty under the Higher Education Act Amendments of 1998, and pension plan rules apply under the Employee Retirement Income Security Act of 1974 (ERISA) and the Internal Revenue Code (Sciscoe, 2006). It is also permissible to reserve the incentive for those whose retirement serves the financial goals of the institution, as opposed to making it available to all employees.

The severe economic recession caught CSU in an exposed position. As president, Burgundy had invested heavily in facilities and positions, leaving the institution little margin for financial error. He has increased enrollments, which has helped revenues, but has had to implement furloughs and not replace departing faculty to balance the last two budgets, given reductions in state appropriations. Even with employing adjuncts and using the relatively few funded graduate students enrolled at CSU as aggressively as possible, the university has struggled to offer required courses, with students and parents beginning to complain—loudly, with legislators listening—that it is impossible to graduate in four years.

A local for-profit institution is beginning to siphon away students, guaranteeing that students will get the courses they need—and charging triple the tuition that CSU does. Burgundy is also learning that such competitors can offer distance programs more efficiently—and probably even better. The satellite campuses, as with Del Mar, that Burgundy launched are stable, as people seem to be following the conventional wisdom and returning to school in response to disruptions in their employment. But the students expected to move onto campus into the new residences the university built have been opting to live at home, with CSU's partner in the project reducing rents and having unfilled rooms—and at risk of bankruptcy. Most of the business spaces that are part of the project are now empty (and only about one-half of them ever attracted tenants).

Burgundy is also finding that doctoral programs are expensive, generating little revenue through funded research, and costing considerably more than undergraduate efforts in the same areas, particularly given the lack of economies of scale at a small research university. And even with the NCAA tournament appearance, basketball continues to attract little interest and athletics is generating substantial deficits, with the football program launch and stadium construction delayed for at least two years. At least the fitness center is a financial success, generating enough revenue to even supplement some other efforts.

Burgundy knows he needs to do something. He is determined not to declare financial exigency, as he strongly suspects it will freeze potential donors, who want to give for projects that advance, not simply maintain, an institution. Given there are no union contracts at CSU or other limiting language in the university rules, Burgundy believes he can target specific units for reduction or closure, isolating the exigency there. He has quietly asked his budget and finance and institutional research heads to run numbers. Neither has exactly the data they require, as their efforts have been more directed to issuing reports for accountability and accreditation.

Burgundy has to go with what data he has. Having consulted with the board of trustees and the senior administration, he is ready to address the campus community by e-mail. He has decided that the university simply cannot continue the furloughs and open positions, which amount to across-the-board reductions, especially with another significant state budget reduction on the horizon. Instead, CSU needs to target lower performing units and the largest line in the budget—senior faculty salaries. One of these areas is sociology, which has several senior faculty members, such as Mendez, who are not productive researchers or even very strong teachers (and are generally annoying). The department also has several underutilized administrators, mostly clerical staff. Burgundy has concluded that he has no obligation to transfer those employees.

CSU is offering early retirement to any faculty member in the department with 20 or more years of service, although the package is not particularly attractive, especially for those with less than 30 years in. It has agreed to move the endowed sociology professor it recently hired, Adam McKay, to communications, shifting the students majoring in sociology also to communications, where it will continue the major until the current students have departed. The university is not

(*continued*)

renewing most untenured and contract faculty in the department, moving a few in needed areas to communications, where it will not grant tenure to Mantooth, given the financial situation. (Mantooth knows she has no real legal rights, given there are no suggestions of a flawed or discriminatory process, and is looking for other employment.)

Several of the tenured faculty in sociology took the early retirement offer, some in the thought that they could sign on as adjuncts elsewhere or even come back to CSU in that capacity. Mendez refused the offer and hired an attorney. His argument is that CSU did not cut various peripheral programs, namely the satellite sites and the significant subsidies to athletics, before deciding to dismiss tenured faculty—and never declared financial exigency, as the AAUP requires. Mendez contends that sociology, as a division with arts and sciences, cannot be isolated within the college—it is not a discrete unit like a dental or nursing school. He also believes that his department was targeted because of its long-standing activism and regular criticism of the senior administration.

The university is ready with a response:

- It was systematic and balanced in its deliberations, deciding to reduce academic programs as a last resort.
- The satellite programs are financially viable and produce needed revenue.
- Athletics are needed for institutional advancement purposes—and operate out of a different financial "bucket."
- Sociology is the third lowest producing department on campus in revenue per full-time faculty member, with no suggestion of improvement on the horizon—and the lowest two producers are mission-essential.

Mendez cannot believe that his tenured position is at risk because, as he views it, the university made several bad investments and lost interest in its academic core.

Financial Exigency at CSU—A Simulation

It is a year later and the state is in a desperate financial situation. State revenues have declined with a downturn in the economy. With insufficient political will to increase taxes and meaningful pressure not to significantly increase tuition, which remains moderate by national standards, draconian budget cuts are necessary. Working with the state university system, the legislature recently approved a package increasing tuition and fees by 20 percent for the coming fiscal year. But as appropriations from the state also declined, Coronado State needs to reduce its budget by $11 million (12 percent) for the coming fiscal year—the third consecutive year of decreases. Additional reductions in the next few years appear likely, with little prospect of these funds eventually being restored.

CSU is reducing its budget during the next year by requiring that all employees take one unpaid furlough day per month, which amounts to a roughly five percent annual pay reduction, saving $3 million in faculty salaries and $5 million overall. It has also increased the proportion of what employees contribute to their health insurance, saving another $1 million each year. CSU is continuing its three-year hiring freeze, not replacing departing or retiring employees, replacing instruction by these full-time faculty members with a combination of larger classes, canceling courses, and adding adjuncts. Doing so has saved just over $2 million in faculty-related expenses and $1.5 million additionally. Additional reductions in administrative expenses, which have already been cut 15 percent over the past three years, make up the difference.

Ron Burgundy, the CSU president, is convinced that the institution simply cannot withstand another round of what are, in effect, across-the-board cuts. Morale across the institution, especially among the faculty, is at rock bottom. The reductions in instruction and administration have reduced capacity below what is minimally acceptable. Classes are overcrowded; the courses that students require to graduate are unavailable; qualified adjuncts are increasingly difficult to secure; it is unreasonable to ask regular faculty members to take on even more students; administrative offices in areas such as student affairs and academic advising are overwhelmed; and deferred maintenance has caught up with the university. CSU has reduced its budget beyond what is required for it to sustain a reasonable level of service—with it unrealistic to even consider advancing as an institution, given the need to simply survive. Burgundy is now willing to declare financial exigency at CSU, knowing that many other institutions in the state, apart from the public research universities, are likely to do, thus removing much of the sting.

The president has convened a task force to address the need to make more targeted reductions for the budget year that begins in 18 months, asking a distinguished professor of higher education from another university to chair it. Burgundy has charged the task force with recommending how to eliminate $4 million in annual expenditures in instruction. He is open to various options, but has emphasized his preference for eliminating at least one academic unit, preferring the approach to further across-the-board reductions. As there are costs associated with any reduction, such as retirement packages for tenured faculty members, the task force must calculate the proposed savings for any reduction involving tenured faculty as 50 percent of their overall salaries. For instance, reducing a unit with $2 million in annual expenditures, with $1 million in tenured faculty salaries, will only yield a yearly reduction of $1.5 million, as one-half of the tenured faculty salaries are not realized as savings. Mergers are also possible, although there are few (if any) areas that would combine neatly. A merger would only allow the reduction of up to 20 percent of tenured faculty in each existing department and cut administrative expenses by 40 percent in each.

CSU is confident that enrollments will remain steady if it engages in program elimination, with students eventually shifting to other programs, and it will realize enough in savings each year to merit such a significant undertaking. State appropriations are not formally connected with credit hours produced, but it is important to minimize declines here as other departments are going to need to teach more to make up for any reductions.

Burgundy has asked the task force to consider the strategic priorities of the university. As expressed in the strategic plan, these include enhancing doctoral education, having launched the doctorate in psychology. There are also doctoral programs prepared to begin during the coming academic year in educational administration and organizational dynamics, the former drawing faculty from educational leadership and educational foundations and the latter from management. The college is planning to establish doctoral programs the year following in teaching (again drawing on foundations), health administration, and international affairs. These three programs have yet to be approved by the state university system. Other priorities include building funded research, strengthening general education and building undergraduate intellectual culture, and increasing fund raising.

The task force should arrive at a set of metrics relevant to deciding which program is or programs are to be eliminated (or reduced or merged). In order to withstand legal challenge from those dismissed, the institution must be able to make a proper showing that a department has been properly targeted. The task force should avoid discriminating on the basis of a category protected under the antidiscrimination laws. The vice president for finance and administration has prepared the tables below for use by the task force. The task force also has available various qualitative data, captured in the last table. The chair of the task force has asked that the group divide into three-person teams to begin its work, considering their metrics and the available data and coming with a recommendation to the entire body. The teams should be prepared to share their financial calculations, remembering to discount faculty reductions by 50 percent and the limitations on savings through mergers. The whole group will then discuss what each team concluded and generate an overall recommendation to the president.

Table 3.1 Faculty Profile, by Number of Tenured Faculty

	TENURED FACULTY	TENURE TRACK FACULTY	LECTURERS AND NON-TENURE TRACK FACULTY	ADJUNCT FACULTY AND GRADUATE FELLOWS	TOTAL FACULTY	TOTAL FULL-TIME FACULTY	TOTAL FULL-TIME WOMEN	PERCENT FULL-TIME WOMEN	TOTAL NON-WHITE FULL TIME FACULTY	PERCENT FULL-TIME MINORITY
Psychology	33	15	5	14	67	53	22	42%	2	4%
Teaching	26	9	4	13	52	39	25	64%	8	21%
Literature	25	10	4	3	42	39	24	62%	2	5%
Educ. Lead.	23	8	3	15	49	34	19	56%	6	18%
Nursing	22	12	15	14	63	49	39	80%	2	4%
Accounting	21	12	3	7	43	36	12	33%	4	11%
Art	21	4	8	12	45	33	15	45%	7	21%
History	21	8	5	3	37	34	15	44%	2	6%
Biology	20	12	5	7	44	37	6	16%	7	19%
Mathematics	18	8	5	8	39	31	10	32%	7	23%
Finance	15	10	3	8	36	28	11	39%	3	11%
Educ. Found.	15	9	5	5	34	29	14	48%	7	24%
Communications	15	9	1	9	34	25	15	60%	3	12%
Chemistry	15	4	2	4	25	21	5	24%	4	19%
Computer Sci.	15	6	5	10	36	26	4	15%	12	46%
Hospitality	14	4	6	22	46	24	17	71%	4	17%
Management	13	11	4	13	41	28	8	29%	8	29%
Economics	13	8	1	2	24	22	4	18%	2	9%
Music	13	4	7	2	26	24	11	46%	2	8%

(continued)

Table 3.1 Continued

	TENURED FACULTY	TENURE TRACK FACULTY	LECTURERS AND NON-TENURE TRACK FACULTY	ADJUNCT FACULTY AND GRADUATE FELLOWS	TOTAL FACULTY	TOTAL FULL-TIME FACULTY	TOTAL FULL-TIME WOMEN	PERCENT FULL-TIME WOMEN	TOTAL NON-WHITE FULL TIME FACULTY	PERCENT FULL-TIME MINORITY
Political Science	12	8	4	14	38	24	11	46%	1	4%
Anthropology	12	3	0	5	20	15	7	47%	3	20%
Foreign Lang.	11	4	8	3	26	23	15	65%	2	9%
Int'l Affairs	10	5	5	12	32	20	8	40%	4	20%
Geography	8	2	2	1	13	12	6	50%	1	8%
Philosophy	8	3	2	0	13	13	3	23%	2	15%
Physics	8	2	5	2	17	15	3	20%	6	40%
Geology	7	3	3	8	21	13	6	46%	3	23%
Health Admin.	5	2	4	3	14	11	3	27%	3	27%
Total	439	195	124	219	977	758	338	45%	117	15%

Table 3.2 Average Faculty Salary, by Full Professors

	AVERAGE SALARY, FULL PROFESSOR	AVERAGE SALARY, ASSOCIATE PROFESSOR	AVERAGE SALARY, ASSISTANT PROFESSOR	AVERAGE SALARY, LECTURERS AND NON TENURE TRACK FACULTY
Economics	$158,325	$131,818	$114,734	$72,800
Management	$156,803	$130,550	$113,631	$72,100
Finance	$149,191	$124,213	$108,115	$68,600
Accounting	$144,624	$120,411	$104,805	$66,500
Computer Sci.	$117,760	$82,665	$66,309	$43,633
Physics	$114,395	$80,304	$64,414	$42,386
Mathematics	$112,152	$78,729	$63,151	$41,555
Chemistry	$109,909	$77,154	$61,888	$40,724
Geology	$109,909	$77,154	$61,888	$40,724
Average	$109,747	$85,203	$69,297	$48,861
Biology	$108,787	$76,367	$61,256	$40,308
Educ. Found.	$107,078	$75,036	$50,708	$41,008
Psychology	$106,526	$80,479	$63,450	$44,650
Educ. Lead.	$104,999	$72,150	$55,118	$44,574
Int'l Affairs	$101,010	$84,670	$67,648	$44,444
Teaching	$99,801	$75,947	$58,019	$46,920
Hospitality	$98,553	$77,540	$63,985	$53,560
Political Sci.	$98,116	$74,126	$58,441	$41,125
Health Admin.	$96,640	$76,035	$62,742	$52,520
Communications	$95,313	$72,008	$56,771	$39,950
History	$94,378	$71,302	$56,215	$39,559
Philosophy	$93,444	$70,596	$55,658	$39,167
Geography	$92,510	$69,890	$55,101	$38,775
Nursing	$91,856	$72,271	$59,636	$49,920
Foreign Lang.	$91,575	$69,184	$54,545	$38,384
Literature	$91,575	$69,184	$54,545	$38,384
Anthropology	$90,641	$68,478	$53,988	$37,992
Music	$88,772	$67,066	$52,875	$37,209
Art	$85,034	$64,242	$50,649	$35,642

Table 3.3 Faculty Salaries, by Total

	SALARIES, TENURED FACULTY	SALARIES, NON-TENURED FACULTY	SALARIES, LECTURERS	SALARIES, ADJUNCT AND GRADUATE	TOTAL SALARIES, ACADEMIC YEAR	SUMMER SALARIES	TOTAL SALARIES
Psychology	$2,381,852	$951,752	$223,252	$112,000	$3,668,855	$398,714	$4,067,570
Accounting	$2,074,598	$1,257,659	$199,500	$56,000	$3,587,757	$428,546	$4,016,303
Management	$1,408,836	$1,249,937	$288,400	$104,000	$3,051,173	$408,614	$3,459,787
Nursing	$1,377,802	$715,634	$748,800	$112,000	$2,954,236	$329,810	$3,284,046
Finance	$1,540,363	$1,081,146	$205,800	$64,000	$2,891,308	$358,783	$3,250,091
Teaching	$1,763,590	$522,168	$187,680	$104,000	$2,577,437	$310,440	$2,887,877
Biology	$1,482,953	$735,078	$201,542	$56,000	$2,475,572	$285,001	$2,760,574
Economics	$1,422,514	$917,871	$72,800	$16,000	$2,429,185	$239,188	$2,668,374
Educ. Lead.	$1,641,838	$440,942	$133,722	$120,000	$2,336,501	$292,530	$2,629,031
Literature	$1,556,714	$545,448	$153,535	$24,000	$2,279,697	$249,940	$2,529,637
Mathematics	$1,378,534	$505,208	$207,775	$64,000	$2,155,517	$252,615	$2,408,132
History	$1,351,434	$449,717	$197,793	$24,000	$2,022,944	$220,186	$2,243,130
Computer Sci.	$1,210,764	$397,851	$218,164	$80,000	$1,906,779	$233,183	$2,139,962
Art	$1,217,629	$202,595	$285,136	$96,000	$1,801,360	$267,793	$2,069,153
Educ. Found.	$1,100,893	$456,374	$205,040	$40,000	$1,802,308	$202,980	$2,005,288
Hospitality	$950,020	$255,939	$321,360	$176,000	$1,703,319	$240,814	$1,944,132
Communications	$981,657	$510,940	$39,950	$72,000	$1,604,548	$202,333	$1,806,881

Political Science	$813,316	$467,527	$164,501	$112,000	$1,557,344	$226,137	$1,783,481
Chemistry	$1,130,046	$247,552	$81,448	$32,000	$1,491,046	$161,933	$1,652,978
Int'l Affairs	$704,708	$338,240	$222,220	$96,000	$1,361,168	$163,340	$1,524,508
Music	$795,334	$211,500	$260,461	$16,000	$1,283,295	$154,725	$1,438,020
Foreign Lang.	$697,739	$218,179	$307,069	$24,000	$1,246,988	$154,725	$1,401,713
Physics	$639,658	$128,828	$211,931	$16,000	$996,416	$110,114	$1,106,530
Anthropology	$751,349	$161,965	$0	$40,000	$953,314	$119,019	$1,072,333
Geology	$540,934	$185,664	$122,172	$64,000	$912,770	$136,023	$1,048,793
Philosophy	$524,157	$166,974	$78,334	$0	$769,465	$77,363	$846,827
Geography	$518,915	$110,203	$77,551	$8,000	$714,668	$77,363	$792,031
Health Admin.	$348,835	$125,484	$210,080	$24,000	$708,399	$73,291	$781,690
Total	$32,186,846	$13,568,479	$5,621,859	$1,752,000	$53,129,185	$6,375,502	$59,618,873

Table 3.4 Expenditures, by Overall

	OVERALL EXPENDITURES	TOTAL SALARIES	TRAVEL	ADMINISTRATION
Accounting	$5,952,784	$4,016,303	$19,705	$1,703,220
Nursing	$4,971,556	$3,284,046	$30,100	$1,435,700
Finance	$4,629,943	$3,250,091	$15,326	$1,324,726
Management	$4,629,943	$3,459,787	$15,326	$1,324,726
Psychology	$3,923,322	4,067,570	$25,009	$295,971
Economics	$3,637,813	$2,668,374	$12,042	$1,040,856
Biology	$3,440,893	2,760,574	$18,629	$575,390
Teaching	$3,406,982	$2,887,877	$17,435	$513,413
Educ. Lead.	$2,970,189	$2,629,031	$15,200	$447,591
Literature	$2,886,973	2,529,637	$18,403	$217,790
Mathematics	$2,882,911	2,408,132	$15,608	$482,084
Educ. Found.	$2,533,397	$2,005,288	$12,965	$381,768
History	$2,516,848	2,243,130	$16,043	$189,868
Art	$2,442,823	2,069,153	$15,572	$184,284
Hospitality	$2,435,048	$1,944,132	$14,743	$703,200
Computer Sci.	$2,417,925	2,139,962	$13,091	$404,328
Int'l Affairs	$2,033,650	1,524,508	$12,000	$497,142
Chemistry	$1,952,939	1,652,978	$10,573	$326,573
Communications	$1,850,624	1,806,881	$11,797	$139,609
Music	$1,776,599	1,438,020	$11,325	$134,024
Political Science	$1,776,599	1,783,481	$11,325	$134,024
Foreign Lang.	$1,702,574	1,401,713	$10,853	$128,440
Physics	$1,394,957	1,106,530	$7,552	$233,266
Geology	$1,208,963	1,048,793	$6,545	$202,164
Health Admin.	$1,116,064	$781,690	$6,757	$322,300
Anthropology	$1,110,374	1,072,333	$7,078	$83,765
Philosophy	$962,324	846,827	$6,134	$72,597
Geography	$888,299	792,031	$5,662	$67,012
Total	$73,453,318	$59,618,873	$382,800	$13,565,831

Note: Some minior expenditure categories included in the overall figure are not included on the table.

Table 3.5 Credit Hours Produced, by Total per Expeditures

	LOWER LEVEL UNDERGRAD. CREDIT HOURS PRODUCED	UPPER LEVEL UNDERGRAD. CREDIT HOURS PRODUCED	TOTAL UNDERGRAD. CREDIT HOURS PRODUCED	GRAD. CREDIT HOURS PRODUCED	TOTAL CREDIT HOURS PRODUCED	CREDIT HOURS PRODUCED PER TENURED FACULTY	CREDIT HOURS PRODUCED PER FULL-TIME FACULTY	CREDIT HOURS PRODUCED PER TOTAL SALARIES	CREDIT HOURS PRODUCED PER OVERALL EXPENDITURES
Political Science	8,410	1,833	10,243	4,846	15,089	1257	629	0.0085	0.0085
Psychology	14,828	4,048	18,876	4,389	23,265	705	439	0.0057	0.0059
Communications	7,525	1,909	9,434	828	10,262	684	410	0.0057	0.0055
Art	9,959	2,520	12,479	—	12,479	594	378	0.0060	0.0051
Anthropology	4,426	1,146	5,572	—	5,572	464	371	0.0052	0.0050
Computer Sci.	8,012	1,212	9,224	2,827	12,051	803	464	0.0056	0.0050
Health Admin.	1,473	2,142	3,615	1,828	5,443	1089	495	0.0070	0.0049
Foreign Lang.	5,754	1,757	7,511	—	7,511	683	327	0.0054	0.0044
Geology	4,674	606	5,280	—	5,280	754	406	0.0050	0.0044
Educ. Lead.	890	3,909	4,799	8,272	13,071	568	384	0.0050	0.0044
Geography	2,877	917	3,794	—	3,794	474	316	0.0048	0.0043
History	8,188	2,597	10,785	—	10,785	514	317	0.0048	0.0043
Literature	9,295	2,979	12,274	—	12,274	491	315	0.0049	0.0043
Music	5,754	1,833	7,587	—	7,587	584	316	0.0053	0.0043
Nursing	6,627	9,542	16,168	3,479	19,647	893	401	0.0060	0.0040
Philosophy	2,877	993	3,870	—	3,870	484	298	0.0046	0.0040
Hospitality	4,839	4,673	9,512	—	9,512	679	396	0.0049	0.0039
Mathematics	8,680	1,445	10,125	—	10,125	563	327	0.0042	0.0035
Chemistry	5,564	979	6,543	—	6,543	436	312	0.0040	0.0034
Biology	9,793	1,724	11,517	—	11,517	576	311	0.0042	0.0033

(continued)

Table 3.5 Continued

	LOWER LEVEL UNDERGRAD. CREDIT HOURS PRODUCED	UPPER LEVEL UNDERGRAD. CREDIT HOURS PRODUCED	TOTAL UNDERGRAD. CREDIT HOURS PRODUCED	GRAD. CREDIT HOURS PRODUCED	TOTAL CREDIT HOURS PRODUCED	CREDIT HOURS PRODUCED PER TENURED FACULTY	CREDIT HOURS PRODUCED PER FULL-TIME FACULTY	CREDIT HOURS PRODUCED PER TOTAL SALARIES	CREDIT HOURS PRODUCED PER OVERALL EXPENDITURES
Physics	3,784	699	4,483	—	4,483	560	299	0.0041	0.0032
Teaching	944	4,484	5,428	4,232	9,660	372	248	0.0033	0.0028
Management	3,525	5,592	9,117	2,827	11,944	919	427	0.0035	0.0026
Finance	3,095	5,592	8,687	1,628	10,315	688	368	0.0032	0.0022
Accounting	3,697	7,190	10,887	1,381	12,268	584	341	0.0031	0.0021
Economics	2,064	4,394	6,457	829	7,286	560	331	0.0027	0.0020
Foundations	617	3,334	3,952	898	4,850	323	167	0.0024	0.0019
Int'l Affairs	928	882	1,810	1,044	2,854	285	143	0.0019	0.0014
Total	149,098	80,930	230,028	32,643	269,337	614	355	0.0045	0.0037

Table 3.6 Departmental Profiles

Accounting	a highly dysfunctional faculty, regularly unable to agree on even the most basic matters; business dean is regularly involved in mediating disputes, with several faculty members having formal disciplinary actions against them for behavior relative to colleagues; several of the strongest professors have departed; a few very good junior hires
Anthropology	an aging faculty, with all of its tenured members over age 52; has not been allocated junior hires over the past several years, with the past three arts and sciences deans not emphasizing the area
Art	the department has been in "receivership" for the past four years, with the associate dean of arts and sciences serving as interim department chair and the department not allowed to make any tenured hires; faculty members are constantly feuding; 15 of 21 tenured faculty members are over 50; the academic quality of the department has been questioned, with reaccreditation of the unit, scheduled for next year, in question
Biology	one of the better departments at CSU
Chemistry	an aging faculty; solid teachers and citizens, in general
Communications	a strong department; recently successfully absorbed sociology in a merger; several faculty members are leaders within the university
Computer Sci.	few leading or difficult faculty members; largest proportion of minority faculty (all but one is Asian American)
Economics	an "up and coming" faculty that has taken advantage of a "buyers market" for faculty members, hiring (and retaining) several junior professors from leading graduate programs; extraordinary long-serving chair, who has successfully raised funds, in partnership with the business dean, to endow a professorship and fund fellowships for accomplished students
Ed. Foundations	a profoundly dysfunctional faculty with almost all of its tenured faculty members in their 50s; an amalgam of educational sociologists, historians, and philosophers (and others who are not a fit within the other two education departments (leadership and teaching); has burned through four department chairs over the past six years, including the last two recruited to run the department, only to depart after a couple of years; largest proportion of non-Asian American minority faculty at the university; several faculty members are essential to programs in educational leadership and teaching, providing many of the courses in these programs
Educ. Lead.	a "tale of two cities" with a few leading tenured faculty (two of them holding endowed positions, both African- Americans) and some of the least productive and most disruptive tenured faculty at the institution; junior hires have been difficult to make; has agreed to offer an off-site cohort-based doctoral program this coming year, an initiative championed by the education dean; among tenured faculty, one-half are over age 55; produces most of the graduate credit hours at the university
Finance	an average department
Foreign Lang.	an unbalanced department, with several French and German professors, but little student interest in the areas; a desperate need for Spanish faculty members, with several hired as lecturers and adjuncts in recent years (perhaps not with enough attention to quality, which is perceived to be mediocre)
Geography	has one-half of the full-time faculty it did just five years ago, with a few stalwarts, who are well respected on campus, keeping the department together; not an area of emphasis within arts and sciences over the past several years
Geology	a newer department, developed in response to local economic needs; adequate performance, but has not reached the status anticipated at its launch
Health Admin.	a strong department at the very top, but struggling at the bottom; quality is uneven, ranging from the best courses at CSU to among the worst; launching a doctoral program (not yet approved) the year after next

(continued)

Table 3.6 Continued

History	an unexceptional, but solid, department; two endowed faculty members and several newer hires with significant potential
Hospitality	a productive department with several entrepreneurial faculty members; close ties with local business community
Int'l Affairs	established as its own unit, apart from political science, early in the history of the university; three endowed professorships and several strong faculty members; recent hires have been less impressive, but the department remains one of the most prominent at CSU; launching a doctoral program (not yet approved) the year after next
Literature	a solid and stable department
Management	an adequate department; a few faculty members have driven the development of an applied doctoral program (a D.B.A.) ready to launch next year; has overcome a history of internal divisions and questions about quality
Mathematics	a solid and stable department
Music	a mediocre department; several senior faculty members are habitual complainers, but are more annoying than disruptive
Nursing	several tenured, tenure-track, and non-tenure significant faculty have departed recently, causing the department to turn increasingly to adjunct faculty; has emphasized appointing lecturers over the past five years; solid core of faculty; few tenured faculty over age 50; second in credit hours produced at the university
Philosophy	an unexceptional department; aging faculty, with tenured members averaging age 56
Physics	similar to philosophy, with several older faculty and no real exceptional or disappointing members
Political Science	an average department with no extraordinary or disastrous faculty members; third in credit hours produced at the university
Psychology	the largest and most prominent department at the university, with its only current doctoral program; two endowed faculty positions and several recent prominent hires; highest number of credit hours produced
Teaching	has been difficult to retain junior faculty, who tend to depart for other positions; a few senior faculty with national reputations; some resistance to being entrepreneurial, although the faculty has agreed to launch an off-site cohort-based doctoral program the year after next, an initiative championed by the education dean (subject to approval by the state system); among the highest proportion of African American faculty at the university

4

STUDENTS

The relationship between institutions and students, once akin to parent relative to child, has evolved into a contractual one prompting various obligations, even if implicitly. Universities and colleges can be subject to tort liability for reasonably foreseeable harm under what is deemed a "special relationship" with their students. Areas of possible liability are expanding as are the boundaries of institutions, but defenses such as assumption of risk and contributory negligence remain. As contractual relationships increasingly define the entrepreneurial university, extending them to students has not proven uncomfortable, as the courts show continued deference to decisions by institutions on academic matters, provided they have followed their own reasonable rules and are not arbitrary, capricious, or discriminatory in their determinations. Review of disciplinary decisions based on behavior is more likely.

Students have leverage not only through contracts, but also given the competitive nature of the higher education market, they also have leverage through asserting various constitutional and statutory rights, an example of which would be the 1990 Americans with Disabilities Act (ADA), with students requesting reasonable accommodations. But there is deference by courts to deliberative processes in making decisions in the area. There are also ADA-related issues with parents attempting to game the system, seeking advantage for their students, and expectations based in broader disability rights present in K-12 education. Students also have privacy rights, as under the Family Educational Rights and Privacy Act of 1974 (FERPA, also known as the Buckley Amendment), which regulates the release of student records, but there are broad exceptions, as with foreign students and when health and safety are implicated. Institutions have had to balance privacy with managing risk, most recently in developing teams to monitor and address student behavior perceived to be a security threat. Public institutions, in particular, have due process concerns, with the question being, as always, what level of notice and hearing is appropriate.

There is no real due process in admissions, given the lack of property and liberty interests at issue, but the Fourteenth Amendment is applicable in that the U.S. Supreme Court has allowed narrowly tailored affirmative action programs based on the educational necessity of diversity. Other constitutional rights arise with concurrent campus disciplinary hearings and proceedings in local courts. Furthermore, free expression by students at public institutions is protected, especially when it occurs in a public forum, with prior restraints and content-based regulation disfavored, but universities and colleges can impose reasonable time, place, and manner restrictions.

Finally, there are emerging First Amendment issues related to accommodating the religious needs of students and with recognition by institutions of student religious groups that discriminate.

Contract Theory and Student Rights

Contractual Rights

The traditional posture of universities and colleges assuming a parental role toward students has evolved into a contractual relationship, with courts willing to consider disputes involving them. Over the past four decades, students have come to be viewed as consumers, having expectations of institutions in providing programs and performing services triggered when they pay tuition and fees. In exchange, creating an implied or express contract, students must fulfill various behavioral and academic requirements, as found in course catalogues and student handbooks (and even marketing materials). Just as public universities and colleges now justify state appropriations through suggesting a return on their investment, higher education is no longer regarded as a privilege for students, but instead as a purchased good, with a contract created upon the acceptance of tuition by the institution.

The traditional *in loco parentis* approach, which both charged universities and colleges with the duties of parents in their supervision of students and provided them with corresponding rights, came to no longer fit higher education with changes in society and expansion of access in the 1960s. The transition away from *in loco parentis* began with the decision of the U.S. Court of Appeals for the Fifth Circuit in *Dixon v. Alabama State Board of Education* (1961), subsequently accelerating in the context of social change, governmental legislation, and judicial decisions throughout the decade, all of which framed students in higher education as adults (Melear, 2003). With the transition from *in loco parentis* to the so-called bystander era in the 1970s and 1980s, courts tended not to impose duties automatically upon universities and colleges, but only when they assumed various responsibilities. Within both frameworks, courts rarely held institutions liable under tort theories (Dall, 2003).

Associated with the present approach is a greater willingness to impose liability, responding to societal demands for greater accountability and the broad perception that campuses are safe. Universities and colleges, while not parents, are deemed to have a "special relationship" with students, assuming a degree of responsibility for their general welfare and thus liability for injuries caused by breaching a duty owed (Burling, 2003). Liability is more akin to businesses relative to customers or landlords with their tenants, requiring reasonable care to discover dangerous conditions and warn invitees about foreseeable dangers, protecting them, as reasonable. It is important to remember that even if there is a relationship, institutions are not insurers. For liability to attach, harm must be foreseeable, which hinges on reasonableness.

Universities and colleges have responded with preventive measures that involve risk identification, assessment, and management (Dall, 2003).

The contract-based "special relationship" doctrine is a better fit than *in loco parentis* with most aspects of the entrepreneurial university or college—an increasingly commercialized environment more organized by contractual relationships. Contractual agreements protect the rights of both institutions and students, supported by the standard assumptions of good faith and fair dealing (Melear, 2003). Implicit in the contract is that students and parents continue to expect universities and colleges to assume a broad role in student affairs, providing a multitude of services and taking responsibility for providing experiences outside of the classroom. Institutions thus continue to have duties toward students based on the "special relationship"—and liability if they fail in them. The relationship is akin to a fiduciary one, in which students entrust the institution to act on their behalf (Melear, 2003).

Framing relationships as contracts similarly protects institutions as in managing risk. In a contractual relationship, universities and colleges can penalize students for a breach, as with suspension or dismissal, upon applying the appropriate due process (considered in Chapter 1). But institutions also must provide the academic programs and support services that they implicitly or explicitly promise. If needed, students can compel performance, as courts are willing to hear matters based in contract on which they once would have deferred to the institution-as-parent. Courts continue to defer to the decisions of faculty and administrators on academic matters (also discussed in Chapter 1)—not substituting their judgment in areas such as grading—but have become comfortable hearing cases framed as contractual relationships between students and institutions (Stoner and Showalter, 2004). Students also have leverage in being able to readily transfer to another university or college, with academic programs having become relatively standardized and courses usually counting from one institution to the next.

Contract theory applies equally at public and private institutions, as both provide services in exchange for payment, and also frames the relationship with contractors and consultants. It is the primary device employed to extend rights, such as free expression, covered by constitutions at public universities and colleges, to those at private institutions that integrate such principles into their own rules. Moving to contract theory requires that institutions regularly audit materials such as catalogues and handbooks, especially on websites, that could be read as a contract, even if not intended as such. Precision in language and consistency across areas maximizes the leverage that universities and colleges can derive through contracts, while reminding them of the promises they have made and to which students may hold them.

Contracts provide a comfortable framework for routine exchanges, as in student services. Universities and colleges have long directly contracted with students in areas such as housing and dining, signing leases and buying meal plans, with courts comfortable resolving disputes via the use of standard contract principles (Melear, 2003).

Because mandatory student fees support them, some student services, such as computing or health centers, may be deemed contractual in nature. As institutions struggle with budgets, effectively unable to raise tuition to cover expenses, both nondiscretionary and discretionary, they increasingly turn to fees. For instance, in constructing facilities such as fitness centers toward remaining competitive with other institutions, student fees provide an option—and most universities and colleges use them, in part, to support athletics. Other student services are read into the broader contract between institutions and students, as with the provision of academic advising, resource centers, and campus security.

Finally, the contractual relationship between students and institutions is not static, as universities and college sometimes need to alter programs and revise policies as circumstances merit, especially given the increasingly competitive and turbulent environment in higher education. When they can demonstrate that such changes are reasonable and necessary, institutions tend to have a more defensible position in a student-initiated breach of contract action. (The same would apply with contractual relationships with employees, discussed in Chapter 3.) Universities and colleges improve their legal position when they provide proper notice and attempt to provide appropriate alternatives toward minimizing hardship on students, as with arranging transfers when closing an academic program or allowing existing students to follow the degree requirements they matriculated under. They are more exposed, as with program closure, when their failure to maintain standards or provide notices has negative consequences for students. Across situations, institutions tend to do well when they follow their own clearly stated procedures and do not act in an arbitrary or capricious manner so as to violate their contractual obligations (Melear, 2003). Basic contractual remedies apply in these situations, with compensatory damages—and punitive ones in extreme cases. Options for injunctive relief—the court requiring an institution to take or avoid some action—are available, but less realistic when it is impossible or impractical to continue a program.

Constitutional and Statutory Rights

Students have certain constitutional and statutory rights relative to institutions. The U.S. Constitution does not expressly reference education, but particularly since *Dixon*, it is clear that students in public higher education have certain fundamental rights. Private universities and colleges can choose to grant such rights, enforceable by students through contract. Additionally, various state and federal statutes apply to public and private institutions alike, as with the antidiscrimination laws detailed in Chapter 2, such as Title VII and the Americans with Disabilities Act. Courts are less inclined to defer to academic judgment on constitutional matters. They might not upset a grading or tenure decision, but they are more comfortable deciding matters related to the free exercise of religion or protections related to search and seizure. Judges who once would have supported, without questioning, decisions made in the "best interests" of a student, may well now review these when constitutional or statutory rights are involved.

Disability. A prominent illustration is the ADA (introduced in Chapter 2), which protects students as it does employees, extending rights and providing a framework for raising legal challenges. As with the other federal nondiscrimination statutes, it applies to both public and private institutions. In order to ensure access for students with disabilities who are otherwise qualified for academic programs, institutions must make the reasonable accommodations it can without undue hardship. Universitities and colleges do not need to make such modifications if to do so would compromise the integrity of their academic programs. Students with disabilities, as accommodated, must still be qualified and perform in mainstream settings, as the purpose of the ADA is not to segregate students with disabilities in special programs, but to enable them to integrate into institutional life.

For instance, a university or college must adapt instructional facilities, if there is a reasonable means to do so, to enable a student with a disability to participate in classes. The same applies to providing additional time to complete admissions tests or course examinations, but only to the extent an institution can do so without compromising its standards. Such accommodations can often be framed as not involving a fundamental or substantial modification to an academic program (Flygare, 2002). Other common accommodations include course substitution; extended time to complete assignments, courses, or degrees; and auxiliary aids, such as interpreters, real-time captioning, note taking assistance, and instructional materials in alternative formats (Kincaid, 2004b). Whether an offered accommodation is reasonable is situational, as with not requiring the modification of a building to make it accessible for those with physical disabilities when the cost is exorbitant. (Construction projects must comply with the ADA, however.) There are also often solutions that are not expensive or disruptive, as with policies that move class meetings to spaces that allow the entry of those using wheelchairs.

Issues of accessibility to computing are increasingly arising (Thomas, 2004). With the Internet becoming so prevalent and thus essential within higher education, institutions must make teaching materials and relevant websites accessible online to students with disabilities, at least to the extent that doing so does not constitute an undue burden (Golden, 2008; Goldgeier, 2004). The ADA and Section 504 of the 1973 Rehabilitation Act apply to distance learning (Przypyszny, 2004), which has only become more prevalent at the entrepreneurial university. Similarly, there are disability issues associated with study abroad programs, clinical settings, and for-credit internships (McKanders, 2004). Although U.S. disability statutes are not applicable extra-territorially, institutions increasingly have sufficient control over programs abroad to merit applying these (Thomas, 2004). The statutes also apply to athletics (Thomas, 2004). Harassment of those with disabilities is another issue that sometimes arises (Thomas, 2004).

But courts still tend to defer to academic decisions by institutions in appeals by students, absent evidence of bad faith, with less deference given to those motivated by other matters (Stoner and Showalter, 2004). The decision of the U.S. Supreme Court in *PGA Tour, Inc. v. Martin*, 532 U.S. 661 (2001) demonstrates the judicial willingness to overturn a decision not to accommodate a professional golfer through allowing him to ride in a cart during competition, emphasizing the need for individualized analysis in such determinations. The decision could be distinguished from academic context, especially given traditional judicial deference (Wilhelm, 2006). In its only decision on disability discrimination in admissions, *Southwest Community College v. Davis* (1979), the U.S. Supreme Court held for the institution in its refusal to admit a hearing impaired student to a nursing program with a significant clinical component, as it was not possible to make a reasonable accommodation in that setting without compromising curricular integrity. There are several employment cases that are instructive on disability accommodation matters, as well as U.S. Equal Employment Opportunity Commission (EEOC) guidance (Babbitt, 2004).

Institutions must ensure that admissions standards do not have an unfair impact upon those with disabilities, similar to the need to make reasonable adjustments to academic programs to ensure admitted students can make the most of their educational opportunities (Kaufman, 2005). It is also unlawful for universities and colleges to question applicants about disabilities or require them to self-identify in the admissions process, but applicants may volunteer such information and institutions may then require documentation (Flygare, 2002). Institutions may admit students with disabilities provisionally, if they do so in ways similar to the way they admit nondisabled students (Flygare, 2002). Those previously dismissed for academic reasons may remain ineligible for readmision even with a subsequent diagnosis (Daggett, 2006). In addition, secondary schools may be reluctant to provide candid appraisals related to learning and psychiatric disabilities. There is also the problem, even with statutory protections and improved sensitivities, that disabilities may be wrongly confused with unacceptable effort or insufficient aptitude (Flygare, 2002).

As discussed in Chapter 2, a disability under the ADA or Section 504 is a physical or mental impairment that substantially limits one or more of a person's major life activities, with a history of such impairment or being regarded as having it considered relevant (Kaufman, 2005). Once again, the ADA defines disability broadly to include not only those that are readily apparent, as with ambulatory, hearing, or sight impairments, but also less apparent challenges such as learning and psychological disabilities. Learning disabilities such as dyslexia—or dyscalculia (incomprehension of simple mathematical functions) or dysgraphia (difficulty expressing thoughts in writing)—as properly diagnosed, fit under the ADA definition (Crockett, 2004; Rose, 2004). The same is true of psychological disabilities such as bipolar, obsessive-compulsive, and attention-deficit disorders (Rose, 2004).

But not all impairments are disabilities. Also, what constitutes a sufficient impairment or disability to trigger the law must be determined on a case-by-case basis—a matter that has only been complicated by advances in medication and technology. Rose (2004) raises the relevant question of determining what constitutes a limiting mental impairment being relative, as there are examples of people compensating for such disabilities through "self-accommodation," as with learning certain academic coping strategies, and being quite successful in higher education and then in professional careers.

Students who claim a disability and request an accommodation must demonstrate that they are otherwise qualified, thus able with the adjustment to meet all essential academic and nonacademic requirements. Once again, universities and colleges are obligated to provide reasonable accommodation, but not substantially modify programs or take actions that would otherwise pose an undue burden upon them (Kincaid, 2004a). Institutions may require that students requesting an accommodation document their disability, considering confidentiality and related concerns (Kincaid, 2004a). It is the responsibility of the student claiming a disability to notify the institution of their status and such students may disclose a disability at any time. They must assist in identifying necessary academic accommodations, and continue to demonstrate qualified status throughout their program (Flygare, 2002). Institutions may require such students to provide supporting medical, psychological, or educational diagnostic tests and professional prescriptions related to needed adjustments (Flygare, 2002; Mansfield, 2007).

When administrators consider accommodation requests through a deliberative process, courts are likely to defer to their well-supported professional judgments that they cannot adjust for a disability without compromising essential requirements (Lee and Abbey, 2008). Universities and colleges cannot use burdensome proof-of-disability criteria nor unnecessarily discourage individuals from establishing that they have disabilities, but they may question the legitimacy of documentation. Even the most financially fragile institutions cannot simply say that they are not equipped to handle learning or psychiatric disorders, and must consider an accommodation if informed of such a disability, with promises made later enforceable (Flygare, 2002).

There are standard concerns about "gaming the system," as with families claiming a student has a learning disability—with supporting documentation from a willing psychologist—in the thought that there are advantages associated with accommodations such as being granted more time to take examinations with little or no stigma associated with doing so. Diagnoses such as dyslexia can be by medical and nonmedical professionals alike, so they can be relatively straightforward to secure. The parents of students with disabilities often have several years of experience advocating for such accommodations, retaining counsel and bringing lawsuits, as they deem necessary. One challenge is that families with experience with the Individuals with Disabilities Education Act (IDEA), which governs K-12 special education, have expectations, given the expansiveness of the law, that exceed requirements relevant to higher education institutions (Thomas, 2004). Rothstein (2007) notes that students in the millennial generation—and their parents—tend to raise more mental illness issues, such as

ADHD, dyslexia, panic attacks, and disorders such as Asperger's syndrome. There is also an emerging field of academic study on disabilities, providing a theoretical and empirical base and increasing awareness and advocacy.

Universities and colleges commonly have offices devoted to services for students with disabilities, compliance with associated regulations, and educating the campus community about such issues (Crockett, 2004). These students should have available the same student services available to those across an institution, including regular opportunities at no additional cost in student housing, financial aid, student employment, career services, fitness and athletics, health care and insurance, transportation systems, computer accessibility, and physical accessibility (Kaufman, 2005). The latter is viewed in the context of the campus in its entirety, thus not requiring every building to be accessible, but instead a reasonable proportion. Additionally, institutions can provide separate programs in areas such as athletics, as appropriate (Kaufman, 2005).

Students with disabilities are also subject to the same rules and potential discipline for violating them as other students. Institutions are not required to alter student conduct codes or excuse misconduct, even if it is linked to an underlying disorder, in contrast with IDEA in the K-12 sector. They only must consider the disability as with any mitigating circumstance (Kincaid, 2004a). The only twist is that the discipline must address behaviors apart from the disability (Bunting, 2004). For instance, punishing an outburst associated with a student having Tourette syndrome is different from discipline for an inappropriate outburst within a student's control. As with other at risk students, those with disabilities can be subject to preventive measures such as mandatory withdrawals and refusals to be assigned campus housing. As always, any determination must be individualized (Lee and Abbey, 2008).

A few institutions have found a market niche in developing and marketing specific programs for learning disabled students. Such an approach underscores that disabilities issues cut across all aspects of institutional life (Kincaid, 2004b). Finally, Murray and Helms (2001) consider the issue of how long accommodations should be applicable in higher education, as with denying requests in the context of graduate education should the student be already deemed employable following his or her undergraduate program.

Privacy. Another set of statutory rights relate to student records and privacy concerns. The Family Education Rights and Privacy Act prohibits institutions from releasing records to unauthorized persons, whether by policy or practice. The intention of the act is to provide students over age 18 with the ability to review and potentially challenge information in their files deemed inaccurate or damaging, as well as limiting access to records to those with an appropriate interest. Universities and colleges must provide students with access to their records and develop appropriate processes to facilitate needed changes or deletions in them (Tribbensee, 2003; Williams, 2007). They are also required to retain transcripts, as well as various admissions, disciplinary, and medical records, with the length of time sometimes mandated (Ambash, 2005).

FERPA applies to both public and private universities and colleges that receive federal funding—and some states also have laws relevant to student records (Tribbensee, 2003). The U.S. Supreme Court held in *Gonzaga University v. Doe* (2002) that the statute does not create an enforceable right for individuals against institutions, as under section 1983 of the Civil Rights Act of 1871, which provides for the enforcement of federal constitutional or statutory rights when state laws are inadequate or unavailable. The case involved a student challenging the withholding by a private university of an affidavit of good moral character required for certification as a teacher. There may be alternative remedies available, such as state law actions for breach of contract, invasion of privacy, and defamation (Sidbury, 2003). There are no real penalties for FERPA violations—the federal government can withhold aid to universities or colleges, but to do so is unrealistic (Williams, 2007).

With FERPA, the two main questions for institutions—namely the official designated, as required under the act, to monitor compliance—to consider are what constitutes a record as covered by the act and who can properly be afforded access to such records. Records include documents such as transcripts. In addressing the latter concern, institutions tend to restrict access to records to faculty and administrators with a clear "need to know," as to enable student advising, limiting advisors and relevant others to reviewing only relevant portions of files. Notes related to student records should also be kept confidential. In practice, universities and colleges should (and tend to) instruct faculty and administrators not to release any information about a student—even basic information to parents—without reviewing it for the applicability of FERPA.

But FERPA allows disclosure when there is a legitimate interest, as to relevant on-campus officials, but also to parents of dependent students, in compliance with a subpoena, in connection with a disciplinary process, and to accommodate health and safety concerns (Khatcheressian, 2003; Tribbensee, 2003; C. R. Williams, 2007). Institutions may also provide access to directory information related to student records to outsiders such as accrediting agencies for use in research and auditing (Tribbensee, 2003). Under the USA PATRIOT Act of 2002 (Uniting and Strengthening America by Providing Appropriate Tools Required to Intercept and Obstruct Terrorism Act) and other legislation, institutions must release information on foreign students— those holding a visa, as with the F-1 for academic study, J-1 for exchange visitors, and M-1 for vocational study—with FERPA providing few effective limits. There are also added reporting requirements (Khatcheressian, 2003). White (2007) notes the challenge with FERPA in not disclosing to parents information on matters such as drug and alcohol abuse, which may lead to tort liability for the institution if something goes wrong, arguing for better balancing of institutional interests with student privacy, perhaps by broadening the health or safety emergency exception.

Additionally, there are privacy rules related to protected health information under the Health Insurance Portability and Accountability Act of 1996 (HIPAA) that apply to university-affiliated health providers, such as a medical center, with FERPA covering other privacy situations such as student medical records. HIPAA, which includes civil fines and criminal penalties for violations, applies to entities within a university or college, although not the entire institution, that transmit "protected health information" in electronic form, as to an insurance provider, in providing health care or conducting research (Scaraglino, 2003; Williams, 2007). Student health centers are likely subject to HIPAA if they are a health care provider, conduct electronic transactions, and treat students and nonstudents (Bianchi, 2006). Finally, institutions that comply with FERPA are exempt, as related to students, from financial services legislation mandating privacy related to customer information, but are responsible for maintaining the confidentiality of information connected with a financial service or product, as with certain financial aid transactions (Williams, 2007).

A related set of privacy concerns involves the Fourth Amendment, which prohibits unreasonable searches and seizures by the state. These can become an issue in residence halls at public universities, at which staff function as state actors. In such settings, there are exceptions to the requirement of obtaining a warrant, as when lives are being endangered or having received consent (although consent from third parties is more questionable) (Jones, 2007). Institutions can take action to maintain an orderly and safe environment or in an emergency, but must balance the Fourth Amendment and statutory rights of students related to privacy. Drug testing, which is essentially a search and seizure, is another concern. The standard for determining whether a drug testing policy is constitutionally valid is whether any intrusion caused by the actual testing, which can be significant, outweighs a legitimate governmental interest in preventing the behavior that the testing is intended to prevent. Such an interest is likely to involve matters such as protecting public safety or sensitive information, as within a pervasively regulated industry.

Students are unlikely to be in such roles. And it is questionable that all but a very few university or college employees are apt to impair the safety of others through their substance abuse, so as to merit testing. Student athletes tend to be an exception, given incentives to abuse drugs to enhance performance and the interest in preserving the integrity of games, as well as their diminished expectation of privacy associated with being an athlete and their ability to withdraw from competition and thus avoid testing. There may also be prohibitions on testing in state constitutions that include a right to privacy, or local ordinances that limit testing; applicable common law causes of actions such as invasion of privacy to challenge testing; or questions one can raise about the reliability of tests.

Certain types of other testing are expressly prohibited by statute for both private and public employers, such as for genetic defects, HIV and AIDS, or psychological traits. There is also a right to privacy read into the U.S. Constitution in *Griswold v. Connecticut* (1965) and other cases in matters related to procreation. Additionally, the ADA protects individuals with certain alcohol- and drug-related addictions from discrimination on the basis of that addiction. But there still may be an interest in avoiding the deficient performance that can be related to the use of drugs, justifying perhaps observation as opposed to testing.

But even monitoring raises privacy concerns, as with the response by many institutions to the 2007 massacre at Virginia Tech. Institutions have begun to have regular meetings to identify and monitor students who could potentially "snap" and injure others, attempting to guide these students into treatment. Universities and colleges are balancing privacy concerns with the need to manage risk, seemingly favoring the latter. Aside from the simple need to maintain safety, there are significant reputational risks that an entrepreneurial university or college simply cannot afford (Stuart, 2009).

Faber College is among the most selective—and expensive—higher education institutions in the country. Its students expect much of both themselves and their college. Faber offers an impressive academic program, with accomplished faculty and ample support services, as well as a rich experience for students outside of class. Over one-half of Faber students spend some time studying abroad, with many doing so multiple times, with individualized experiences increasing in popularity. The college also has an increasingly active undergraduate research program, matching students with faculty to engage together in scholarly work. The program is a favorite of the Faber president, Vernon Wormer, who arrived at the college two years ago.

There are now well over a hundred student organizations at Faber, some devoted to intellectual pursuits, but most to service. Given the dearth of night life in the small town for which the college is named, social life tends to revolve around the sororities and fraternities that the college would prefer to close, but that alumni champion and that remain popular. About one-quarter of Faber students are varsity athletes, most of them recruited, but none of them on athletic scholarship, which is not allowed in NCAA Division III. Under dean of students Robert Hoover, Faber also invests heavily in student services, with one of the highest ratios of administrators to students in the nation. Like other universities and colleges, it has also invested heavily in student facilities, building a new fitness center, student commons, and a residential complex in the past five years, along with a science building and addition to the library.

Faber students tend to know how to get the most out of their college experience, with Hoover and the dean of faculty Donald Day now discussing almost weekly whether they are going too far. For instance, the undergraduate research experience office is overwhelmed with requests for placements with faculty, only some of whom are actively involved in research, the students having come to believe that admission to graduate or professional school depends on participating in a project. A few students have even become assertive with faculty members,

(continued)

as with insisting they be included as an author of a published paper, again having heard this plays well on an application. There has also been an explosion in the number of student organizations at Faber, with students similarly viewing founding their own group as essential. Perhaps the diffusion of organizations is partly to blame on Faber and its peer institutions, as word got around a few years ago that they tended to be smitten with founders-as-applicants.

Hoover and Day are beginning to ask whether such an individualized approach is really within the contract between the institutions and its students. They realize that the students are paying a premium to attend Faber, partly because of the high level of service they receive. But individualized demands threaten to overload the system. Not only do students want to do their own thing, but they also insist on having Faber administrators being closely involved with them doing it. Administrators have begun to joke that students seem to view the proper role of student affairs administrators as "staffing" them. Not only have institutions nationally grown more entrepreneurial, Hoover and Day have concluded, but so too have elite students. And there is little they can do about it, except hire more staff in response to various boundaries expanding.

The students come by their expectations honestly, as many of their parents are equally aggressive. Kenta Dorfman is illustrative. Like most Faber students, her parents took a very active role in the college search that she began well before her senior year in high school. Few Faber students work during summer, as with Dorfman, instead participating in internships, volunteer work, and summer academic enrichment programs—and thereby adding lines to their resumes. Like many parents, Dorfman's have also paid for multiple standardized admissions tests preparation courses; retained private counselors to assist in identifying institutions and preparing applications; and approached the financial aid process with great purpose upon her admission. They are also involved in the daily life of their child while she is at college. Dorfman thinks nothing of calling her parents on her mobile phone to manage a routine situation, seeking instant resolution, a type of occurrence that has become almost cliche among students at Faber and other elite colleges.

Some parents have gone so far as to secure a diagnosis for their child as learning disabled, perceiving an advantage to be had in receiving additional time to complete tests and other accommodations. There is even a coach at Faber who is encouraging her athletes to seek diagnoses, wanting the extra academic latitude she sees it providing. There has been a marked increase over the past decade or so in such accommodations at Faber, but administrators there appreciate (and are pleased) that some of it is attributable to improved identification of actual learning disabilities. Faber is committed to assisting these students in whatever ways it reasonably can. But what it has found is that there is little it can do to challenge a questionable diagnosis, especially if made while a student is in high school.

Parents also have exhibited unrealistic expectations of Faber in ensuring campus safety. The college, guided by Hoover, has resisted developing a "watch list" of students who have exhibited signs of being potentially dangerous to themselves or others. But they are also fearful of being exposed to significant liability if there is an incident, because they have not developed such a list while peer institutions have. There is also significant reputational risk that comes with an occurrence. Being perceived (or misperceived) as a less-than-safe environment is an obvious disadvantage in the highly competitive market for the most accomplished high school students. Some parents, like the Dorfmans, essentially demand that the college be an insurer. The situation has gone beyond the "good old days" of trusting administrators and faculty to act in the best interests of students—and even past reassurance, to something, it seems sometimes, more like validation.

Admissions and Financial Aid

As in hiring in employment, institutions may not unjustifiably discriminate in admissions on the basis of immutable characteristics such as race or gender, with the antidiscrimination statutes discussed in Chapter 2 available to those alleging a violation. The Equal Protection clause also applies at public institutions, disfavoring preferential treatment for a member of any one group, absent such a compelling reason as affirmative action when appropriately crafted. Enforcement is by federal agencies, such as the Office of Civil Rights of the U.S. Department of Education, or there can be private actions for nominal, compensatory, and punitive damages, with the latter two requiring a showing of compensable injury (Meers and Thro, 2004). At private universities and colleges, certain religious or single-sex settings merit an exception within the antidiscrimination laws.

Due process concerns, considered in Chapter 1, may also arise in admissions. But because there are not property or liberty interests attached to being an applicant for admission to a university or college, rights to notice and hearing are few (if any). Given the specialized academic judgment associated with admissions, courts are inclined to defer to institutions when there are not procedural defects and decisions appear to be reasonable (Stoner and Showalter, 2004). In other words, in substantive areas like admissions, when universities and colleges follow their own rules and do not appear to make arbitrary or capricious decisions, courts are likely to allow their determinations to stand.

Race-based affirmative action programs in admissions are an exception to equal protection, justified by a compelling state interest and needing to be as narrowly tailored as possible to serve that need. In its 2003 decision in *Grutter v. Bollinger*, which involved affirmative action in admissions at the University of Michigan Law School, the U.S. Supreme Court held that the education benefits of enhanced diversity were such a sufficient interest and the program was properly limited. The court preserved its ruling in *Regents of the University of California v. Bakke* (1978), which enables universities and colleges to consider race as a factor in the admissions decision, but does not allow them to consider applications from underrepresented groups in a separate pool or establish quotas. Race can be a "plus" factor weighed by an admissions committee at a selective institution similar to a prospective student residing in a region underrepresented in an entering class (perhaps Idaho) or having participated in an unusual extracurricular activity in high school (maybe playing the oboe). *Gratz v. Bollinger*, the companion case to *Grutter*, rejected institutions applying numerical formulas to such determinations, particularly when they overemphasize race so as to markedly improve prospects for admission. *Grutter* holds that if race is going to be a "plus" factor, admissions needs to be qualitative, with a review of the entire file.

Affirmative action programs in admissions remain constitutionally permissible, as in *Bakke* and *Grutter*, provided they satisfy the most stringent standard of judicial review (strict scrutiny) through meeting its compelling interest and narrowly tailored conditions (discussed in the context of employment in Chapter 2). In *Grutter*, the court was persuaded by empirical evidence of the profound need for a university or college to have the intellectual environment and educational benefits enabled only through enrolling a diverse student body. It emphasized the advantages of furthering understanding across races and diminishing persistent racial stereotypes. But the broader justification of remedying societal discrimination has not been held to be a compelling interest, leaving the arguably weaker one of diversity (Ancheta, 2008), which is not to say that racial literacy resulting from exposure to diverse environments should not be valued in higher education (Kaufman, 2007). Nor would justifications such as maintaining racial balance or providing role models likely be sufficient (Meers and Thro, 2004). Bases in remedying the present effects of identified past discrimination within the institution are stronger, provided there is specific evidence and not merely a generalized assertion (Meers and Thro, 2004).

The University of Michigan also met the second condition with its Law School program, achieving its desired ends through neither directly nor indirectly insulating certain groups from consideration in the same applicant pool with all candidates. Such narrow tailoring requires individualized consideration, reading each application individually, not isolating applications from competition. It also demands that race alone is not the defining feature of an application, with everyone having the chance to highlight his or her contribution to diversity and that contribution not simply being assumed for anyone (Meers and Thro, 2004). There should also be, as at Michigan, good faith consideration of the viability of nonracial alternatives, no undue burden to nonminorities, and limited duration and periodic review of programs (Meers and Thro, 2004). There is little judicial direction as to what are possible race-neutral alternatives, but there is guidance available from the U.S. Department of Justice, Department of Education, and Commission on Civil Rights, as well as private organizations such as the College Board (LaNoue and Marcus, 2008). LaNoue and Marcus (2008) recommend considering the principles of program evaluation, as with established formal policies and standards, identification and evaluation of multiple race-neutral policies, articulation of underlying facts, empirical data collection and analysis, measurement against established benchmarks, transparency in and documentation of the policy making process, and periodic review.

The decision in *Parents Involved in Community Schools v. Seattle School District No. 1* (2007) overturned a race-based school assignment plan intended to achieve racial balance in a K-12 setting, as race being essentially the sole determining factor violates the compelling interest and narrowly tailored standards (Coleman, Palmer, and Winnick, 2007). But *Parents Involved* suggests that there are compelling interests, analogous but distinct from higher education, in promoting diversity that can properly be pursued through appropriate race-conscious means. Courts do not always make fine distinctions between higher education and K-12 settings, but the decision should not upset allowing affirmative action in higher education admissions (Olivas, 2009). In *Grutter*, numbers alone did not drive race-conscious policies and the diversity sought materially advanced institutional goals. Additionally, *Grutter* reflected individualized review in which race is only one of several factors, considered possible race-neutral alternatives, and offered a transparent and understood approach to diversity and access (Coleman, Palmer, and Winnick, 2007).

Across selective institutions, there is the situation analogous to affirmative action in applicants connected with influential alumni and donors and recruited intercollegiate athletes receiving a sometimes significant preference in admissions (Shulman and Bowen, 2002). Entrepreneurial universities and colleges grant these preferences for practical reasons, knowing it is part of the costs of raising private funds and sponsoring sports teams. Neither public policy nor civil rights litigation has questioned these because discrimination in favor of those with family or social connections or exceptional athletic abilities does not violate Equal Protection or the federal antidiscrimination laws. In contrast, there have been challenges to affirmative action in public policy. The University of California Board of Regents effectively ended affirmative action in 1995, with a resulting decline in already deficient miniority enrollments (Chacon, 2008). States such as Texas and Florida have shifted to a formula admitting a certain percentage of students from each high school in the state, attempting to diversify their classes without direct preferences (LaGrand, 2009). As admissions has become more contested at state flagships nationally, given their combination of relatively low price and generally high prestige, with applicants who once would have easily won admission now being turned down, affirmative action for minority students provides an easy target.

There are arguments in opposition to affirmative action, as in those based on resentment by groups that perceive themselves to lose out in the process and the alleged stigma attached to beneficiaries in their own eyes and those of others (Horn and Marin, 2008; Levine, 2006). There are allegations that "phantom minorities," for whom ethnicity or race has played no real role in their lives, exploit the benefits of affirmative action (Thomas, 2007). Carey (2005) contends that diversity is not so compelling as to justify the use of any type of racial discrimination. But higher education enrollments have diversified significantly post-*Bakke*, with affirmative action at least somewhat responsible. Jabaily (2008) argues that institutions have responded to *Grutter* with increased formality, which has encouraged viewing race consciousness more as colorblindness, with traditional discretion becoming mechanized and normalized, as with emphasizing standardized test scores (Small, 2008). Moran (2006) cautions against either colorblindness or strict racial proportionality, contending that the flexible *Grutter* approach offers a useful middle ground. In dicta in *Grutter*, Justice O'Connor expressed the aspiration that affirmative action be no longer needed in 2028 (25 years after *Grutter* and 50 years after *Bakke*), emphasizing the inherently temporary nature of such efforts (Heller, 2008; Kurlaender and Felts, 2008; Yun and Lee, 2008).

Miller and Toma (forthcoming) frame the diversity that results from affirmative action as a strategic imperative in higher education, with not only the credibility of the industry dependent on pursuing it in robust ways, but also the competitive interests of individual universities and colleges. They connect addressing diversity with the standard institutional aspirations of pursuing prestige and seeking resources. With intense competition in the recruitment of the most desirable students, faculty, and administrators, leading candidates from underrepresented groups are particularly sought after. Such as they are able, institutions accordingly tend to make needed investments, as through attractive scholarship packages, to achieve the diverse environments to which they aspire, both to realize their longstanding values and in positioning for prestige. Universities and colleges thus do not only pursue diversity because it is right. It also contributes to their overall ambitions in becoming more prestigious and therefore more prosperous.

Race-based scholarships in the interest of enhancing diversity are permissible, but have been challenged, as in *Podberesky v. Kirwan* (1991). In that case, the federal appeals court held that an institution can make such awards, if it can generate particularized findings of the present effects of past discrimination at the institution itself, the scholarship program has a legitimate remedial purpose in that context, and it is sufficiently narrowly tailored (Meers and Thro, 2004). U.S. Department of Education guidelines deem such race-exclusive scholarships to be permissible, as are privately funded race-conscious scholarships that do not limit scholarship opportunities for other students (Small, 2008). But judicial guidance at the appellate level is limited to *Podberesky*. Elson (2009) contends that institutions are tending to move away from race conscious scholarships, but that they would be upheld under *Grutter* if they can demonstrate a connection with the need for diversity as a compelling interest, as well as exhibit sufficient narrow tailoring. The latter would result from flexible and individualized consideration where race is one of several factors, no undue burden on nonminorities, and race-neutral alternatives considered. Finally, it is acceptable to have conditions connected with any scholarship, such as maintaining grades or demonstrating need.

Podberesky offers the reminder that affirmative action in admissions needs to be accompanied by the provision of resources to enable and encourage students from underrepresented groups to attend (Nelson, 2005). Entrepreneurial universities and colleges tend to provide such resources, understanding that not doing so compromises the success of their diversity efforts. Such financial aid programs are important in influencing enrollment decisions, both for obvious practical reasons and symbolic ones in sending a message of institutional commitment to realizing the benefits of diversity (Meers and Thro, 2004).

There is no obligation, as under the Americans with Disabilities Act, to implement an affirmative action program for students with disabilities. Nor can there be quotas that limit the number of such students admitted, even if institutions are conscious of the expense associated with accommodating disabilities. And institutions should take care that ostensibly neutral policies do not have a disproportionate negative impact on these applicants. Once again, students with disabilities still must be otherwise qualified for admission, with institutions needing only to make those reasonable accommodations needed to enable an applicant to be fairly considered. Similarly, admissions policies based on age need to have a rational relationship to a legitimate state purpose to conform to constitutional standards. Admissions at private single-sex colleges are exempted from the standard equal protection principle and federal legislation addressing sex discrimination, such as Title VII, based on the benefits that these institutions afford women or minority students. Single-sex public institutions, such as the Citadel and the Virginia Military Institute, both providing military-based education, were unable to justify excluding women, particularly in the context of the successful effort in doing so at the federal military academies.

Finally, there are various other regulations associated with admissions, as with immigration, discussed in Chapter 5, and residency requirements for in-state tuition have been upheld, unlike for welfare benefits, medical care, and voting rights (Llewellyn, 2006).

Faber College receives four applications for each high school senior it admits to its annual class of around 450 students. The college is need-blind in admissions, offering places without regard to the ability of an applicant to pay and arranging financial aid packages accordingly. Faber receives enough applications that its class is balanced each year pretty much to the extent it wants, with an optimal mix of students from different regions of the country and desired proportions of minority and international students, for instance. About

(continued)

40 percent of its class is nonwhite or nonnative, an increase from 25 percent only 15 years ago, with only modest increases among African American, Hispanic, and international students—and a doubling of Asian American students to around 17 percent.

But only 7 percent of Faber students come from households below the U.S. median income. Scholastic Aptitude Test (SAT) scores, which average around 1350 at the college, tend to correlate with family income, so the pool of qualified lower income students is rather small. There are also cultural barriers, as lower income students may not attend expensive institutions even if granted attractive financial aid packages. Accordingly, critics charge that diversity across elite higher education has come to mean "rich kids of all colors."

Faber can thus afford its need blind financial aid policy, despite having an adequate, but not overwhelming, endowment from which to draw scholarship money—it knows that poorer students are less likely to attend, even if admitted and funded. The dean of admissions Lawrence Kroger has long contended that the college would actually prefer to have more of the lower income students that it recruits and admits attend, valuing the diversity they would bring. Admissions at Faber is not only a strategic exercise in attracting the most accomplished students, but is also an expression of its core beliefs as an institution.

But Kroger knows there is also a business side to admissions. About two-fifths of the applicants to Faber are deemed "special applicants," meaning they receive preferences due to race or ethnicity, or status as legacies or children of large donors, recruited athletes, or those with artistic or musical ability. Admitted minority students, excluding Asian Americans, tend to score about 150 points lower, on average, on the SAT than students from outside the special applicants group. Such figures have prompted legal challenges in public higher education, as in *Gratz* and *Grutter* at Michigan.

Other special applications have received little attention. Like other elite institutions, Faber depends on its continued success in fund raising. The easy illustration is thus the likelihood of Faber admitting the child of a $50 million donor, even if the applicant has modest credentials. Being from a very wealthy family is a "plus factor," as the college knows it needs to maintain its relationships as there may well be more large donations in the future. The more interesting question for Kroger and his colleagues is what preference the offspring of the $100,000 donor should receive. Or what about the applicant whose parents have only first given to the institution months before? Admissions can be need blind, but it is not, in effect, income blind—and it is only something of a meritocracy, with some applicants being more equal than others.

A subgenre of the donor issue is the children of celebrities and prominent politicians. Both groups tend to send their children to elite institutions in considerably higher proportions than the rest of the population. Some of this is attributable to the cultural capital that these families possess. But institutions like Faber also know that the buzz that tends to accompany enrolling the child of someone regularly featured in *People* magazine can be considerable—and useful in enhancing the profile of the institution. When a celebrity's child expresses interest, Faber tends to respond aggressively, just as it does with special applicants.

Affirmative action is not only driven by values such as fairness, but also the strategic necessity of institutions enrolling an appropriate number of minority students so as not be perceived as exclusionary. Lest they be targeted, even private institutions need to make a case that they are reasonably representative of society, at least in terms of race and ethnicity, if not socioeconomic status. Having "affirmative action" for such categories as the children of celebrities—granting them a preference in admissions—similarly has strategic purposes for institutions, generating useful publicity.

Among more prominent programs, as in Division I, athletics has the same purpose. At Division III Faber athletics is participatory in nature, with no expectation of generating revenue or even all that much notice. It is, in essence, another student activity. But the nature of coaches and athletes is to want to win—and Faber is committed to recruiting the competitors that it requires to continue to be successful. For instance, Donald Schoenstein, the men's lacrosse coach, must recruit elite athletes for Faber to compete in its league, even at the Division III level. He knows that he cannot promise admission to those he is recruiting, but also counts on admissions reserving, in effect, slots in the entering class for the athletes he needs to bring in each year. There is also the understanding that the college will stretch, as much as possible, to admit recruited athletes and provide them with competitive financial aid packages.

These athletes tend, on average, to have lower admissions numbers—about 100 points lower on the SAT. They also tend to cluster in certain more applied majors at Faber, not often in the humanities or sciences. But even Division III athletics has uses for institutions that may justify making such accommodations. At less selective institutions, sports teams are a way to fill the class, offering modest scholarships to those, particularly men, interested more than anything else in competing in athletics at the next level. At Faber, it may be as simple as keeping pace with competitors, varsity athletics being a staple of American higher education. It is not really an option not to have athletics—and Faber does not want to be embarrassed relative to its peers by or questioned by its alumni about losing persistently.

Discipline and Liability

Discipline

The decisions of the U.S. Supreme Court in *Regents of the University of Michigan v. Ewing* (1985) and *Board of Curators of the University of Missouri v. Horowitz* (1978) articulate the principle that courts should defer to the reasonable judgments of universities and colleges on academic concerns. The more recent decision in *Grutter* (2003) reinforced respecting professional expertise in matters of educational importance. In *Grutter*, the Court deferred to what it deemed the careful and deliberate efforts of faculty and administrators in devising educationally appropriate means to accomplish goals identified as significant (Stoner and Showalter, 2004). Stoner and Showalter contend that, given the unusual and complex nature of academe, courts have long recognized that even if they could hear from all of the constituents involved, they would be unlikely to completely understand their needs and interests. But institutions must still act in accord with express or implied contractual obligations, as with following their own reasonable rules in areas such as due process, not making arbitrary or capricious determinations, and not acting in a discriminatory manner (Melear, 2003; Stoner and Showalter, 2004).

Although courts have chosen to not substitute their judgment for that of experts in academic affairs, deference is not absolute. Judges are more comfortable making determinations on behavior, as with vandalism or underage drinking, as these are more akin to the criminal matters in which they have direct experience (Stoner and Showalter, 2004). Courts will also step in where institutions appear to be acting contrary to public policy—or making decisions driven less by academic judgment than other factors, such as discrimination. For instance, in *United States v. Virginia* (1996) the court substituted its view for that of the Virginia Military Institute in requiring the college to admit women (Stoner and Showalter, 2004). Furthermore, contract theory, applicable at both public and private institutions, provides an opening for students arguing matters such as courses or programs not having met representations made in catalogues, adhered to external standards, nor adequately provided needed training or certification upon graduation. Courts are more reluctant to apply the substantive due process rights, such as privacy or economic rights, that are often connected with procedural due process. The latter addresses the manner in which the state restricts property and liberty rights, but not the substance of the policies themselves (Baker, 2003).

In governing student discipline, institutions tend to have conduct codes. Such codes should include minimal procedural due process protections, as with those required under the U.S. Constitution at public institutions. But they are not measured by the standards associated with criminal procedure, as with the requirement of proper legal representation and assurance of the confrontation and cross-examination of witnesses (Baker, 2000; Stoner and Lowery, 2004). Codes should nevertheless treat different students with equal care, and with concern, honor, fairness, and dignity (Stoner and Lowery, 2004). Some institutions have an honor code, perhaps most prominently at

West Point, in which students themselves are responsible for reporting and addressing those who "lie, cheat, or steal" (Buchanan and Beckham, 2006; McCabe and Trevino, 2002). Conduct codes invite questions of whether they are rationally related to a legitimate state interest and thus consitutionally permissible, and courts have been vague in articulating standards in the area (Baker, 2003). There have also been academic bills of rights (discussed in Chapter 3) proposed by conservative advocacy groups intended to ensure expression rights in campus environments claimed to be hostile to students' so-called traditional values, which opponents contend conflict with academic freedom and judicial deference (Cameron, Myers, and Olswang, 2005).

Standards resulting in student discipline for violations must be clear enough to be understandable, as a constitutional principle, with even written rules not surviving challenge when they are so vague or broad that they can be interpreted in multiple ways. In contractual contexts, the standard covenant of good faith and fair dealing requires institutions to adhere to their own rules (Berger and Berger, 1999). There are also problems when standards or policies contradict one another, are extraneous to institutional missions, or inconsistent with external laws. Additionally, institutions lose credibility when they enforce rules and apply standards in an inconsistent manner from student to student, as with rarely enforced rules being inherently suspect when unveiled in a specific disciplinary case.

In situations potentially resulting in discipline, due process (explored in Chapter 1) is determined case-by-case. These rights to a sufficient hearing and enough notice to prepare an adequate defense are grounded in the Fourteenth Amendment at public universities and colleges and commonly included in institutional rules at private and public institutions (Geller, 2007). The property and liberty interests that give rise to due process under the Constitution can be present in severe cases. For instance, dismissal for serious academic integrity violations may cause a stigma to attach to an individual and make enrollment elsewhere difficult, indicating a liberty interest. Not allowing a student who has completed his or her academic program to graduate or failing to certify a graduate for professional licensure may suggest a property interest, as the action by the state can be framed as the state taking something that student earned. While the U.S. Supreme Court recognized judicial deference to academic decisions in *Ewing*, it also held that a property interest merited a court reviewing a student dismissal matter.

In arguing that there are property and liberty interests inherently involved in disciplinary suspensions and dismissals—and thus procedural due process rights—Dutile (2001) contends that processes should include a hearing conducted before unbiased decision makers. The procedure should allow the student to confront adverse and present favorable evidence, and should conclude with formal findings and appeal rights. Berger and Berger (1999) similarly maintain that students should have broad rights in disciplinary proceedings, whether attending a public or private institution and drawing upon constitutional or contractual rights. The question should always be what process and outcome does fairness require. But Berger and Berger conclude that practice among institutions, even in the most serious matters, commonly does not afford the right to counsel, leaves insufficient time to prepare, and does not subsequently provide a transcript or written record. There is more often the right to call and confront witnesses, and there is usually a right to cross examination, but there may not be an advocate trained in its practice (Berger and Berger, 1999).

Different types of situations require different procedural approaches, with all actions demanding appropriate substantiation and documentation. Dismissals obviously require more process than less significant disciplinary cases. But students should, at minimum, have some opportunity to prepare and present their side of the story. Doing so does not demand a formal trial, but typically does require access to information underlying the matter, the ability to challenge facts presented during a hearing, and an option to appeal a negative decision in a meaningful way. The question of the right to counsel is difficult to resolve, but in serious matters, students usually can opt to have an attorney present as an advisor, with certain parents willing to provide one (Janosik, 2005). With increases in selectivity and price, parents have more interest in protecting what they have come to see as their investment in higher education for their child. There are also interests among students and parents with maintaining confidentiality and expediting processes (Janosik, 2005).

Institutions are not precluded from dismissal as an option in situations involving students with disabilities, as with engaging in behavior that threatens the safety or performance of others, or when the student commits a violation of policy that would normally lead to dismissal (Munsch and Schupansky, 2003). IDEA, which governs primary and secondary special education, tends to be more restrictive relative to students with disabilities, but universities and colleges are typically granted deference upon indications of their careful consideration, with it appropriate to account for the likely recurrence of the difficulty in making a decision (Munsch and Schupansky, 2003). The issue of conditioning readmission upon taking medication presents a challenge—and doing so may be poor policy—although it is likely more reasonable to consider how a student might modify his or her troubling behavior through other means (Munsch and Schupansky, 2003).

There is also the matter of concurrent judicial proceedings and disciplinary actions, as with the issue of sometimes needing to postpone disciplinary hearings when criminal charges connected with the same incident are likely or pending. The concern is with self-incrimination, as protected by the Fifth Amendment, as statements in one setting can be raised in the other (Geller, 2007; Swope, 2005). Although institutional proceedings have little influence on judicial ones, court determinations do tend to influence campus hearings (Swope, 2005). Universities and colleges may—and often do, but are not required to—postpone their own actions, especially if rules trigger an automatic expulsion for failing to testify at a hearing (Swope, 2005). There may be cause for interim suspension pending the resolution of certain cases, with institutions advised to have established policies and processes (Geller, 2007). Additionally, there are not the same evidentiary standards in institutional and criminal actions (Swope,

2005); there tend to be different orientations toward approaching matters between the courts and student affairs (Capone, 2005); and double jeopardy (being charged twice for the same offense) is rarely a successful defense (Geller, 2007). Finally, given complications such as self-incrimination, the right to counsel is more important when there is a concurrent disciplinary hearing and criminal proceeding (Swope, 2005).

Another issue in disciplining students is whether universities or colleges can and should punish misbehavior that occurs off campus, including that not directly related to their academic programs (Friedl, 2000). Institutions tend to have the right to develop and enforce disciplinary rules related to off-campus conduct, provided there is a nexus between the misbehavior and a vital interest of the institution and the rules are expressly stated in relevant codes (Capone, 2005; Geller, 2007). But not every student offense in town is necessarily connected with the educational mission or health and safety concerns of the local university or college (Capone, 2005; Friedl, 2000). These issues regularly arise with athletes associated with prominent teams, attracting media attention and commonly resulting in suspensions or expulsions from teams. Additionally, federal legislation, such as the 1990 Crime Awareness and Campus Security Act (CSA), requires institutions to publish statistics related to crime, with definitional questions arising about on- and off-campus problems (Burling, 2003; Geller, 2007).

Issues on campus, as with searches, are generally more straightforward. The Fourth Amendment applies to searches by those representing the state, as with residence hall staff at a public university. Searching a residence hall room without a warrent is permissible when there is consent or an item is in plain view (Geller, 2007). Enforcing the responsible use of computing and other electronic communications, as with inappropriate material on the Internet, is a related concern, with emerging norms and rights related to privacy and accessibility (O'Donnell, 2003). There are also concerns with preventing harassment, violating copyright or licenses, spoofing (constructing electronic communications so they appear to be from someone else), or snooping (viewing another's files without official reason) (Sermersheim, 2003). Institutions can potentially be vicariously liable as a publisher or distributer, with the standard when it knew or should have known, which recognizes that institutions have limited control over activity on their networks (Sermersheim, 2003).

Additionally, there is the question of whether withholding or revoking a degree is appropriate in some extreme cases (Geller, 2007). Institutions have such rights, provided they follow due process, as with withholding degrees improperly earned, when there is good cause such as fraud, deceit, or error (Connell and Gurley, 2005). But the law is not as settled when there is a nonacademic reason, such as social misconduct or nonpayment of a bill. In such instances, traditional deference is less likely and greater procedural safeguards are typically required (Connell and Gurley, 2005). Capone (2005) raises the issue of disciplining a student for a serious offense who is no longer enrolled, with the only real remedy being withholding or rescinding a degree.

Finally, earlier criminal conduct by students may be relevant in the admissions process. Institutions may ask for such information in applications for admission, financial aid, and housing, justifying it based on potential liability if there is a later problem, such as a rampage (Geller, 2007). But there are also factors such as an open admissions policy or the practical ability to obtain and process such information (Geller, 2007). Furthermore, arrests are different from convictions, so universities and colleges may ask about charges, but cannot make them the sole determinant of a decision and need to provide the applicants with an opportunity to explain (Geller, 2007).

Liability

Just as suspension and dismissal results from students not meeting their obligations under standards and policies, institutions can be liable to students for not fulfilling their responsibilities.

Sexual harassment, discussed in the context of employment in Chapter 3, involving a student as victim, provides an illustration. In a private action by a plaintiff under Title IX, an institution can be liable for damages when an instructor or another student harasses a student, provided an official with authority to address the problem had actual knowledge of it and was deliberately indifferent (Harris and Grooms, 2000; U.S. Department of Education, 2001). Both quid pro quo (as with exchanging sex for grades) and hostile environment (as with persistent inappropriate comments) apply to students (U.S. Department of Education, 1997). For instance, a sexual relationship between a coach and athlete can be simultaneously a quid pro quo issue, if the relationship influences playing time, and thereby creates a hostile environment problem, because the entire team experiences the effects of the relationship (Cole, 2003; Reaves, 2001).

As in employment, the standard is not consent, but whether the behavior is unwelcome by the target. Inappropriate behavior alleged to create a hostile environment is only actionable when severe and pervasive—an isolated inappropriate joke is unlikely to meet this standard, but an abundance of hugging and touching on a sports team can rise to the level of a hostile environment (Cole, 2003; Reaves, 2001). Relevant variables include how often and long the conduct occurred, the nature of the student (as with his or her age), the impact the behavior had on him or her, the position of the harasser or harassers over the student, where the behavior occurred, and whether it was part of a pattern (U.S. Department of Education, 1997). In reporting the results of a student-to-student sexual harassment investigation to the target, as required under Title IX, FERPA privacy protections are overridden. There are standard due process rights, discussed in Chapter 1, for those accused.

Although Title VII and IX do not specifically protect sexual orientation, hostile environment, as with persistent taunts associated with sex stereotyping, is covered as it denies a student the right to participate in or benefit from an educational program (U.S. Department of Education, 2001). Once again, the unwelcomeness standard applies, with institutional liability possible when there is actual knowledge and indifference.

Institutions can also be liable based on their responsibility, grounded in implied contract, for the safety of their students while under their aegis. Universities and colleges have a duty to protect students, to the extent that it is reasonable to impose that obligation. Institutions may be liable, in failing to meet appropriate standards of care, for criminal acts committed against students or injuries suffered by them while they are engaged in programs and activities. The latter situation is akin to liability in a landlord–tenant relationship, applying a reasonableness standard in determining the duty to protect those whom they invite on their property. Liability requires an affirmative duty or special relationship being breached to cause an actual injury, with the need also for a causal nexus between the responsibility and the harm (Bickel, 2007). Increasingly, there is a special relationship assumed in higher education between institutions and students, especially when alcohol, hazing, and suicide are involved (Humphries, 2008).

Findings of institutional liability are commonly predicated on findings of foreseeability, duty, and causation. Foreseeability is whether an institution knew or should have known about a risk of harm to its students. Duty is the reasonable care owed, as in inspecting premises to discover possible dangerous conditions and warning about foreseeable dangers. Causation is whether the injury resulted enough from the actions or omissions of the defendant to merit liability. Courts are less likely to find a university or college liable in situations in which it can demonstrate that it had no real influence over the activity that caused the harm or the locale where it occurred. When institutions have a stronger connection, as with harm involving institutional employees or campus facilities, there is more likely to be affirmative duty to protect students against harm, resulting in liability for injuries for which they are the proximate cause. Defendants may seek a reduction in damages based on the contributory negligence of the individual injured or another responsible actor. There are also intentional torts, imposing strict liability on responsible defendants (as in workers' compensation and product liability), and vicarious liability (which is imputed fault to an employer) (Bickel, 2007).

Institutions are exposed to tort liability in a variety of areas, which are only becoming more diffuse as the boundaries of universities and colleges expand as they assume more responsibilities as in areas such as residence life and student organizations, fitness centers and recreational sports, and academic internships and externships. They develop rules to limit risk, as with ensuring trained drivers, as well as employ devices such as release forms that indicate assumption of risk in recreational sports, conduct orientation and room inspections in housing, and take precautions at special events as with risk management checklists (Novak and Lee, 2007; White, 2005). There are also issues associated with violence, as in sexual, interpersonal, and hazing contexts. Responses need to be preventive, while also being: comprehensive and multicomponent (addressing multiple types of violence, all-campus constituents, and on- and off-campus settings); strategic, targeted, and empirical; coordinated and synergistic, with efforts complementary and reinforcing one another; and multisectoral and collaborative across stakeholders and disciplines (Langford, 2007).

There are also arguments available to institutions based on assumption of risk, as in areas such as the use of alcohol by students (Lake and Epstein, 2000; White, 2005). But with the increased involvement of institutions in mental health care, they also assume a potentially greater risk of liability (Huebinger, 2008). Lake and Epstein (2000) argue that societal views have shifted toward greater willingness to extend accountability for high-risk activity, as with alcohol liability laws targeting hosts, resulting in increased emphasis by institutions on preventive strategies. Risk management during football tailgating provides an interesting illustration. Foreseeability is a significant consideration in determining the extent to which an institution owes a duty of reasonable care—that it knew or should have known that an invitee may be exposed to injury—but there is certainly some assumption of risk by participants. In taking a preventive approach, as through focusing on crowd control, institutions can make a case for reasonable care (Miller and Gillentine, 2006).

With the Virginia Tech and Northern Illinois massacres in 2007 and 2008, respectively, institutions (and commentators) have directed considerable attention to preventing and responding to rampages by students and others. Virginia Tech underscores the limited information that universities and colleges sometimes have available, with the severe problems the student perpetrator had long been experiencing only formally identified relatively shortly before the shootings (Humphries, 2008). There was also the issue with the management of the perpetrator's condition requiring outpatient treatment that depended on him making and keeping appointments. Institutions have established teams responsible for threat assessment and intervention, but there are significant challenges associated with collecting, analyzing, and communicating information, as well as balancing privacy and safety and aligning with disability laws (Dunkle, Silverstein, and Warner, 2008; Humphries, 2008). What is possible to do is a real question, as well as what constitutes a proper institutional response, whether in heeding warning signs, responding to the immediate peril, or during the aftermath of an incident (de Haven, 2009). Also, situations that involve violence differ greatly in type, as with insider versus outsider and targeted versus random acts (de Haven, 2009), and gender-based violence can be a prelude or warning, as with peer sexual assault (Cantalupo, 2008).

Universities and colleges tend to default to nondisclosure, even though FERPA has an exception for health and safety emergencies, including permitting notification of parents or family. It also allows disclosure to a subsequent institution—and has no realistic consequences, as with fines, even if violated (Tribbensee, 2008). As for liability associated with a rampage, the issues are foreseeability and the duties that arise, within the context of the special relationship assumed between institutions and students (Humphries, 2008). Universities and colleges are likely to argue that violence is not foreseeable and they are thus not responsible, despite any special relationship they might have (de Haven, 2009). An institution today can no longer claim the defenses once available under *in loco parentis* or during the bystander era, with some duty assumed based on a special relationship and thus the potential for liability (MacLachlan, 2000). Recovery requires significant negligence, but there is incentive for institutions to settle, whether to avoid negative precedents and reputational risk or because of pressure from insurers, providing plaintiffs with leverage (de Haven, 2009). Cantalupo (2008) argues that ignoring campus crime problems such as rampant gender based violence, yielding to pressures related to image and avoiding negative publicity, constitute actual notice but deliberate indifference, and thus increase the likelihood of liability.

Devices such as background checks before admission remain unusual and tend to involve practical complications and ethical questions, but are sometimes employed in selected cases, as with athletes at some institutions or in health related professions (Dickerson, 2008). In admissions, institutions need to balance whether an applicant is otherwise qualified with a reasonable accommodation with whether he or she is a direct threat due to mental illness (Rothstein, 2009). The ADA has an exception when a mental disability is a direct threat, but institutions need to make an individualized inquiry, finding actual substantial risk and not simply yielding to subjective fears (Hubbard, 2001). Once again, there are typically limits on information available. Another issues is that upon graduation institutions must certify medical and law graduates, which may prompt students to defer receiving treatments (Rothstein, 2009).

Hazing remains a concern in higher education, especially in athletics and fraternities and sororities, with issues that are similar to rampages, as with institutions likely to be named as defendants and liability dependent on foreseeability under a special relationship theory (MacLachlan, 2000). Even when institutions have policies, inaction or lack of appropriate action upon becoming aware of the problem, as determined case-by-case, invites liability (Somers, 2007). Universities and colleges also assume certain risk in sponsoring activities known to provide the setting for hazing. Even accurately defining the concept can pose challenges (Somers, 2007). There may also be potential liability under a negligent supervision theory, with a duty to protect and failure to supervise as a proximate cause (MacLachlan, 2000; Weddle, 2004). An additional challenge in hazing is that there is the possibility of courts applying a landlord–tenant or business invitee approach, both potentially less favorable for institutions (Crow and Rossner, 2002). There is legislation in several states that addresses—and even criminalizes—the problem, as well as less sympathetic societal and institutional attitudes, especially related to the connection between alcohol and hazing (Burling, 2003; MacLachlan, 2000). Institutions have generally responded, as they have in relation to other student organizations, with enhanced risk management programs (Novak and Jackson, 2007).

Another area of potential liability based on responsibilities to foresee risk is in student suicides. Lake (2008) notes that the law is still uncertain on institutional exposure in the area, also making the point that suicide and rampages are sometimes connected, as at Virginia Tech and Northern Illinois. The issue involves identifying those at risk of suicide and deciding how to address the problem once aware that it exists, as with notifying police, considering voluntary or involuntary treatment or hospitalization, mandating involuntary leave, or arranging for close supervision (Jed Foundation, 2007). There are also issues of reentry—as well as those particular to graduate, professional, distance-learning, and international students. Institutions must consider complicated matters associated with the best interests of both the student and community, such as what the threshold for intervention should be, whether to inform friends and others involved with the student, and if the student is able to participate in a study abroad program or off-campus internship (Jed Foundation, 2007). There are also difficulties not only in collecting relevant information but also in sharing across complex organizations (Konopasky, 2008).

A particular challenge with potential suicides is how to address students who do not voluntarily withdraw or seek treatment following an attempt, with various procedural responsibilities and practical limits associated with potential disciplinary and nondisciplinary responses to students who are at high risk of hurting themselves. The choice for institutions can be between risking liability and violating rights, as with violating due process or the antidiscrimination laws in areas such as forcing eviction from campus housing or withdrawal from the institution (Kaveeshvar, 2008). Even with mandatory counseling, students can ignore appointmens or disregard treatment (Konopasky, 2008). Additionally, there are more students reporting problems, as well as advances in medication and treatment and parents wanting a more activist approach by universities and colleges. But suicide is individualistic in nature and defies ready detection and prevention (Kaveeshvar, 2008; Wei, 2008).

Once again, the special relationship between institutions and students triggers a duty to protect, with foreseeability determining potential liability (Lake and Tribbensee, 2002; Sokolow et al., 2008). As with rampages and hazing, institutions would generally prefer to avoid the analogy to a landlord's duty to maintain safe premises. But arguments by universities and colleges that they have no duty are not likely to be persuasive (Kaveeshvar, 2008). Even if there is an established duty, a plaintiff needs to establish breach and causation, and there may be contributory and comparative negligence issues (Sokolow et al., 2008). There are also privacy concerns in making disclosures and taking action, but an increasing presumption that favors tracking students and warning broadly, recognizing that acts such as rampages or suicides may not be foreseeable, but where there are warning signs, there may be a duty (Kaveeshvar, 2008; Sokolow et al., 2008). Konopasky (2008) maintains that a duty to prevent suicides is unrealistic, but a duty to notify is less so and could employ FERPA's emergency exception. But simply calibrating notifying relevant community and family members can prove tricky (Lake and Tribbensee, 2002). Finally, grief management involving both families of victims and the overall campus community also requires institutions to manage risk, as with requests for specific information from family members that may later weaken legal positions (Franke, 2007).

The special relationship between institutions and students has extended the boundaries of the entrepreneurial universities and colleges. Among academic programs, study abroad is a prominent example, with institutions increasingly emphasizing these efforts for both educational and strategic reasons. Although internationalization remains rather limited in American higher education, short-term study abroad programs, in particular, have increased in popularity (American Council on Education, 2002; Hayward, 2000). The potential for institutional tort liability is similar to back home, as with premises liability. But matters such as where a lawsuit is heard and what law is applied may complicate matters for programs operated by a partner institution abroad (Johnson, 2006; Robinson, 2000; Schultz, 2005). Additionally, U.S. disability or civil rights laws do not apply abroad apart from settings in which an American institution controls a given study abroad program, as opposed to a student attending a foreign university or an institution contracting with a foreign university (Kanter, 2003).

With facilities abroad, as in other areas where liability is possible, institutions have focused on risk management, including considering local laws, as applicable, in areas such as corporate status and taxation, contracts and leases, environmental responsibilities, intellectual property, employee rights and working conditions, salaries and benefits, and insurance coverage (Hall and Ferguson, 2000; Harding, 2000; Hoye, 2005; McCreath, 2005; Schultz, 2005). These tend to differ based on whether a program is an extension of the institution, involves a contract with another institution or organization, is a loose relationship between an institution and a provider, or is a hybrid of these (Hoye and Rhodes, 2000; Hoye, Rypkema, and Zerr, 2005). With the latter two, there is the possibility of vicarious liability for the negligence of the partner (Hoye et al., 2005). Ferguson (2005) concentrates on managing risk associated with such issues as control of academic matters, sufficient financial resources, available exit strategies, and accreditation.

There is also the need to manage risk in developing a student services infrastructure with programs abroad. There are countless practical issues, such as difficulties in communication; risks of natural disasters, terrorism, or political upheaval; the potential of being the victim of property or violent crimes; the possibility of being jailed; and health emergencies. A serious incident can be devastating for the psyche of a university or college community and pose significant reputational risk, raisng the stakes (Hoye et al., 2005). Furthermore, challenges in study abroad include students misperceiving themselves to be "invincible" and that certain constitutional rights extend abroad, as well as alcohol and drug related issues (Simonelli, 2005).

These can only be managed to a degree through required insurance; waivers, releases, and indemnification agreements; and orientation sessions and applicable warnings. But Simonelli (2005) offers the reminder that waivers mostly have symbolic value. Connell and Savage (2003) list various other limitations on their enforcement, as when an activity is in the public interest, cannot be obtained elsewhere, or is required; there is a significant disparity in bargaining power between the parties;

the release seeks to avoid liability for willful or grossly negligent acts, or expresses the exculpatory intent in ambiguous and inconspicuous language. In discussing risk management in wilderness settings, Ritchie (2005) adds that programs need to consider that some cultures believe fate determines outcomes, thus minimizing impulses toward prevention. There are approaches, such as participant selection, reconnaissance trips, orientation sessions, and documentation, as well as encouraging development of cultural awareness and leadership abilities, but none is infallible (Hoye et al., 2005; Ritchie, 2005). The reality is that the boundaries of the entreprenurial university or college—and thus the possibility for liability—have expanded into territory in which institutions have less control.

Internships, whether optional or required, raise similar issues. These have only become more prominent across higher education, as students at selective institutions, especially, often have several such experiences on their high school resumes—and expect to prepare similarly for employment following graduation. Institutions continue to be responsible for students engaged in off-campus projects in accord with the special relationship, with duties enhanced when work is more connected with academic programs and facilitated by faculty or administrators, such as field placements for teachers (Butler, 2003; Foster and Moorman, 2003). When students are acting more independently, there remains a duty of care, but it may be more akin to a business relationship with the institution, thus diminishing its responsibilities. Universities and colleges are not insurers, even when they have supervisory responsibilities, but reasonable expectations to protect against foreseeable harm ramain (Butler, 2003). Finally, interns have limited employment rights, as with not being afforded employee status under the 1938 Fair Labor Standards Act (FLSA), so there is no required pay and it can be difficult to take advantage of employment discrimination or workers' compensation laws, although there may be tort remedies available for severe harassment or discrimination (Yamada, 2002).

Institutions have fewer liability concerns related to athletics spectators. They may be responsible for field-rushing injuries when such occurrences are foreseeable, as with past experiences, encouraging rowdy behavior, or insufficient security coverage (Misinec, 2005). But there are also assumption of risk defenses available, as with the classic situation of teams not being responsible for a spectator being struck by a baseball, or even trespass theories applicable (Denner, 2004). Denner argues that there may be more of a duty to athletes than to fans.

In the end, Hoye (2007) contends that institutions best avoid liability by integrating proactive risk management into the campus culture, as society has become more litigious and courts are less likely to exempt universities and colleges for their negligent conduct. Institutions are more exposed, whether in traditional tort litigation, such as personal injury, premises liability, and property damage—or with respect to other more exotic theories, such as negative supervision and instruction, intentional torts (misrepresentation and intentional distress), constitutional and contractual due process claims, and failure to warn and protect against reasonably foreseeable harm to students, licensees, and others caused by third parties.

Unlike most Faber students, Mandy Pepperidge comes from a middle class background. Her parents are a middle school teacher and an insurance sales-person, having met while attending a regional state university, with her father earning a masters degree in education over several years taking evening courses. Pepperidge would have never even considered a private college—much less an elite one with a $55,000 annual "sticker price"—except for the guidance of Dave Jennings, a counselor at her public high school.

Jennings, who serves several hundred students, might not have identified Pepperidge, who was a straight-A student, except for her 1480 SAT score. He was able to direct her through the admissions and financial aid process, with her receiving a package that brought her price down to about twice what she would have paid to attend her parents' alma mater. She would be able to keep her student loans under $10,000 per year—and was convinced that Faber would be worth it, having fallen in love with the campus upon visiting after being admitted.

Upon arriving at Faber, Pepperidge felt a bit overwhelmed. Her assigned roommate, Barbara Jansen, had attended an elite private school in New York and knew what seemed like every third student on campus from some connec-tion back home, such as summer camps, riding lessons, ballet school, or family friends. Barbara was rarely around, spending time at the sorority (Tri Pi) she pledged as a legacy and jetting to New York on weekends (and even once to the Caribbean for a long weekend). Pepperidge, meanwhile, enjoyed her classes, but felt that her classmates had been better prepared for college work than was she. She also had made a few good friends through her work-study job at the dining commons and around the residence hall.

At the end of her first semester, a professor noticed some suspicious passages in a course paper, raising the matter with Pepperidge and then referring it to a panel of faculty, administrators, and students charged with hearing such cases. She apologized to the professor, letting her know that she was aware of the protocols involved in citing passages pulled from the Internet, but had allowed herself to be sloppy when rushing to meet several deadlines that arrived at once, promising not make the same mistake twice. Pepperidge informed her parents of the pending hearing and they advised her to tell the truth and take responsibility for her actions. After a proper hearing, during which Pepperidge was able to tell her side of the story, the panel referred her to an academic counselor and warned her that a second offense would result in suspension or dismissal.

Later that year, in looking into a matter involving another student, the aca-demic integrity office stumbled upon the information that Jansen had paid Pepperidge, who was saving for a study abroad trip to Tanzania she hoped to take following her sophomore year, to complete some assignments in a Spanish language course they were both taking. Scheduled to appear before the same

(continued)

panel as before—and informed of the possibility of being dismissed for a second violation of the academic integrity policy—Pepperidge was at a loss. A Faber staff member reached out to her to explain the process and make sure she was coping, but all she could think to do was to ask her parents to accompany her to the hearing. Presented with the evidence, she admitted to the wrongdoing. The panel recommended her dismissal from Faber. She subsequently was able, upon explaining her transcript, to gain enrollment at a small state university near home.

Jansen's hearing followed. Her father, a Wall Street investment banker, had arranged for Eric Stratton, the family's personal attorney and a partner in a prominent New York law firm, Otis and Day, to handle her defense. Stratton knew that the facts were against his client, particularly after Pepperidge admitted to Jansen paying her. Her best hope was to find a material defect in the process and convince at least some on the panel that the case must be dismissed on those grounds. At worst, he figured he could avoid suspension or expulsion by casting doubt over the integrity of the process.

Faber did not allow counsel to speak at hearings, but Stratton was able to script Jansen, who proved to be quite capable in her own defense, redirecting the discussion back to how the academic integrity office learned of the alleged wrongdoing, once attempting to frame it as akin to a warrantless search. (The faculty members on the panel rolled their eyes at that one, having discerned Jansen's strategy—and having noticed that more students were coming into hearings with counsel.) A divided panel decided not to suspend or dismiss Jansen, assessing the same penalty as Pepperidge received for her first offense. The decision was a relief, but Jansen was never really that stressed about the process, not allowing it to interfere with enjoying her sorority formal the previous Saturday. She knew that her father had spoken with President Wormer, suggesting his interest in making another six-figure gift to the college.

First Amendment

Like other constitutional protections, the actual First Amendment applies only to restrictions on protected activity by public universities and colleges, functioning as the state. As with other constitutional rights, these are not absolute, as the state can make exceptions under appropriate circumstances. First Amendment protections do not apply to private institutions, but students and others derive some similar rights from certain institutional rules and contractual relationships, both formal and implied.

Expression

With institutions managing public perceptions more carefully, there are increasing pressures to regulate speech that has the potential to embarrass them or provoke controversy, risking disappointing those who provide funding. Public institutions, when they have a rational basis, can impose reasonable regulations on expression, as with limiting the time, place, and manner of its occurrence to minimize disruption of normal activities. For instance, a university or college may restrict holding a protest that uses amplified speech planned during finals week near classroom buildings in which students are taking exams. But any regulation must leave open ample alternative channels for communication. If there is a limitation or denial, institutions need to be clear on the nature and their reasons (Langhauser, 2005). Additionally, prior restraints on speech are disfavored, as with banning the above protest altogether, but are not invalid provided they are limited to determining whether an activity will cause a substantial disruption. A substantial disruption need not be a fait accompli, but simply the fear of a protest is insufficient grounds for a prior restraint.

Regulations by public universities and colleges specific to content are also disfavored, as held by the U.S. Supreme Court in *Clark v. Community for Creative Non-Violence* (1984) and *Ward v. Rock Against Racism* (1989) (Langhauser, 2005). An example of an inappropriate content-based regulation is to restrict speech to that of a "wholesome nature," as was the situation in *Shamloo v. Mississippi State Board of Trustees* (1980), or might apply in attempting to maintain decorum at an athletic event (Wasserman, 2005). A public institution may not prohibit speech simply because persons who hear it may be offended by the message. In order to satisfy First Amendment concerns, any content-based regulation of speech must be narrowly tailored to protect a compelling state interest by the least restrictive means (Shekleton, 2005).

According to the decision of the U.S. Supreme Court in *Perry Education Association v. Perry Local Educators' Association* (1983), the ability of the state to regulate speech depends on the type of forum involved. A public forum is a place commonly devoted to assembly and debate, as with a campus mall or the public streets, with regulation or exclusion of expression in such settings required to be necessary to serve compelling state interest and narrowly drawn to achieve that end. A designated public forum is transformed from a public forum by purposeful government action, with the same strict scrutiny requirements. An example is a "free speech zone" established near a campus auditorium hosting a presidential debate to allow those protesting to be noticed, but to keep them from disrupting the event. A nonpublic forum is neither a public forum nor designated forum, with the state only requiring a reasonable basis to limit expression, provided that regulation does not involve an effort to suppress speech merely because officials oppose the speaker's view (Bird, Mackin, and Schuster, 2006; Capone, 2008; McDonald, 2002). As a limited public forum, the same auditorium can be opened for expressive activity and limited to campus groups, wherein reasonable and viewpoint neutral regulations are acceptable, provided they are narrowly tailored (Bird et al., 2006). Deeming a campus a public forum thus means restrictions would require content-neutrality, narrow tailoring, and adequate alternatives—with a non-public forum creating more options for institutions (Davis, 2004).

O'Neil (2008c) posits that academic settings may be freer for expression than in the broader society because of principles such as academic freedom, which proscribes limits only when views are so extreme that they demonstrate a lack of competence in a subject, as with a Holocaust denying modern European historian. There is also the tradition of judicial deference based in the unique and valuable contributions that higher education makes to society, similar to the press and religious organizations, thus supporting an argument for special treatment under the First Amendment (Horwitz, 2007). But universities and colleges are also stricter in regulating expression, as with plagiarism and regulations on time, place, and manner that are particular to the academic setting. Additionally, there is concern over reputational risk at entrepreneurial universities and colleges, as with making decisions influenced by political correctness. An example, is the pressure to dismiss Ward Churchill from his tenured position at the University of Colorado for unpopular statements following the September 11, 2001 attacks (Horwitz, 2007). Greenup (2005) argues that it is inappropriate for a public institution to prohibit controversial speakers on campus for both legal and educational reasons, as a university is both a public forum and a marketplace of ideas.

But expression that lacks any real value can be regulated based on content, such as sexual or racial harassment or defamation. These encompass some speech activities, but may be seen outside of the boundaries of the First Amendment (Marcus, 2008). Also unprotected is obscenity, which appeals only to prurient interests; depicts sexual conduct in patently offensive ways; and lacks serious literary, artistic, political, or scientific value. The same is true of fighting words, which by their very utterance inflict injury or incite an immediate breach of the peace; incitement of imminent lawless action, as with burning a classroom building; and a true threat of bodily harm (Bird et al., 2006). What is termed "hate speech" is also not protected. Hate speech is expression not intended to communicate ideas or information, but instead only to humiliate or wound through grossly negative assessments of persons or groups, as those associated with factors such as race or gender. Activities such as threats or intimidation aimed at particular individuals or groups take on the attributes of conduct, as opposed to speech, and are not protected as expression. Despite such exemptions, it is important to remember that the presumption is toward allowing expression (Bird and Mackin, 2006).

The challenge in regulating nonproductive expression is that institutions must draw rules narrowly enough to prevent prohibiting protected speech—that involving the exchange of ideas and thus protected under the First Amendment. Additionally, rules can neither be overbroad nor vague. The overbreadth principle requires that standards be sufficiently narrowly tailored to avoid sweeping within their coverage activities that would be constitutionally protected. The vagueness standard requires that regulations be sufficiently clear so that persons can understand what is required or prohibited and act accordingly (Coleman and Alger, 1996). An illustration is a sexual harassment policy that limits patronizing remarks or dismissive comments may be so broad and vague as to defy common understanding (Majeed, 2009).

A related challenge is that the application of regulations in areas such as sexual harassment can impinge on free expression rights, as with the situation of an institution being too quick to frame any negative expression connected with gender as sexual harassment (Coleman and Alger, 1996; Lasson, 1999; Majeed, 2009). Majeed argues that institutions are also misapplying employment law principles to the student-to-student situation in this area, not recognizing differences such as power imbalances being lacking, as well as conflating Title IX with Title VII. The proper standard is that behavior needs to be so severe, pervasive, and objectively offensive as to effectively deny equal access to resources and opportunities at an institution, as held in *Davis v. Monroe County Board of Education* (1999). But Lasson (1999) contends that while there may be political correctness risks, and that speech codes present difficulties in drawing lines, as with allowing certain Afro-centric and anti-Semitic speech, certain regulation may be merited as the First Amendment is not absolute. It has careful exceptions in areas such as obscenity and allowable reasonable time, place, and manner regulations.

Public universities and colleges have more latitude in regulating private commercial activities on campus that involve "expressive" products or limiting certain advertising (Shekleton, 2005). Expression also tends to be more limited, as a practical matter, in areas such as athletics, where there are codes of conduct for athletes and employees that are justified by the public profile of the enterprise. But even in athletics, restrictions such as on criticizing the athletic department would not be permissible (Heckman, 2003). Additionally, loyalty oaths to the constitution are still required in many states for professors and other teachers, and are extended to private institutions in some states (albeit on probably dubious grounds) (Chin and Rao, 2003). Finally, O'Neil (2008d) contends that courts have been inconsistent in responding to institutional limits on avant garde visual art and dramatic productions. There has been more reluctance among universities and colleges to support expression here than in other areas, with external pressures testing the resolve of the academic community, even when naturally inclined to support artistic freedom.

Once again, private universities and colleges are not subject to constitutional provisions such as the First Amendment. A private entity, such as an employer, is able to chill and prevent speech just as much as government actions, thus justifying approaches that encourage speech (Chemerinsky, 1998). Although there are challenges with extending formal free expression rights into the private sector, there are civil rights statutes that regulate private conduct, as well as state statutes, as with the Leonard Law in California, which prohibits public or private institutions from disciplinary sanctions on students on the basis of speech that would be protected if engaged in outside of campus (with religious institutions exempt) (Eule and Varat,

1998). Catholic universities have limits on their expression issued from the Vatican, as with the requirement that they function consistent with church doctrine under *Ex Corte Ecclesiae* (Burtchaell, 1999; Russo and Gregory, 2001). Faculty members thus need to balance traditional academic freedom with requirements of the church, with Catholic members of the university owing a personal fidelity to the church and non-Catholic members required to respect the Catholic character of the university (Russo and Gregory, 2001).

Publications

Student publications at public institutions receive full protection under the First Amendment. Under the decision in *Papish v. Board of Curators of the University of Missouri* (1973), the First Amendment provides a shield even when what students write is in poor taste or causes a substantial outcry. Laws prohibiting libel and obscenity and regulating advertising also apply in common ways, with liability for such matters attaching to institutions based on the degree of control that they exercise over the publication. As with expression, prior restraints associated with publications are disfavored. As entrepreneurial universities and colleges tend to be more conscious of controlling messages, employing public affairs staffs to do so, student publications can prove frustrating, as they do not need to align what they write with institutional purposes. Courts are likely to view unfavorably attempts by public institutions to control or influence student publication. Institutions can thus only eliminate or change funding to an institution-supported student publication for reasons unrelated to substance. They can regulate some noneditorial activities, as with prohibiting discrimination in staffing. These conditions also apply to student publications supported by student fees managed by student governments.

The public forum analysis discussed above may apply to student publications, with an independent newspaper deemed in the public forum having greater autonomy than one in a nonpublic forum, as with an internal publication, which would invite influence by administrators (Melear, 2007, Rooksby, 2007). There is also the challenge with expression posted on the Internet, as on a faculty webpage controlled by the institution, which requires balancing academic freedom with institutional interests in regulating certain speech (O'Neil, 2008c). Monitoring e-mail messages by public universities and colleges may be less of a concern because they are available under freedom of information statutes as public records, thus essentially having similar privacy expectations to paper correspondence. There are also concerns associated with electronic communications, especially given the popularity of social media among students, which is usually outside the control of universities and colleges. As with faculty, there is the need to balance regulation of student communication with the presumption of expression (O'Neil, 2008c).

Assembly

Even when they may disagree with the purposes of a group, public universities and colleges likely need to recognize the rights of students under the First Amendment to organize. As defined by the U.S. Supreme Court in *Healy v. James* (1972), institutions may restrict the right to organize when student groups are not willing to adhere to reasonable campus rules, when the assembly would interrupt classes or substantially interfere with the opportunity of other students to attain an education, or when it would be illegal for the group to assemble. But the presumption is toward viewpoint neutrality—once a university or college recognizes one group, it should afford the same rights and privileges to others who meet basic conditions (Schulman, 2006).

For instance, the Court in *Widmar v. Vincent* (1981) held invalid an institutional restriction, grounded in Establishment Clause concerns, against student religious groups meeting on campus. Given that the university allowed other student groups such rights, it was discriminating on the basis of expression. But institutions need not provide forums for religious groups not otherwise generally available to student groups, create a forum if one does not exist, or provide access to facilities that are not part of the forum. Also, there can be some regulation, particularly when it is not based on content, if there is evidence that a religious group will dominate the open forum, or in the situations described in *Healy*.

Similar conditions apply to funding student groups. In *Rosenburger v. Rector and Visitors of the University of Virginia* (1995), the U.S. Supreme Court held that the university violated the First Amendment in failing to award funding from student activity fees to a student journal that served religious purposes. The definition that the university applied to religious activities to avoid potential problems with the Establishment Clause—efforts that "primarily promote or manifest a particular belief in or about a deity or an ultimate reality"—was too broad, as it would include discussion of philosophers and poets, for instance. In *Board of Regents of the University of Wisconsin v. Southworth* (2000), the Court also favored viewpoint neutrality, holding that mandatory student fees to fund various student groups are allowable, even if some students object to the viewpoint of certain organizations receiving funds. Such fees tend to be allowed when they are for educational purposes, particularly if these outweigh achieving political or ideological goals associated with the group. In other words, only when a group becomes a vehicle solely for a particular viewpoint, it is acceptable to disallow mandatory activity fees (Brady, 2008). Fees allocated must thus be viewpoint neutral under *Rosenburger*, with mandatory fees allowable under the same principle—so long as the university opens and supports a forum, it can require that student fees support it (Mawdsley and Permuth, 2008).

Private universities and colleges have more latitude in limiting the establishment and recognition of student organizations, but still must exercise care. In *Gay Rights Coalition of Georgetown University Law Center v. Georgetown University* (1987), one of the few assembly cases brought against a private institution, a Catholic university attempted to exclude an organization it felt violated its religious tenets. The outcome required it to provide the organization with facilities, services, and funding afforded to other student groups, but allowed it to avoid formally recognizing the group. Public institutions are obligated, if they recognize any groups, to treat them the same if they obey rules and applicable laws and are not disruptive, whether under *Widmar, Rosenburger, and Southworth* (Thro, 2008). Values and pressure may compel private institutions, particularly more secular ones, to follow the same basic policy.

There is also the issue of student religious organizations desiring to exclude certain groups, perhaps gay and lesbian students from a Christian organization or women from a Muslim one, in violation of institutional nondiscrimination policies (Mawdsley and Permuth, 2008). In a 2010 decision, *Christian Legal Society v. the University of California, Hastings College of the Law*, the U.S. Supreme Court upheld a decision by Hastings to withhold official recognition, based upon a policy requiring nondiscrimination, to a Christian group that expressly required members to forswear unrepentant participation in or advocacy of a sexually immoral lifestyle, which it defined as sex outside of heterosexual marriage. The court was influenced by the fact that the Hastings rule did not prohibit the group, but simply did not provide a subsidy.

The issue becomes difficult as forcing organizations to accept members is problematic, both as a practical and constitutional matter (Schulman, 2006). Thro (2006) argues that when the religious beliefs of a group are counter to nondiscrimination policies, a university or college can likely prohibit the group if there is racial or other prohibited discrimination, but not when there is simply a negative opinion about the conduct of a group. Similarly, even though a politically incorrect student group at a public institution may espouse viewpoints and advocate practices that are offensive to campus community—as with racist, sexist, or homophobic rhetoric or views that mock Christianity or other religions—it is important to remember its constitutional rights (Russo and Thro, 2007; Thro, 2008). Institutions have more latitude in excluding groups for discriminating based on race or gender than areas such as religion, but are not compelled under the U.S. Constitution to give any special treatment to religious groups (Russo and Thro, 2007). Also, the analysis may be different in different kinds of forums (traditional public form, designated public forum, and nonpublic forum) (Mawdsley and Permuth, 2008).

Schulman (2006) notes that association rights may sometimes outweigh nondiscrimination, citing decisions, such as *Boy Scouts of America v. Dale* (2000), that did not require a private association, pursuant to a state public accommodations law, to include a gay assistant scoutmaster when that conflicted with its messages and viewpoint—and thus its expression. But institutions have leverage, he argues, as with viewpoint neutral nondiscrimination policies and accommodations rules that govern conduct as opposed to speech, thus avoiding First Amendment problems. Also, *Dale* may be read narrowly, given the circumstances of the case. Volokh (2006) asks whether the state may extend funding only to groups that do not discriminate, which might exclude certain student groups in higher education, as well as organizations such as the Boy Scouts, the Catholic Church, or Orthodox Jewish synagogues. There is no government duty to subsidize organizations, just as private groups can do what they wish. But when it does, groups are required to be neutral in their viewpoint and not discriminate. Such antidiscrimination conditions on subsidies must be religion-, viewpoint-, and content-neutral. For instance, if the state subsidizes secular conduct, it must subsidize religious conduct in parallel areas. Finally, the Solomon Amendment mandates that military recruiters have the same access to campuses as others and their access does not violate freedom of association and expression for those at institutions (Secunda, 2007; Thro, 2006).

In the end, universities and colleges have an interest in maintaining a certain environment. But students have perhaps a stronger set of rights under the First Amendment, causing attempts by universities and colleges to suppress unpopular student organizations to be deemed inappropriate. An institution must overcome a significant presumption favoring the right of citizens, including students, to organize and assemble. As with expression, when such behavior is contrary to protecting the image of a university or college, constitutional rights will outweigh reputational concerns.

Religion

In addition to the mandate that universities and colleges do not discriminate against student religious organizations, there is also the matter of accommodating student needs when their religious beliefs conflict with institutional requirements or prerogatives. As in employment, detailed in Chapter 3, institutions need to make reasonable accommodations, but only to the extent that they do not cause undue hardship—a situation paralleling the application of the Americans with Disabilities Act. Accommodations, when requested by students, might include scheduling around religious observances or adjusting course requirements that significantly burden the sincere religious beliefs of a student.

For instance, a devout student in a drama course may object to participating in sexually suggestive scenes, with the faculty member then determining if an alternative approach is consistent with maintaining the integrity of the course. Such determinations should be about the sincerity of beliefs and not their validity. But a student need not be accommodated whenever requested, as some proposed alternatives will not meet the reasonableness and hardship standards. Certain courses tend to challenge students intellectually and personally within the context of an academic discipline—and simple discomfort with such an approach, even if on religious grounds, is unlikely to justify an accommodation (Rose, 2006).

Furthermore, whenever a given rule allows some exception for a secular reason, religious reasons should be afforded the same consideration (Rose, 2006). For instance, a rule requiring first year students to live on campus is likely to have exceptions for secular reasons, perhaps exempting students with families or those from the immediate area—and would have to accommodate parallel needs based in religious principles. Challenges are determined by whether the secular and religious exceptions similarly challenge the integrity of the rule.

Finally, Lupu and Tuttle (2008) offer the situation of displaying the cross at a public university chapel. There is an Establishment Clause problem if the government is understood to promote the practice of one religion or imposes unnecessary burdens on those who do not participate in that religion. But there is precedent that allows public display of religious images and messages provided they only acknowledge our common religious heritage and are not positive endorsements of the religious content of the message.

Despite having spent a 20-year career in admissions, Doug Neidermeyer was always anxious before the weekend when those applicants offered Blutarsky fellowships—and their parents—visited campus. Established five years ago, the Blutarsky fellowships are intended to enable Faber to attract the very best students nationally. The college not only offers them a full scholarship, but also structured opportunities to work on research with leading faculty, special study trips abroad each year led by prominent alumni, and arranged internships each summer with prominent corporations and nonprofit organizations.

In preparation for the weekend each year, Neidermeyer had his staff scrub bulletin boards of signs that either lacked aesthetic appeal or included messages that might not appeal to parents. An example of the former was an announcement for an upcoming concert by the band, Omega, that misspelled the words "embarrassment," "humorous," and "ignorance." One of the posters in the latter category was nicely presented, but removed because it announced a speech sponsored by a student organization, Diversity Through Exposure (DTX), by Gregory Marmalard, who had recently attracted national attention for attacking the motives of soldiers serving in the Iraq War.

When they noticed that their posters had been removed, both Chip Diller, the Faber student who fronted Omega, and the head of DTX, Clorette DePasto, upon asking around, quickly learned that Neidermeyer's staff was responsible. They complained to Robert Hoover, the dean of students, who was accustomed to hearing such concerns, and he brought it up with Neidermeyer. Both agreed that the Omega poster was a reasonable enough "time, place, and manner" restriction, as serial misspellings on a poster by Faber students were more embarrassing to both institution and band than humorous and harmless. They asked Diller to redo the posters, even offering him the use of the photocopying machine in the student activities office. He agreed.

Hoover had not known of the Marmalard talk—and was not pleased. He was willing to work with students to bring all views of speakers to campus, although admittedly struggling in doing so when they represented far right wing opinions. But he made it clear to student groups, both during orientation and in a written handbook, that they needed to consult with his office about matters such as arranging security before inviting speakers that might reasonably spur antagonism. He asked DePasto to visit his office. She was furious that the campus "thought police," as she termed it, "confiscated" the signs and was preventing "all the little princesses and their Ken doll boyfriends on this campus from hearing the truth."

Hoover was conflicted. Having been active in the protests supporting divestment in companies doing business in South Africa during apartheid, he was sympathetic to what DTX was attempting to do. But he also understood both the reputational risk concerns that Neidermeyer raised—that all the visiting parents would want to discuss was why Faber was "sponsoring" the likes of Marmalard, who had been regularly lambasted on conservative radio and FOX News. If it was only that, Hoover might have taken a stand in favor of DTX, but his staff kept coming back to their concern that outsiders would pour onto campus and there would be violence if Marmalard spoke. He suggested to DePasto that DTX delay the speech until the coming fall, allowing matters to calm over the summer. She refused, growing even angrier, arguing that the concerns about safety were a pretext. Hoover wondered the same thing himself—was it really unreasonable for Faber to secure the site and was safety just a convenient excuse?

President Wormer, who was Secretary of Defense prior to arriving at Faber, sided with Neidermeyer. Several faculty, who were still not entirely comfortable with someone as president from outside academe, soon became aware of the issue and supported DTX. Faber was now being singled out in the conservative media as a test case for "political correctness." Wormer, who was beginning to hear from board members and prominent donors, few of whom were sympathetic, demanded that Hoover act quickly, leaving the decision to him, but making his opinion well known. (The president was not going to have a decision attach to him that was certain to be unpopular with the disappointed side, which would be the faculty and left-leaning students, he was reasonably sure.) Hoover decided to prevent the speech—an act akin to a prior restraint at a public institution.

DePasto and DTX had no constitutional recourse. Because it is a private institution, Faber is not subject to the First Amendment. Had it been, the college would have had to defend the reputational risk and imminent danger justifications, convincing a court that one or both was a compelling interest. The student group did have a contract action available, given Faber had longstanding institutional policies favoring free expression—allowing reasonable time, place, and manner restrictions, but disfavoring prior restraints unless there are extreme circumstances. The American Civil Liberties Union has agreed to file an action on behalf of DTX for an injunction that would compel Faber to uphold its contractual obligations under the prior restraints provision. The college is prepared to argue that the Marmalard speech fits within the extreme circumstances exception. It may even contend directly that as its finances depend on continuing to raise funds, and thus not alienate donors, the court should weigh their negative reaction.

Assessing and Managing Threats at Faber—A Simulation

In response to the risks, including liability for the institution, of an incident on campus involving violence, threatening behavior, unwanted pursuit, or harassment—whether a threat to self (as with suicide) or threat to others (as with a rampage)—Faber has formed a standing threat assessment and management team. The team meets regularly to identify student behavior suggestive of later problems, developing a plan to monitor or address the situation, as merited. (There is a parallel group at Faber to consider employee behavior, although the two functions are often combined at other universities and colleges.) Approaches may include voluntary or involuntary counseling or treatment, voluntary withdrawal or suspension until the student is able to safely return to the campus community, or expulsion from the institution. The team may also refer matters to the town police or county sheriff.

The Faber team includes the following members (with their basic orientation in parentheses):

- vice president for student affairs (chair) (lead process and ratify decisions)
- associate vice president for academic affairs (academic integrity)
- director of public safety (security)
- director of counseling and psychiatric services, Faber Health Center (a licensed psychiatrist) (treatment)
- associate dean of students for student support services (a certified counselor) (empathy and referring students)
- university counsel (liability)
- director of student judicial affairs (due process)
- director of housing and residence life (student welfare)
- director of student life (student emotional development)
- associate vice president of finance and administration for human resources (documentation)
- director of academic advising and registrar (student records)
- representative from the faculty senate (faculty welfare)
- assistant to the president (reputational risk)
- director of the disability resource center (disabled students)
- director of international student services (international students)
- associate director of athletics (athletes)

The deputy chief of police of the town of Faber and the deputy sheriff of Faber Country are ex-officio members of the group. The student support services office makes referrals to the counseling center and providers of other resources. There is also a staff member, reporting to the vice president for student affairs, responsible for coordinating the activities of the team.

For the simulation, each member of the group should assume a role, working from the top of the list and stopping when everyone has been assigned. If there are more members of the group than roles, there can be multiple representatives of the offices toward the top of the list. If there are fewer, those assigned roles should integrate an office at the bottom of the list into their sphere of responsibilities, as with the athletic department reporting to the vice president for student affairs.

Upon convening, the team reviews cases, considering its response and concluding with an action plan for each. The response may be to: (a) do nothing; (b) investigate the matter further, assigning it to the relevant office to prepare a report for the next meeting; (c) refer the student to the counseling center (for either voluntary or involuntary treatment) or student support services, including assigning an administrator to be responsible for monitoring the situation; or (d) recommend action such as suspension or dismissal. There are due process considerations associated with option (d), but referrals to counseling or support services do not have such requirements. A student who resists counseling, once referred, is reconsidered for another response.

The team understands its obligations to maintain student privacy, but has taken a broad view of the health and safety exception to FERPA and tends to notify parents, as warranted, as part of its response. It is also charged with considering who to notify on campus or in the community about a given situation, again respecting student privacy. Those contacted may include other students, faculty members, administrators, or the local police. Finally, the threat assessment team is called into action in crisis response situations, convening to assess a situation and make recommendations to President Wormer.

Please address how the team would choose to address each of the situations below. If referral or monitoring is advisable, please indicate who would be responsible and what would be involved. If notification to parents, law enforcement, or members of the campus community is merited, please develop an approach. For variety, have a different member of the team present each situation.

- During the second week of the academic year, the roommate of a first-year student reports to his resident assistant that the student is posting "disturbing" quotations and images on his Facebook page. The material suggests a preoccupation with violence, but the student has not made specific threats toward anyone. The roommate indicates and the resident assistant confirms that the student has not made any friends and only leaves the room to go to class. There are also concerns about his personal hygiene, as he has taken to wearing the same clothes each day. While in the room, the student tends to watch DVDs of war movies.
- A fourth-year student in an art history class aggressively confronts her professor at the end of class after receiving a poor grade on the midterm examination. The student blames the professor for her performance, making some alarming statements overheard by several students as they are leaving the classroom. The professor reports to her department chair that the student exclaimed: "I'm not going to let you get away with this" and "You haven't heard the last of

me—if I don't do well in this class, I'm ruined and you'll regret what you did to me." She also yelled at the students listening to his outburst: "What are you idiots listening to—I know who you are."

- Public safety responds to a call from a residence hall front desk reporting that a third-year student has apparently overdosed on nonprescription medication. The student is transported to the local hospital by ambulance, where she is treated and receives a psychiatric evaluation. She is not deemed to be a threat to herself by the mental health staff at the hospital, and is released to return to campus after an overnight stay. Public safety notifies the threat team of the situation.

- A student sends an alarming e-mail message to his professor. His class attendance has been sporadic throughout the semester and he has not turned in his past several assignments. In his message, the student reveals that he is a veteran who returned home from Iraq about a month before enrolling for the current semester. He reports that he is experiencing flashbacks and depression, but has not been to the VA for treatment. The student is not asking for any assistance, but just wants the professor to know why he has done so poorly in class. The student lives off campus with three roommates. The only record the college has related to his military service is that he was honorably discharged.

- A student reports that a fellow student, his former girlfriend—they broke up a month ago, after seeing each other for six weeks—has been "bumping into him" frequently, often several times a day, as at the fitness center, dining commons, laundry room, and even at the Wal-Mart located several miles away. He has reported to his residence hall faculty member-in-residence that he thinks she may be stalking him. He is more annoyed than concerned at this point, not believing that she is, as he puts it, "the crazy or violent type."

- A third-year student, having returned from a study abroad trip to the South Pacific, has decided to only wear a loin cloth and flip flops, whether to class or around campus. The dining hall director reports him, noting that he seems to be popular with the other students. Winter is approaching, however.

- A resident assistant responsible for two first-year football team members reports that they appear to have had a brand seared onto their upper backs. Responding to his question about it, the students contended it was just part of being on the team and they volunteered for it, explaining how the first-year players decided together to brand each other as a show of commitment and unity.

- A second-year student lost a striking amount of weight at home over the summer and has continued to do so having returned to school. She is working out several hours each day and rarely visits the dining commons. The students with whom she was close last year report, via their resident assistant, that she is withdrawn and has resisted their attempts to connect with her. One of these students has gained 75 pounds since arriving at Faber last year and is snacking obsessively.

- A third-year student has seemingly dropped everything to devote himself to a 37-year-old professor at the college. He has moved in with her, is no longer in contact with his friends, and is not attending classes regularly. The professor, recently tenured, separated from her husband over the summer. Both the student and the professor claim the two are roommates and there is no amorous relationship between the two. The student's parents have contacted the college multiple times to register their displeasure.

- A group of eight students, calling themselves "the Senate," have taken to meeting nightly in the residence hall room of one of them, taking steps to maintain secrecy. No one knows what they are doing, except that they usually order in pizza at around midnight.

- A student claims inspiration from recent political protests and insisting that it is necessary for his own safety, has taken to wearing a pistol around campus. He is complying with all relevant laws and thus has the right to carry the weapon. The student has become so strident in discussions about current affairs that he is constantly attempting to initiate that his fellow students have taken to avoiding him. He has a seeming obsession with the U.S. president, mentioning him in conversations many times a day, often out of context. His class performance has begun to decline because he is more interested in discussing his political philosophy than in addressing the question at issue.

- A resident assistant has apparently joined a religious cult, changing his last name on his Facebook page to "Savior," which it appears all members of the group do. He does not appear to be attempting to convert the students on his floor, but information on the Internet indicates that the foundation of the group is attracting new members. There is no history of violence associated with the group.

As a possible postsimulation exercise, those participating could develop their own scenario, modeled on the ones above and the trickier the better, suggesting how the threat team would respond. Another exercise would be to consider how the crisis response team at Faber would respond to one of these situations, were it to escalate.

5

REGULATION

The passage of antiterrorism measures and the tightening of immigration have led to an increase in federal compliance and reporting requirements across higher education, with both posing challenges for the research enterprise. Research continues to demand an extensive infrastructure devoted to maintaining compliance with regulations that address direct and indirect costs, research integrity, human and animal subjects, taxation, and emerging areas such as biosafety and the use of human tissues. With technology transfer, there are further issues with conflicts of effort and conflicts of interest, as well as challenges associated with preserving tax-exempt status. Greater attention is paid to transparency, both in accounting and consumer protection, the latter represented by the conclusions of the 2006 Commission on the Future of Higher Education (the Spellings Commission) and other accountability measures posed by the federal government, the states, and private accreditors and regulators. There has also been debate about undocumented students, to whom states can deny in-state tuition and scholarships, but not access.

Intellectual property rights broadened with the passage of the 1997 Digital Millennium Copyright Act, which addressed complications in copyright arising from the Internet. There continues to be a copyright exception for fair use, but there are arguments that there has been a "privatization" of knowledge, with a decline in what is available in the public domain. Similarly, there is more aggressive enforcement of intellectual property rights, as with media corporations threatening to prosecute peer-to-peer file transfers among students. The TEACH Act (the Technology, Education, and Copyright Harmonization Act) of 2002 has extended classroom rights to online education, but institutions have claimed ownership over content, arguing that faculty create it as work-made-for-hire.

Finally, the most pronounced illustration of private regulation over higher education involves athletics, with National Collegiate Athletic Association (NCAA) compliance requirements connected with recruiting and eligibility, as well as standards imposed in areas such as admissions that are a deviation from norms of institutional autonomy. Institutions are also subject to Title IX, with federal policy and judicial decisions mandating equality of opportunity for women in athletics. Athletics is not unlike the rest of the university in that aspects of it are becoming increasingly—and even essentially—professional in nature, with significant revenues and expenditures connected with commercial involvement, but needing to maintain the perception (and formal status) of amateurism.

Compliance and Integrity

The federal government requires that universities and colleges comply with various regulations, many of these connected with conducting and commercializing research. Following the September 11, 2001 attacks on New York and Washington, the U.S. Congress added to these compliance requirements, including acts addressing bioterrorism prevention (as with biological agents and equipment), export controls (as with technologies) and foreign nationals (as with participation in certain research), and educational records privacy (as with access to telephone and e-mail records) (Keith, 2004).

The Bioterrorism Preparedness and Response Act of 2002 (BPARA) covers certain biological agents and their required registration, as well as background checks and safety concerns (Bienstock, 2004). Export controls primarily concern proprietary research that is restricted for national security reasons, with limitations on foreign students and researchers working on projects involving technologies or data subject to BPARA (Carr, 2006; Kearney, 2005; Keith, 2005a). But they exclude fundamental research or work in the public domain, which enables research universities to conduct most activities without constraints (Carr, 2006). There are also issues with partnering with a foreign institution in a country subject to restrictions, as well as applicable international traffic in arms regulations (Claus, 2005). Knowledge leakage violations can involve serious penalties, both significant fines and imprisonment.

The USA PATRIOT Act of 2002, most notably among these post-9/11 statutes, reaches computing and libraries at universities and colleges, with enhanced federal surveillance capacities and means to facilitate sharing of sensitive information with intelligence agencies and law enforcement (Strickland, Minow, and Lipinski, 2004; Tribbensee, 2004). The legislation underscores that privacy is not an absolute at libraries and in computing, with the need to balance it with federal obligations and liability concerns (Strickland et al., 2004). Additional compliance and reporting requirements even reach university and college credit unions under expanded money laundering statutes (Larose, 2004). A particular challenge in higher education is that international graduate students working in laboratories have broad access to information and technology that may prove valuable to foreign governments.

Also in response to 9/11, the federal government tightened immigration requirements, which has had a meaningful impact on universities and colleges. The policy had the effect of limiting the graduate assistants and postdoctoral fellows available to staff the laboratories that had come (and continued) to rely on them for affordable labor, as well as tightening access to the international undergraduates who are being recruited increasingly aggressively by institutions. The primary contemporary issue related to immigration is with undocumented students (Olivas, 2004). These individuals do not have guaranteed access to resources that make higher education possible, such as scholarships and loans. Such rights are assured in primary and secondary education under *Plylar v. Doe* (1982), but higher education is not deemed to be a fundamental right (Huang, 2007). (There is also the practical problem of needing to provide a social security number to attain financial aid.) Undocumented students can also be denied in-state tuition and other public benefits under two 1996 federal statutes, the Illegal Immigration Reform and Immigrant Responsibility Act (IIRIRA) and the Personal Responsibility and Work Opportunity Reconciliation Act (PRWORA) (Huang, 2007; Wheelhouse, 2009).

There are questions raised about whether states can prohibit undocumented students from attending public universities altogether. The concern is less of a legal issue, given reasonable interpretations of IIRIRA and PRWORA prohibit only the state providing additional consideration that it would not give a documented student or a citizen (Ruge and Iza, 2005). It is more of a political issue, as some disagree with using tax dollars to support undocumented students and are concerned about them circumventing U.S. immigration law (Huang, 2007). While in-state tuition can be denied, it can also be allowed for undocumented students under state statute, as in California and Texas. It is also allowable to afford in-state tuition based on a uniformly applied residency requirement, as in Texas where graduation from a state high school is allowed as a qualifying standard (Maki, 2005; Ruge and Iza, 2005). (Fung [2007] argues that such state statutes are preempted under federal law, and that IIRIRA does not allow benefits that are denied those living in another state.) As access to K-12 education cannot be denied to undocumented students, some students do not know they are undocumented until they ask their parents to fill out financial aid paperwork requiring a social security number.

There is proposed legislation, the Development, Relief and Education for Alien Minors Act (DREAM Act), that would offer undocumented minors a six-year conditional path to citizenship upon earning a college degree or completing two years of military service (Maki, 2005). Texas already offers a similar policy, treating undocumented students as citizens for tuition and financial aid purposes if they have resided in the state for three years, graduated from a Texas high school, and promise to seek legal status as a permanent resident (Wheelhouse, 2009). Even without such state legislation, undocumented students can pay out-of-state tuition, as international students commonly are charged, although there are practical limits, as these students often lack resources (Maki, 2005). Private institutions can admit undocumented students and provide them with financial aid, but there are issues such as the students not being able to work part-time or necessarily being able to secure employment following graduation, as they lack needed papers. Private scholarships are allowable at public and private institutions, as from philanthropic organizations or even through fund raising by individual students within their local communities, provided they do not ask for documentation.

For nonimmigrants involved in higher education, there are several categories of status, as with short-term visas for business or academic activities (B-1 visas) or tourism (B-2 visas), with citizens of certain countries exempt from the need to obtain one. Students enrolled full-time at a recognized institution can obtain an F-1 visa, with rules related to their ability to be employed and adequate financial resources to cover expenses. Foreign professionals, such as professors or researchers, can gain status on a H-1B visa for three-year increments not exceeding six consecutive years. There is also the J-1 visa for exchange students, short-term scholars, medical residents, and others, with the requirement that they show the intention to return home following their time in the United States. The visa has a three week minimum and five year maximum. Additionally, there is also the O-1 visa for individuals of extraordinary ability; R-1 visas for religious workers; and status for Canadians and Mexicans under the North American Free Trade Agreement (NAFTA). Furthermore, there are options for obtaining permanent residence, either a waiver for certain exceptional workers or a labor certification, which requires an employer to advertise a position to gauge the interest of U.S. workers. Those with permanent residence status can be employed permanently and can change positions at will. Finally, there are requirements that employers verify that someone they are hiring is authorized to work in the United States, using the I-9 form, and institutions enrolling foreign students must designate an officer charged with monitoring and compliance in the area (Rhoads and Konrad, 2007).

Two other areas requiring compliance are employee safety and fair labor standards. The Occupational Safety and Health Administration (OSHA) can investigate a university or college for violations of its regulations. There are monetary penalties for violations, and information acquired during an investigation can be used in subsequent civil actions and criminal prosecutions (Barber, 1991). The Fair Labor Standards Act of 1938 (FLSA) applies to public and private universities, with the Department of Labor able to inspect relevant payroll records and conduct interviews toward substantiating a complaint. Issues are often related to whether employees are properly deemed exempt (salaried) or nonexempt (hourly), as with calculating comp time and overtime for nonexempt employees (Flygare, 1999).

As discussed in Chapter 2, the U.S. Department of Education (USDOE) can investigate allegations of discrimination, as in employment, under the various anti-discrimination statutes, such as the Americans with Disabilities Act or Title VI. Complaints tend to be vague to protect the privacy of the complainant, with institutions required to produce documents and provide relevant people for interviews. The USDOE encourages negotiation toward a voluntary resolution, but will seek to compel compliance, if merited by its findings, when conciliation efforts fail (Jewett and Rutherford, 2005; Johnson and Schoonmaker, 2004).

Another broad area attracting recent attention is corporate disclosures and consumer awareness. The 2002 Sarbanes-Oxley Act is related to the accuracy and reliability of corporate disclosures under the security laws in the interest of protecting investors. Its spirit is consistent with the aspirations of academe, even though not expressly intended for nor applicable to the area, as in eliminating conflicts of interest; establishing effective checks and balances; and insisting on disclosure, transparency, and openness. It encourages board of directors independence, with audit committees, and annual audits of financial statements and risk assessments by outside consultants. There is also whistleblower protection (Oxholm, 2005). University and college trustees, who often are from corporate backgrounds, tend to be familiar with the legislation, and some of them encourage implementation of its principles at their institution.

Similarly, federal higher education policy is increasingly focused on accountability and consumer protection, as with the Spellings Commission and the 2008 Higher Education Act reauthorization. Both endeavor to increase access to information about higher education toward producing more informed consumers and keeping institutions honest about costs and pricing (Morgan, 2009). There are also some protections against selling bogus degrees and transcripts, but such activity is only increasing with online possibilities, and state and federal laws are underdeveloped (Johnson, 2006). As discussed in Chapter 4, the Health Insurance Portability and Accountability Act (HIPAA) requires compliance related to electronic health care transactions, which can apply to certain kinds of research and practice at universities that incorporate a health care facility (Boswell and Barefoot, 2005). Finally, as employers, universities and colleges are required to maintain various records—personnel and compensation, nonprofit status, financial aid, grants and sponsored research, law enforcement, and licensure and accreditation—with the length of time sometimes mandated (Ambash, 2005).

Compliance with sponsored research regulations also requires an extensive administrative infrastructure (Dobkin, 2005). Private foundations, federal or state governments, or private corporations may sponsor research, each with a slightly different set of processes and expectations, as with fast and targeted results for the latter or compliance concerns with governments (Bienstock and Colecchia, 2005). There are multiple sources of applicable law and regulation pertaining to sponsored research:

- These include various research integrity rules, as captured in the uniform Federal Policy on Research Misconduct (2000) from the presidential Office of Science and Technology Policy, and Public Health Service (PHS) and National Science Foundation (NSF) regulations on conflicts of interest in research.
- There are federal human subjects regulations, as with the Common Rule that applies across 17 agencies, and specific policies enforced by the Department of Defense (DOD) and Food and Drug Administration (FDA) that require an independent review committee to approve and monitor research, with a goal of protecting volunteers (Colecchia, 2005; Rice, 2005); standards for animal research, as from the U.S. Department of Agriculture (USDA) and PHS (and various state laws in addition to the federal Animal Welfare Act and Health Research Extension Act of 1985) (Shiels, 2005); HIPAA (Blau, 2005); and various FDA rules on clinical trials and drug studies.
- The Internal Revenue Service (IRS) promulgates taxation rules on corporate sponsored research; there are cost reimbursement and financial regulations from the Office of Management and Budget (OMB).
- There are export controls under the U.S. Department of Commerce; biosafety and biosecurity regulations and requirements from Health and Human

Services (HHS), the Centers for Disease Control and Prevention (CDC), and the USDA; and various federal hazardous waste laws (Vercauteren, 2007)

- The Bayh-Dole Act of 1980 (University and Small Business Patent Procedures Act), discussed in greater detail below, addresses the commercial development by universities and colleges of the products of federally funded research (Bienstock and Colecchia, 2005).

- Regulations exist related to the use or control of human tissues, as through cadaver donations, organs and other tissues harvested postmortem, retention and banking of tissues during standard medical procedures, or retention of tissues collected as part of primary research studies. These regulations address various consent, privacy, and rights concerns, as well as the commercial value of tissues collected (Barnes, Heffernan, and Hermes, 2005).

The Federal Grant and Co-Operative Agreement Act (1977) applies to most federal procurement contracts, grants, and cooperative agreements with universities and colleges. Federal acquisition regulations (FARs) and OMB circulars provide guidance on policies, as with determining costs that are appropriately charged, both whether and where they can be assigned (Irwin, 2005). Federal grants allow institutions to charge direct costs, as interpreted by OMB circular A-21 (2004) and the National Institute of Health's (NIH) *Grants Policy Statement* (2003). Costs can be allocated if incurred solely to advance the work under the sponsored agreement, if it benefits both the sponsored agreement and other work of the institution in proportions that can be approximated through the use of reasonable methods, or is necessary to the overall operation of the institution and deemed to be assignable in light of the principles in the circular (Kenney, 2005a). There are issues related to defining closely related work, the timing of charges to sponsored projects, deviation from approved budgets, carryover of funds to another budget period, funding meetings and conferences, and direct charging of administrative and clerical costs (Kenney, 2005a).

Another set of issues relate to salary and benefits payments to researchers and others, with requirements that compensation be reasonable within relevant markets and consistent with overall institutional policies, with bonuses and incentives possible but restricted (Kenney, 2005b). (The NIH has a salary cap for what it will reimburse under its grants.) Universities and colleges tend to be serious about compliance, while pursuing advantage as much as possible. The behavior of institutions is tempered by prominent examples of institutions being audited for being overly aggressive in charging direct costs and rules such as on accounting for and determining faculty effort. But given the benefits of securing grants and contracts, institutions have become increasingly entrepreneurial, delving into voluntary cost sharing, incentives to faculty who secure funding, and various partnerships with industry (Kenney, 2005b).

Such researcher-university-industry commercialization efforts, driven by Bayh-Dole, enables institutions to capture title to the outputs of federally funded research. They require complicated contracts that address issues such as the ownership of intellectual property, and involve issues such as the right to review articles before publication, maintaining confidentiality and limiting dissemination of research results, and ownership of biologic specimens and future use of data (Adams, 2005; Irwin and Dries, 2005; Parker et al., 2005; Porter, 2005). (The Small Business Innovation Research Program [SBIR] encourages firms of more modest size to become involved in commercial development.) For instance, the corporate partner may be more interested in minimizing potential reputational risk and commercial harm than in the advancement of science through publishing the results of the work.

Various other practical matters arise in such collaborations, as with institutions that construct research facilities with tax-exempt bonds not being able to use the facilities for private activities beyond a *de minimis* degree without incurring tax liability (Durant and Hammersla, 2005). Similarly, a university performing research with the purpose of product commercialization may be subject to unrelated business income tax (UBIT), just as an institutional insider could have a sufficiently significant economic or financial interest in a partnership business so as to trigger an excess benefit penalty (Durant and Hammersla, 2005). There can also be product liability concerns, complications with transferring various compounds, challenges with cross-national collaborations, and difficulties with terminating the partnership (Adams, 2005; Durant and Hammersla, 2005; Henning, 2005; Keith, 2005b; Porter, 2005).

Given commercial and professional pressures, research misconduct is a concern. The National Science Foundation (NSF) and PHS define the concept similarly, as fabrication, falsification, or plagiarism in proposing or performing, reviewing, or reporting funded research, not including honest errors or difference of opinion (Parrish, 2006). Fabrication is making up data; falsification is manipulating it to inaccurately represent the record; and plagiarism is appropriating the work of another without due credit. The NSF rules assign to institutions primary responsibility for preventing and detecting research misconduct, as well as for investigating and adjudicating allegations, with the agency mandating the process followed and ensuring that federal interests are protected. Under PHS standards, a finding of research misconduct requires a significant departure from accepted practices of the relevant research community, committed intentionally, knowingly, or recklessly, with the allegation being proven by a preponderance of the evidence—the fact at issue is more probably true than not (Patti, 2005). There is also protection for whistleblowers against retaliation.

There are various types of conflicts of interest involving researchers, which usually arise from complicated fact patterns and often occur in connection with faculty startups (Bienstock and Colecchia, 2005). Various federal agencies, institutions, and professional organizations have standards, with federally funded work subject to statutes (Shea et al., 2004). Common situations that involve individuals include financial conflicts through receiving excessive consulting fees, earning bonuses for enrolling study subjects, accepting inappropriate honoraria or travel expenses, holding an equity or ownership interest in the commercial sponsor, having an intellectual property interest in the resulting product, enjoying philanthropic support from commercial sponsors, and receiving credit for published work without having participated in its production (Broccolo and Lutz, 2005). Institutions can also be involved in conflicts, as with holding an equity stake in a partner company (Shea et al., 2004).

Preserving the exemption from taxation afforded to higher education is complicated by the increasingly commercial nature of entrepreneurial universities and colleges. The standard is that functions, including auxiliary ones such as dining and housing, are exempt because they are essential to the operation of the institution and sufficiently connected with educational purposes. Institutions must also comply with regulations on the federal financial aid that their students receive, such as Pell Grants and federally guaranteed loans, the latter not being dischargeable in personal bankruptcy (Hoke, 2006; LeMay and Cloud, 2005; Welnicki, 2005). There is also private lending, which often is more expensive for students (Milligan, 2008).

Finally, additional federal regulations relate to various tax provisions providing subsidies for individuals involved with higher education, as with tax credits (such as the Hope Scholarship Credit and the Lifelong Learning Credit), the "above the line" deduction for qualified tuition and related expenses, and prepaid tuition programs (Section 529) (Pike, 2007). There is some deductibility for training in order to maintain or improve skills, but not for entering a new trade or business (Musselman, 2007). Pike (2007) argues these are flawed as a tool for delivering financial aid, given their administrative complexity; the cash flow issue, as benefits come later; and (especially) upper-income families enjoying most of the benefits (Ryan, 2008; Smith, 2008; Stegmaier, 2008). There are also tax implications for individuals related to institutional policies such as retirement buyouts (Fuehrmeyer, 2009).

Globo University (GU), the flagship public institution in its state, has research expenditures of $600 million annually, ranking in the top 25 nationally and constituting about one-third of the annual budget at the university. It has emphasized research in the biological sciences over the past two decades, leveraging its medical, veterinary, and agriculture schools, in addition to its programs in engineering. The Globo University Research Foundation (GURF), established in 1982, has an aggressive technology transfer program, supporting several ventures that involve GU faculty and being involved in various corporate partnerships. President Peter LaFleur, entering his second decade in the position, is an aggressive fund raiser who has doubled the endowment over his tenure to $1.5 billion and raises around $200 million per year in private donations. The proportion of the budget Globo receives in annual state appropriations has been steadily declining, and is now below 20 percent of its nearly $2 billion budget (about 40 percent of which is associated with medical research.)

Tuition at the university has not risen in proportion with increasing expenses. The state has a merit scholarship program, which provides tuition and fees for higher achieving high school graduates—and 95 percent of first year GU students enroll with scholarship support. Because any tuition increase is thus passed to the state through the scholarship program, increases have been modest. Globo has attempted to increase its out-of-state, graduate, and professional enrollments to compensate, but there is political resistance to increasing the former beyond the current 18 percent. Enrollment is 35,000, with 22,000 undergraduates, almost all attending full-time, with about 1,500 students enrolled part-time in masters programs offered at four satellite facilities across the state. Primarily because it is able to keep so many accomplished high school graduates in state, but also due to its increasing research and endowment, GU ranks in the top 15 among public institutions in the annual *U.S. News and World Report* survey (42 among all institutions last year). The average SAT score for freshmen is approaching 1300, having increased by 150 points since 1995. About one-tenth of the Globo undergraduate students are in the honors program, with 30 students, named Dwight Fellows, receiving packages that enable the university to recruit successfully against the leading national public and private universities and colleges.

Like other presidents, LaFleur focuses fund raising on supporting scholarships, capital projects, and endowed professorships. The university has tripled the number of endowed faculty positions over the past decade, with 200 professors now holding chairs. GU has concentrated these in the biological sciences and other areas with significant funded research potential. Scholarships are directed toward honors and minority students, with African American undergraduate enrollments increasing to the 9 percent LaFleur targeted at his inaugural. The technological infrastructure at the university is well developed—another LaFleur priority—and the institution has built its global presence, now ranking among the top 10 nationally in short-term study abroad programs. Globo has 15 graduate programs ranking in the top 10 nationally, with its law, business, and medical schools in the top 30.

Although it has made significant progress, the institution is not without its challenges. The endowment and annual state appropriation both declined markedly during the recent economic downturn, with the former recovering slowly and the latter being cut by 8 percent last year (about $29 million lower than the $363 million the previous year) and 18 percent over the past three years. But these funds remain crucial, with LaFleur devoting considerable attention to legislators and others in the state capitol.

Research funding has become even more important, with Globo investing in needed administrative infrastructure, nearly doubling over the past several years the number of people reporting to the vice president for research, White Goodman. The several areas for which he is responsible include: commercial

(continued)

development of technology, business and economic development, sponsored programs, internal grants and contracts, fiscal affairs, facilities management, legal services, human subjects and animal care and use, and biosafety and quality assurance. The university has launched, also reporting to Goodman, several institutes and centers in emerging research areas. It has also developed an "incubator" for startup companies connected with university research, providing venture capital, facilities and equipment, and support services—and eventually commercial development through the production of marketable products. Most of these startups are faculty-institution-industry partnerships, with each having an equity stake. Globo has been particularly successful in negotiating licenses for patents held by the research foundation, with $25 million annually in licensing revenue, ranking Globo in the top 20 among institutions nationally.

Globo has worked with Kate Veatch, who arrived five years ago as an assistant professor, in pursuing the commercial applications of her work in bioinformatics (the application of statistics to molecular biology). She has attracted over $5 million in federal grants for her laboratory, with several other institutions taking notice. Globo encouraged her not to take an Ivy League position last year through an aggressive counteroffer. Veatch had been working with the technology commercialization office, having established a startup firm, Kateco, to move her work analyzing mutations in cancer to market. The institution provided venture capital, taking a two-thirds interest in the firm.

Working with the sponsored programs office, she has secured grants to cover the salaries and benefits of the nine people in her laboratory as direct costs, and developed protocols to comply with various associated requirements. (The institution negotiates indirect costs with various federal agencies, using the percentage to cover the expenses related to accounting, personnel, purchasing, facilities, depreciation, utilities, etc.) Veatch had an issue last year when she attempted to charge more of her salary and benefits to various grants than was allowed, resolving it in cooperation with the research office. There is also the struggle to avoid conflicts of effort, balancing her activities and those of her team between her university work and efforts associated with Kateco. Veatch has attempted to develop policies and processes here, but bright lines have been difficult to establish, with her team rarely able to document their "whereabouts" with precision.

There have also been conflict of interest issues recently, particularly as a leading biotech corporation, Gordon Technologies, has taken an interest in Veatch's research. They have indicated an interest in investing in her efforts, working with research office staff, but also offering her direct funding for one of her "side projects" for which she has been unable to attract federal support. She has also signed a consulting contract with Gordon, with questions raised about whether its fees are excessive, as well as whether recent first-class overseas travel covered by the corporation was appropriate. In compliance with federal rules, the institution has opened an investigation through its research integrity office. Along with the direct costs issue, the inquiry has aggravated Veatch.

The agreement with Gordon depends upon demonstrating certain results—and she has warned her researchers that any allegation of fabrication, falsification, or plagiarism could destroy the relationship. She is less concerned about federal taxation issues, but those in the research office have carefully considered whether a partnership with Gordon would compromise the exempt status of the institution, prompting having to pay unrelated business income taxes or the corporation benefitting from the use of a university built with tax exempt bonds. The university has constructed several such buildings devoted to research over the past several years. One of these, devoted to the study of infectious diseases, opened in 2000. In 2002, the university had to close most of the building because it was not in compliance with new bioterrorism regulations, hindering the progress of several funded research projects. It took three years to reconfigure the building, which required essentially gutting it.

Globo also had to develop policies and processes to comply with the USA PATRIOT Act because many of its laboratories depended on international graduate students and postdoctoral fellows to function, as is the situation with Veatch's group. For instance, the Federal Bureau of Investigation (FBI) office in town became quite interested in tracking, as it can under the legislation, foreign students working in areas in which national security could be implicated through the transfer to foreign governments of information and technology. Given the computing resources needed to do her work, Veatch's laboratory attracted interest. Globo concluded that there was no realistic option other than to provide the information requested. There was also the immediate challenge of tightened immigration restrictions causing particular problems in employing these individuals. The university had research funding, but struggled to find the (inexpensive) labor needed to operate various projects.

Globo has also had to invest in various accountability efforts, as in federal research compliance, which requires staffing at the laboratory level as well as centrally in the research office. The state has expanded reporting requirements, with those across the institution having to complete ever more forms and narratives, with the university establishing an institutional effectiveness office, now with eight full-time staff members, essentially to comply with such demands. Even with all of the data it is now regularly collecting, the institution did not have the information it really needed to make targeted budget cuts during the recent financial crisis, as the state is interested in different figures from those that often have direct utility in managing an institution, especially a research university that is so different from the other campuses in the state higher education system.

(continued)

The state recently instituted a customer service initiative and the chancellor of the state higher education system has introduced various other private sector management approaches, all of which seem to have attendant paperwork. The Globo board of trustees is comprised primarily of people with business backgrounds, with the chair encouraging the institution to adopt transparency principles in its accounting from the Sarbanes-Oxley legislation, even though it does not apply to higher education. Much of the work at the institution is already subject to open records laws, presenting a particular management challenge when efforts involve sensitive subjects. For instance, the recent search for a new research vice president became a matter of public record as soon as the outside search firm completed its work, passing a list of finalists to the university. Finally, the fund raising foundation staff has needed to expand as the institution has attracted more private funds, with questions related to maintaining tax exempt status becoming more complicated as the institution has grown more complex.

Intellectual Property and Technology Transfer

Intellectual property laws protect copyright (original expression), trademarks (signature), trade secrets (know-how), and patents (inventions) (Cochran, 2005; Williams, 2005). The author of a creative work of original expression has certain exclusive rights under copyright law of reproduction, creation of derivative works, and distribution (or display, performance, or broadcast) (American Association of Universities, 2005; Cochran, 2007; Harper, 2005; McDonald, 2007; Sun and Baez, 2009; U.S. Copyright Office, 2007a). Digital information has required copyright law to adapt, with changes in reproduction, publishing, and distribution—and often the blurring of distinctions among these—prompting questions about private use and fair use (National Research Council, 2000). The Internet complicates issues as varied as the ownership of online course materials (discussed below); protecting individuals against defamation, obscenity, and harassment from anonymous senders, given the lack of government regulation in cyberspace; ensuring privacy and increased security related to managing information; and due process complications when jurisdiction in intellectual property is based on geography and the Internet is not (Hawke, 2001).

Copyright

Copyright protection extends to original work in any tangible medium of expression—writing, music, drama, choreography, painting, photography, sculpture, etc.—but does not cover facts or concepts by themselves, only when they have been collected and organized in some meaningful way. Certain work in the public domain or government publications is not protected at all, and there are major exemptions in academe to copyright restrictions for fair use, libraries, and face-to-face and distance teaching, and in providing Internet service (Harper, 2005; McDonald, 2007). Nevertheless, institutions can be subject to vicarious or contributory liability for actual or statutory damages for infringements by employees, contractors, and students, as when they have knowledge of violations and supply the means to carry forth the infringement. But there is a good faith defense based in intentions related to fair use (Blum, Cahr, and McDonald, 2007; Harper, 2005; Harper, 2007a). Universities and colleges can similarly be deemed liable when they do not remove materials after being informed by the copyright holder, but are also in the position of protecting their own intellectual property, as with others infringing upon trademarks (Hawke, 2001).

The author is the owner of a copyright (with joint ownership where there is more than one author), but a work-made-for-hire within the scope of one's employment resides with the employer (Harper, 2005; McDonald, 2007). Research collaborations can require agreements to share intellectual property, including copyrights (McElwee, 2007). Copyright is secured upon creation of a work, with filing notice of copyright no longer required, although it is sometimes beneficial, creating a record that can aid in recovery in infringement actions (Cochran, 2005; Latourette, 2006; McDonald, 2007; U.S. Copyright Office, 2007a). It lasts for a set period of time, depending on the situation, as with the life of the author plus an additional 70 years for works created after 1978 (Cochran, 2007), with the work then entering the public domain (Hirtle, 2007).

The Digital Millennium Copyright Act of 1998 (DMCA) is generally perceived to have broadened protections for copyright holders (Colbert and Griffin, 2007). A challenge in collecting is that copyright is national in origin—there is no international copyright—and violations sometimes occur offshore, especially given the nature of the Internet. But there is some reciprocity for member countries with treaty relationships, as with the Berne Convention (U.S. Copyright Office, 2007b). There is also the concept of moral rights, which allow creators to protect their personal, as opposed to pecuniary rights, with the Visual Artists Rights Act of 1990 covering moral rights to the fine arts (Harper, 2005; Kwall, 2000). Kwall (2000) argues that moral rights may provide more protection than copyright laws in the university setting in the case of coauthorship disputes. Jensen (2003) suggests the need to develop a copyright culture, as opposed to relying solely upon regulation, especially given the nature of the Internet being difficult to manage.

The fair use exception allows use of a portion of a copyrighted item. It is determined by considering, in combination: the character of the use (educational versus commercial), nature of the content (factual versus creative), how much is used (small versus substantial), and the impact on the market (modest versus competes with sales of original) (Harper, 2005; Hawke, 2001; McDonald, 2007; Sun and Baez, 2009). For instance, given its nature, there are likely to be few fair uses of software, even if used for educational objectives, for factual purposes, in modest amounts, and with limited impact—it is not workable to break off a small piece of software for fair use. In contrast, photocopying a chart from a reference book for use in the classroom may qualify as fair use. Using copyrighted material outside of fair use requires receiving permission through a collective rights organization such as the Copyright Clearance Center (CCC) or directly from the copyright owner (Harper, 2005). Coursepacks, collections of readings copied from various journals and books and assigned to students by professors, or purchasing software site licenses, are illustrations.

Libraries operate in an increasingly complicated copyright environment, with the emergence of electronic reserves, web-based digital image and audio collections, and new means to reproduce materials for users. Fair use applies, with misperceptions about its limits being common (Hoon, 2007; Latourette, 2006). As reserve readings have moved into electronic formats, libraries have initiated means to ensure copyright compliance, as with negotiating electronic licenses and restricting access to authorized users (Alford, 2002).

Another set of exceptions are for classroom use, which the TEACH Act extends to distance education. Fair use under TEACH is conditional on using a volume of materials akin to traditional settings, access being limited to enrolled students, with various "downstream" controls such as removing material following a session or course and not allowing a student to copy a streamed presentation (American Association of Universities, 2005a; Colbert and Griffin, 2007; Crews, 2000; Drooz, 2007; Hoon and Drooz, 2007; Latourette, 2006). Distance education raises a variety of contractual and intellectual property concerns, including working with outside vendors, exclusive arrangements, ownership of content, intermingling of intellectual property, use of university name and marks, educational quality and integrity issues, access for those with disabilities, and faculty conflict of interest (Alger, 2007). There are also potential complications in areas such as accreditation (Lindsay, 2007), accommodation for students with disabilities (as through auxiliary aids such as captioning) (Goldgeier, 2007; Przypyszny, 2007), and plagiarism using online resources (which is also a concern in other than online settings) (Bender, 2007).

Primary among these issues is the question of faculty rights to the online material they produce (Alger, 2007; Latourette, 2006). Institutions increasingly claim that they own the rights to distance education materials under the work-made-for-hire doctrine when faculty members develop courses in connection with their compensated efforts as university or college employees. In asserting the right to use faculty-created material into which they have invested resources, institutions contend that they are concerned about competition from their own faculty, who might take the course to a rival institution (Harper, 2007c; Laughlin, 2000). But there is also a tradition of faculty assuming that they own such work. Shared ownership agreements have accordingly become recognized as a sensible solution to balancing faculty sensibilities and the commercial interests of institutions, establishing matters such as who gets paid when others use materials (Harper, 2007c; Euben, 2000; Klein, 2004; Laughlin, 2000). (Also, faculty members simply arguing that work is done outside of office hours has the disadvantage of individuals losing representation and indemnification by the institution should there be an investigation or litigation.)

The American Association of University Professors' (AAUP) *Statement on Distance Education* (1999a) asserts faculty rights, arguing that universities and colleges have not traditionally sought ownership over course materials, with the work-made-for-hire doctrine thus inappropriate and university and college instructors exempt from it (Harper, 2007c; Euben, 2000). The AAUP is interested in ensuring that values continue within the online environment, such as faculty influence in program decisions, academic freedom determined in course content and delivery, sufficient student–faculty interaction, voluntary involvement by faculty, recognition of additional time needed to develop courses, and adequate technical assistance (Euben, 2000).

Faculty interests in research and scholarship are more assured, as with agreements for electronic publishing between authors and university presses, which preserve traditional prerogatives (Hoon, Kaplan, and Harper, 2007). McSherry (2001) questions whether instructional and scholarly efforts should be owned at all, as treating academic work as "property" undercuts a working covenant that has long sustained intellectual life. But with the commodification of higher education—considering external markets along with traditional values—property becomes the only language available for talking about knowledge. There may be an academic exception to work-done-for-hire principle that may enable faculty to resist losing control of their work, but it requires framing their efforts as property, which raises conceptual difficulties similar to the alternative (McSherry, 2001).

Contemporary copyright and other intellectual property ideas, particularly as applied within higher education, have attracted critisism. Sun and Baez (2009) contend that intellectual property law simultaneously enables and disables the higher education community, especially the premise of ownership over knowledge allowing it to be privatized and commodified, which is in conflict with traditions related to public purposes. For instance, university patent activities can advance knowledge and encourage its production, while also restricting and inhibiting it in the interest of protecting commercial prospects, as with trade secrets and trademarks. They argue that environmental pressures (economic, political, and social forces) and prevailing factors (legal parameters, technological advances, and competing interests) shape intellectual property policies and practices in higher education, enabling the commercialization of research, teaching, and other activities. These create the environment for faculty work related to course materials being framed increasingly as work-for-hire by institutions. (With patents, discussed below in the context of technology transfer, there are also questions of ownership between faculty and institutions and academe and industry.)

There are also various practical frustrations, as with universities and colleges being expected under the Digital Millenium Copyright Act to control students and others in peer-to-peer networks connected with pirating intellectual property, or simply in seeking access to intellectual property, having the same challenges as others (Sun and Baez, 2009). An illustration of the latter is a single creation or invention having many interests involved, each qualifying for protection, creating a thicket of multiple patents that potential users must navigate (Sun and Baez, 2009). Many such challenges are attributable not only to strengthening of intellectual property protections, but also rights holders becoming more assertive in protecting them (Netanel, 2001). Lemley (2007) argues that framing intellectual property as akin to real property is flawed because copyright is inherently more regulatory in nature; Netanel (2001) is concerned that the broader prerogatives of holders create greater burdens on free expression; and Sun and Baez (2009) note that public universities and colleges can privatize and commodify knowledge, while continuing to hold themselves immune for intellectual property violations, even shifting risk to their employees, who can be sued in an individual capacity. There is also the argument that the state subsidizes higher education to a significant degree, as through financial aid and research funding, thus allowing institutions to act as entrepreneurs but without incurring much risk.

Others have contended that asserting more robust intellectual property rights, as under the DMCA, erodes the public domain—the so-called information commons—that is so important in the dissemination of information, including about science and culture and especially through the Internet (Bollier, 2007; Boyle, 2003). Boyle (2003) connects more expansive copyright protections with the neoliberal ethos and departures from public purposes that increasingly characterize American higher education. McCormick (2006) writes that institutional policies may have a chilling effect on academic freedom and technological innovation (Electronic Frontier Foundation, 2006). For instance, the Google library project of digitizing portions of books for free availability over the Internet has clear public benefits, but there is controversy over copyright issues and significant opposition from the publishing industry. Google makes a fair use argument because the copying does not involve the entire book, has no profit motive, mostly digitizes nonfiction work, and publishers can elect to opt out (Band, 2007; Harper, 2007b). The situation underscores just how difficult it is to balance the legitimate interests of copyright holders with advancing innovation within settings such as higher education or the enjoyment of content by individuals across formats (GarnerG2 and the Berkman Center, 2005).

Perhaps the most notable illustration of the increasingly aggressive stance in protecting copyright and trademarks is the "cease and desist" letters and "take down" notices under the DMCA sent by copyright owners, as to students caught using file sharing to download content on university or college networks (Heins and Beckles, 2005). As Internet service providers, institutions assume the risk of contributory or vicarious liability, but there is Eleventh Amendment (governmental immunity) protection and the DMCA prohibition against suing ISPs (Blum et al., 2007; Harrison, 2006). The challenge is that fair use is unpredictable because it is so case specific, with misperceptions that it is both narrower and broader than it in fact is. It requires flexibility because new formats, such as iTunes, appear constantly, rasing sometimes difficult questions (Harrison, 2006).

Patents

Similar to copyright, patents are exclusive rights granted by the federal government for a limited (but lengthy) period of time in exchange for a public disclosure of an invention, which is an original and useful process, composition, or device, or an improvement of an existing one. (Some biological materials, such as cell lines and antibodies, cannot be patented.) Institutions have increasingly become involved with patents through technology transfer activities.

The 1980 Bayh-Dole Act enables universities or colleges to secure rights, often in conjunction with the researcher, in the products of research, including patentable work, funded by the federal government (Kettner and Decker, 2005). Doing so is conditional on the transaction serving the public good through encouraging the practical application of research. Institutions must also comply with relevant federal obligations, such as NIH guidelines or taxation regulations, as discussed above (Kettner and Decker, 2005). Under Bayh-Dole, a nonprofit organization such as a university or college usually cannot assign the rights to an invention to a for-profit entity and must itself promote its utilization, commercialization, and availability, as through securing a patent (Kettner and Decker, 2005). Institutions may require their researchers to disclose inventions subject to Bayh-Dole (Kettner and Decker, 2005), but must share revenues with the inventor, with a remainder allowed to go to support research and education generally (Hulsey, 2005). Such efforts typically involve partnerships, with the CREATE Act of 2004 (the Cooperative Research and Technology Enhancement Act) encouraging cooperative research among universities, the public sector, and private enterprises through freely sharing information and flexibility in structuring partnerships, including removing constraints on public entities (Miller and Warren, 2005).

Research universities commonly have research foundations, established through their governing board under section 501(c)(3) of the Internal Revenue Code, to which they can assign inventions, investments, and donations that would be difficult or impossible for the institution itself to hold (Donley and Wingo, 2005). For instance, they can avoid state limitations on investing in private entities. Foundations are defined as a supporting organization formally connected with the institution, functioning for its benefit, and at least operated in connection with it (and perhaps operated, supervised, or controlled by it) (Cerny, 2005). Like research foundations, there are separate entities that institutions establish to manage resources generated through fund raising. At some public universities and colleges, private funds can be used for broader purposes than can state monies, such as for entertaining. Foundations have some utility in limiting liability, but do not have the sovereign immunity defense available. Research foundations typically have express policies on the use of funds, services performed, investments, licensing, and conflicts of interests (Donley and Wingo, 2005).

Research foundations can also provide options in arranging the startup ventures that faculty often launch toward finding a commercial outlet for their research.

Through foundations, institutions often negotiate an equity stake in these enterprises, prompting various questions—whether to take one, how much to take, what to do with it, etc.—as well as the need to consider the potential for conflicts of interest. Conflicts can involve the division between or among those entities involved in research funding, graduate assistants, university facilities, or intellectual property (Biancamano, 2005; Carney, 2005). Equity interests can also raise disagreements involving the desire of both researchers and institutions to manage the enterprise; securities law issues related to raising money from investors; concerns associated with offering stock (as applicable), as with insider trading and voting rights; and exposure to taxation for the otherwise tax exempt university or college (Astle, 2005; Donohue and Wright, 2005). Startups also require institutions to become quasi venture capital firms, evaluating business plans before choosing to invest—and seeking investors themselves (Kelly, 2005). Universities have developed research parks and other "incubators" to encourage startup ventures, assuming the risk that they will recoup their investment.

When startups become successful, foundations have the option to license the intellectual property produced (Anderson, 2005; Bills, 2005; Blakeslee and Bakalyar, 2005). Doing so requires attention to protecting institutional reputation, defining the business arrangement, adhering to government regulations, minimizing legal exposure, and managing contractual obligations (Blakeslee and Bakalyar, 2005). Subleasing can prove complicated, as with situations that involve sharing income across those entitled to it (Anderson, 2005). Warren and Holloway (2005) raise the concern of licensors who are attempting to go beyond the scope of protection of a patent in an anticompetitive way, thus raising antitrust concerns. They also discuss whether reach-through licenses, which are new technologies based on the licensed one, can be treated under the same licensing conditions that cover the original license. Licenses might be for either the products of research or various patentable means to conduct research, such as methods, equipment, and software (Warren and Holloway, 2005). There can be issues, as in software contracts, with the ownership of site licenses, warranties and liability, export controls, and payment and termination (Classen, 2005; Hammersla and Blakeslee, 2005).

Confidentiality and trade secrets issues can also arise with these arrangements. Trade secrets are valuable information not known outside of the organization, with measures taken to preserve secrecy and investment. Rights are often created through express agreement, but these can sometimes be implied, and can be passed to others, as with the sale of a firm. Violations can be based on state or federal law, as with the Economic Espionage Act of 1996, as well as the common law, as with breach of contract or even tort actions for misappropriation of trade secrets. A related issue is non-compete agreements established to restrain departing employees in their future work (Donley and Nelson, 2005). Patent infringement is punishable with compensatory damages (to replace the loss), indirect damages (the value of the infringing device), and punitive damages (to punish knowing violations), with settlements sometimes negotiated. In academe, there may be an experimental use defense. While rarely employed, the defense distinguishes between the use of patented material and its study, the latter being exempted from infringement (Caltrider and Davis, 2004; Dreyfuss, 2004).

There are various taxation and liability issues associated with ancillary joint ventures such as for-profit subsidiaries and spin-offs—and there can be not-for-profit spin-offs. Taxation concerns arise with royalties, equity interests, unrelated business income, financing with tax-exempt bonds, and valuation of patents (Cerny, 2005). For instance, performing research associated with a public–private partnership in a bond-financed facility can give rise to tax liability for the institution (Griffiths, 2005; Harding, 2005b; Hyde, 2005; Weyl and Rodgers, 2006). There can also be unrelated business income taxation (UBIT) issues related to entrepreneurial activities by nonprofit organizations such as universities and colleges, as well as taxes required on royalties paid to faculty members and investors, if deemed to be additional wages (Harding, 2005a; Farmer and Scally, 2004; Griffiths, 2005).

A common criticism of the technology transfer enabled by Bayh-Dole is that it may create an "anticommmons effect," with resources being underutilized given a plethora of competing legal interests in them and actors unable to resolve their diverse interests in an efficient manner. For instance, Bayh-Dole has led to multiple startups and several patent holders, each of whom has a vital piece of technology needed to create a commercial product, but no single entity existing to develop commercial possibilities downstream (Armstrong, 2004). Despite such complications, research universities have embraced technology transfer. With limits on increasing tuition and continued declining appropriations, institutions are pursuing research more aggressively, given its perceived potential to generate significant revenue (Gordon, 2004). In addition to the financial incentives for establishing partnerships, there are also strategic ones, as with leverage for individual researchers, remaining competitive with other institutions, and advancing local economic development (Biancamano, 2005; Carney, 2005).

Finally, institutions commonly trademark certain symbols, as with names or logos, creating a property right on their use. A trademark expressly distinguishes a product, broadly defined, from those produced by others. University or college trademarks can prove quite valuable, as with licensing fees paid to institutions by athletic apparel companies.

Through work funded from her federal grants, Veatch and her team discovered a process with particular commercial promise. Doing so provided Globo University with the ability under Bayh-Dole to participate in the commercial development of the work. It had already funded her startup company, taking a two-thirds equity interest, and subsequently negotiated a partnership with Gordon Technologies, offering the corporation one-half of the Globo share and thus one-third of the firm, creating three equal shares along with the one that Veatch holds. She was not entirely pleased, feeling somewhat compelled
(*continued*)

into the situation by the university, but she appreciated the possibilities associated with direct support from Gordon, which is an aspect of the arrangement. She accepted $4.5 million in funding from the corporation to develop the commercial applications of the process. The agreement among Veatch, Globo, and Gordon assigned management responsibilities to the institution, including the ability to negotiate the licensing of various products.

Veatch and the research office were soon at odds over approaches. The university was interested in securing a large up-front payment from Gordon, sacrificing smaller later payments, but also minimizing risk if the product did not prove successful commercially. It also had concerns about the ability to secure rights to the other patents needed to commercialize the product. Veatch was convinced that the product would be a runaway success. She was eventually proven correct, and is now accusing the university, as advised by various consultants it retained, of being too timid and lacking sophistication in its negotiations with Gordon. The university contends that Veatch is an "exemplary researcher, but has neither the temperament nor the capacity to manage" and proved "so difficult to work with and even outright hostile" that Gordon would only enter into an agreement if she was not directly involved in its business aspects. Veatch admits that she can be demanding and even somewhat narcissistic, but that such characteristics are what make a successful scientist.

The university accepted $12 million up front from Gordon, estimating that later years will yield about $3 million annually. It only informed Veatch of the agreement once it was finalized, contending that it was within its rights under the contract and concerned that she would poison the deal. Veatch's attorneys and consultants estimate the annual value of the product to be more in the $18 million range, with the potential for the amount to escalate. Instead of receiving $4 million initially and $1 million per year, as at present, Veatch would have earned $6 million or more annually. There are also trade secret clauses in the agreement that limit Veatch in certain respects, as with her effective ability to do work related to her discovery with another corporation. She has brought a $400 million lawsuit against the university, with the parties are engaged in settlement discussions.

The university has been more aggressive in pursuing its intellectual property rights under copyright. It has asserted ownership rights to the material developed by faculty for online courses, claiming that work-done-for-hire belongs to the university. It has offered faculty members a one-quarter interest in any later proceeds from the work, in exchange for them formally signing away any rights. Patches O'Houlihan, a 30-year professor in educational technology, has refused to sign and intends to bring an action against the institution. He views the situation as the last straw in what he calls the "corporatization, commercialization, commodification" of university work—and is looking to make a stand. Most other faculty members, particularly those newer to higher education, have accepted the university's offer, always having experienced the university in the manner to which O'Houlihan is reacting. They also appreciate that the arrangement indemnifies them against liability.

The university has also been on the receiving end of more robust infringement enforcement, with several of its students receiving "cease and desist" letters from various commercial rights holders for what they claim is illegal downloading. Although Globo is the Internet service provider, its counsel is comfortable that it is shielded under the Digital Millennium Copyright Act and other applicable provisions. But the students are subject to personal liability, with fair use defenses seemingly unavailable.

State and Private Regulation

States have significant influence over public higher education through coordination and appropriations, but direct regulation tends to be more minimal. There are open meetings and records laws (also called "sunshine laws") in all 50 states intended to encourage openness and disclosure in the operation of state agencies, including public universities and colleges. Different laws prompt different responses to questions such as what aspects of a public meeting must be held in the open, whether it is all discussion, some discussion, or only voting. Faculty or staff meetings are typically not covered. Certain disadvantages can accompany the positives of openness and disclosure, specifically the need for public institutions to conduct sensitive matters in public, such as search processes related to senior positions. Related state legislation addresses matters such as conflicts of interest, competitive bidding on contracts, and whistleblower protection. Certain federal legislation has similar aims, as with the requirement that institutions regularly disclose campus crime statistics. There are also local regulations on matters such as zoning, property taxation, and voting by students that is relevant to universities and colleges.

Institutions may also be subject to state law as it relates to fund raising, as with trusts and estates statutes. Private philanthropy is deductible, so there are also taxation implications, albeit usually federal. For instance, gifts of personal property must be appraised to determine their value, and donated securities, annuities, or insurance are subject to various regulations. There can even be problems with federal and state environmental laws associated with a gift of real property. On a more practical level, donations can be overly restrictive in purpose, not be aligned with institutional missions, or can impinge upon the ability to accept other gifts. Fund raising can also pose reputational risks, as with a discredited donor or a disfavored purpose.

Private accreditation is another form of regulation applicable to higher education institutions, whether of programs, conducted by disciplinary associations such as the American Bar Association (ABA), or of the entire university or college coordinated by one of six regional accrediting agencies, such as the Southern Association of Colleges and Schools (SACS). When legal problems arise, they tend to be in connection with programs or institutions being denied accreditation. Accreditors are not subject to constitutional provisions such as due process, and antitrust challenges are unlikely to be successful. But accreditors do have to follow their own reasonable rules, not make arbitrary or capricious determinations, and not unlawfully discriminate. (Antitrust laws are intended to avoid agreements or practices between and among entities that unduly limit competition or efforts by a firm to dominate a market through mergers or driving out competitors, each of which tends to inflate prices.) Even if accreditation agencies were deemed to be state actors, given that they perform a quasi-governmental function—for instance, accreditation is required for participation in federal student loan programs—an institution would still have to prove due process violation. But it is unlikely to have been unduly denied a property or liberty interest, discussed in Chapter 1, as accreditation processes tend to be orderly and detailed, including ample notice to prepare, opportunity to be heard, and rights to appeal.

The other major area of private regulation of higher education is in athletics, primarily through the National Collegiate Athletic Association (NCAA). In *NCAA v. Tarkanian* (1988), the U.S. Supreme Court held that the NCAA is not a state actor and therefore not subject to constitutional due process requirements. Antitrust laws do apply to the association, as the court held in *NCAA v. Board of Regents of the University of Oklahoma* (1984), removing NCAA limits on the number of times a given team can appear on television. The NCAA operates under the presumption that institutions will maintain direct control over athletics, comply with the rules of the association and cooperate in taking corrective action when violations are found, and assist the NCAA enforcement staff in any investigation and provide complete and truthful information (Connell, Harris, and Ledbetter, 2005). When significant problems are identified, institutions generally conduct their own investigations, self-reporting minor violations. The NCAA has its own procedures for investigations, with notification, multiple opportunities for institutions to respond, and appeals (Connell et al., 2005). In many respects, these are more comprehensive than would be required under constitutional due process. Findings of more serious rules violations can trigger penalties such as loss of scholarships, vacating wins involving athletes later deemed ineligible, and bans from postseason competition.

The NCAA has extensive rules associated with the recruitment and admission of athletes as students and their academic progress while enrolled. The basic principle is that athletes cannot receive benefits additional to those typically available to students. For instance, the athletic department is prohibited from covering personal travel expenses and telephone bills for its athletes. The same is true of under-the-table payments from boosters or agents, whether to recruits or those enrolled. The NCAA preserve the principle of amateurism, which is essential to maintain the connection with the academic enterprise that enables advantages such as being exempt from taxation or workers' compensation. Athletes may not receive compensation beyond a scholarship covering tuition and standard living expenses. That relationship between athlete and institution enables framing as amateur what can be an essentially commercial and professional endeavor in sports like football at more prominent programs (Crosset and Masteralexis, 2008; Toma, 2003).

As institutions tend to stretch to admit athletes, even at highly selective universities and colleges (Bowen and Levin, 2005; Shulman and Bowen, 2002) and especially in prominent programs, the NCAA has imposed minimum admissions requirements with Proposition 48 in the 1980s and Proposition 16 in the 1990s. Disparate impact challenges have failed, even though the rules had a disproportionately negative effect on African Americans (Bruton, 2002; Pennsyl, 2008). There are more recent requirements that mandate a core high school curriculum, making sufficient year-to-year progress while enrolled, and punishing institutions with poor graduation rates. Accordingly, the NCAA has a remarkable amount of influence over institutions that otherwise jealously guard their admissions and curricular prerogatives. There are also some federal mandates associated with athletics, as with reporting gender equity and financial data, as well as similar NCAA requirements (Keen, 2007).

Various legal and other challenges to NCAA rules have generally been unsuccessful. For instance, pressure to compensate athletes, even those in the very few areas that generate revenue, has not yielded change (Brooks and Davies, 2008; Dennie, 2007; Eckert, 2006). The amateur ideal makes such arguments more difficult, as it does with advocacy for covering athletes under workers' compensation (Tiscione, 2007), providing them with security beyond their annually renewable scholarships (Hanlon, 2006), eliminating restrictions on when athletes can be eligible for professional drafts (Pitts, 2008), or avoiding NCAA mandated drug testing on privacy grounds. Other challenges have been more successful, as with litigation to enable an athlete with a learning disability to receive an accommodation under the ADA for having taken alternative courses to the NCAA high school core curriculum.

There are several contextual factors relevant to NCAA regulatory influence over member universities and colleges. Despite increases in the number of women participating as athletes, there is still a dearth of women in positions of influence in athletics (Carpenter and Acosta, 2008; Porto, 2008), with the same true of African Americans (Gordon, 2008; Louis, 2007). Discrimination against gays and lesbians is also common (Osbourne, 2007). However, the NCAA does afford extensions in eligibility to athletes who become mothers (Brake, 2008; Larche, 2008; and McCarthy, 2007).

Additionally, there is significant stratification among institutions in resources directed toward athletics. For instance, in Division I, among the 120 programs in the Football Bowl Subdivision, the range in annual athletics revenues is from over $100 million to under $10 million (Schmit, 2007; Toma, 2009). The NCAA signed a $10.8 billion, 14-year contract with CBS and Turner in 2010 to broadcast the annual men's basketball tournament, thus continuing to have ample resources available. Although the NCAA regulates different sports similarly, teams that generate considerable interest, as with leading football programs, operate in a much more commercialized environment, generating considerable resources and spending aggressively. Sports in other contexts, as with Olympic sports at major programs or football in smaller ones (as in Division III), which constitutes the vast majority of athletics, function more like student activities.

Athletics programs are influenced by the application of Title IX to address persistent inequities associated with gender. Compliance with Title IX requires that an athletics program has either participation in substantial proportionality to enrollment across the institution of women relative to men, a history and continuing practice of program expansion for the historically underrepresented gender, or has fully and effectively accommodated the underrepresented gender (Pieronek, 2005). Relevant factors also include equal treatment of equivalent sports (men's swimming and women's swimming, for instance) in areas such as scheduling and equipment (Fields, 2007; Pieronek, 2003), but there can be compensation difference between coaches, as in men's and women's basketball, where the environment can differ significantly (Gaal, Glazier, and Evans, 2002). As plaintiffs, women have generally been successful in Title IX litigation, beginning in the 1990s when the Clinton administration facilitated enforcement (Pieronek, 2000; Suggs, 2005). There is a debate over whether advances for women have come at the expense of opportunities for men, as with men's teams being eliminated or rosters being capped for the purpose of reaching substantial proportionality (Pieronek, 2003).

Finally, apart from NCAA regulations, criminal behavior, including minor local violations, involving athletes on prominent teams tends to capture public interest, with attendant reputational risk for institutions (McCart, 2008; Spies, 2006). The same is true of fan misbehavior, which is difficult to regulate given free expression rights (Jacobs, 2006; Kaufman, 2009; Tiffany, 2007).

The athletic program at Globo University ranks in the top 10 nationally in revenues and expenditures, with both figures approaching $90 million annually and the department holding $50 million in reserves and spending $20 million each year on football. Unlike most other programs, even larger ones, Globo does not receive an institutional subsidy through either student fees or a direct transfer. About one-third of its budget comes from donations, mostly to ensure the right to initially purchase or continue to purchase football tickets, for which there is a lengthy waiting list. Coach Pepper Brooks, entering his 25th season, has won two national and eight ADAA conference championships (but has been 9-4 the past two years, with discussion of him being on the "hot seat"). Brooks earned $3 million in compensation last year, almost entirely from various outside sources embedded in his contract with the university, ranking in the top 10 nationally. His nine assistant coaches make about the same figure among them. These figures have increased markedly in recent years—and there is no sign of the trend abating.

The athletic department receives over $20 million annually in revenue from conference and bowl game broadcast contracts, primarily connected with football. Licensing income approaches $8 million per year, with the Globo Pirates name, logo, and colors nationally recognized; the program earns $10 million annually for selling Internet and local broadcast rights; and Globo partnered with a global apparel corporation beginning in 1990, transferring to its rival two years ago, signing a $70 million, 10-year contract. It also has various other corporate sponsorships amounting to $7 million annually, with "ribbon boards" circling the facing of the mezzanine of its 95,000-seat football stadium that flash advertisements through games. Skyboxes and other premium seating at the football stadium yield another $5 million with most of the amount paid by individuals being tax deductible. As with its contract with Brooks, these arrangements involve elaborate contracts, with athletics matters commonly requiring specialized outside counsel. Nevertheless, given the institution can frame football as amateur, it retains the standard tax exemptions applied to higher education institutions.

The athletic director, Cotton McKnight, who earns nearly what the Globo president does, is recognized nationally as a savvy administrator. He has built a program that competes for conference and national championships across teams, including the 22 Olympic sports that the institution offers. These programs require little attention, with head coaches pleased to make around $100,000 annually and younger assistants willing to work for one-third of that. He has also stabilized the men's basketball program, generating modest revenue, but nothing approaching the $60 million annually that is directly attributable to football. McKnight's greatest concern is avoiding scandal, as with running afoul of NCAA compliance rules and being penalized, with its competitive, financial, and reputational consequences. Earlier in the decade, the institution endured severe NCAA sanctions related to under-the-table payments connected with Me'Shell Jones, who won the Heisman Trophy before entering the National Football League draft following his junior season. The scandal did not directly implicate Coach Brooks, but did force McKnight's predecessor to resign. Also, NCAA rules that govern the admission of athletes and their academic progress are less stringent than Globo University standards. The situation tends to be reversed with smaller athletic programs, which are often at less selective regional institutions.

McKnight is less concerned, as a daily matter, with maintaining the appearance of amateurism—and thus tax-exempt status—in a football enterprise that

(*continued*)

is essentially commercial in nature, as he simply needs to comply with NCAA rules. He tends to dismiss antitrust arguments by smaller Division I athletic programs associated with access to lucrative bowl games, as the smallest of the 120 Football Bowl Subdivision (FBS) institutions have one-fifth (or even less) of the budget of his program, with much of that subsidized by university funds—it is an apples versus oranges difference. But like others associated with high profile programs, McKnight is attentive to the occasional chatter from those in Congress sympathetic to the smaller programs threatening to regulate the commercial aspect of college football, including through the taxation of activities such as bowl games. He is also not concerned with calls to compensate athletes, knowing that the NCAA and the football conferences will lobby against such efforts—and that the idea is likely to be impractical, with the need to maintain parity across teams causing such an approach to be overly expensive for even the wealthiest athletic programs. Similarly, he knows that unionization among athletes is doomed, given the power dynamics in athletics and the unwillingness of athletes to displease their coaches.

McKnight has managed Title IX obligations by offering three more women's sports than men's, adding one every few years to meet the continuing practice of program expansion standard. There was a lawsuit earlier in the decade, with the women's basketball coach bringing an equal pay action under Title IX, contending that she was entitled to the same salary as the men's coach. The court decided that the nature of the respective positions was sufficiently different, with greater competitive pressure and outside obligations associated with the men's position. There have been other lawsuits, primarily having to do with challenging dismissals as sexual harassment, and religious and other discrimination, but the program has been able to settle these.

Globo, the BCS, and Antitrust—A Simulation

The Bowl Challenge Series (BCS) (fictitious, but based on reality) is comprised of the 11 conferences in the Football Bowl Subdivision of NCAA Division I (FBS, formerly Division I-A) plus Notre Dame and the couple of other programs that compete as independents. The BCS exists to allocate slots into the four major bowl games—the Fiesta, Orange, Rose, and Sugar—and the BCS National Championship Game. The two teams atop the BCS standings, which combine rankings by computers and experts, receive an automatic berth in the championship. The champions of the BCS automatic qualifying (AQ) conferences (the ACC, Big East, Big Ten, Big 12, Pac 10, and SEC) receive a guaranteed BCS bid, with Notre Dame earning an automatic bid if it finishes in the top eight. Globo University is the member of an automatically qualifying conference, having appeared in four BCS bowl games over the past 11 years. The champion of a nonautomatic qualifying (non-AQ) conference receives an automatic bid if it is ranked among the top 12 or ranked in the top 16 and higher than at least one champion of an AQ conference. Typically, non-AQ conference teams need to finish the season undefeated to be in a position for a BCS game invitation, while AQ conference teams often have multiple losses. There are four additional at large bids. No one conference can earn them both of these and a non-AQ conference may earn one of them.

Each of the BCS AQ conferences receives about $18 million annually, with another $4.5 million if a second conference member participates in a BCS bowl. For instance, if both Alabama and Florida earn one of the 10 BCS slots, the SEC will receive about $22.5 million. The other conferences—Conference USA, the Mid-American, Mountain West (MWC), Sun Belt, and Western Athletic (WAC)—divide among them about $9.5 million annually as a result of joining the BCS. If any of the teams in these conferences receives a bid to play in one of the five BCS games, the five non-AQ conferences earn another 9 percent of BCS revenue. BCS revenue comes from selling television rights, earning $125 million annually for four years from ESPN-ABC under a new contract (with the Rose Bowl under a separate agreement). ESPN-ABC broadcasts the games on ESPN, a cable network, raising questions associated with access. ESPN is available in 98 million U.S. homes, about 86 percent of all households with television. Ninety-five percent of people who watched the BCS title game on a broadcast network, FOX, last season had cable or satellite service.

There have been threats of an antitrust lawsuit against the BCS, most prominently by the attorney general of Utah, on behalf of the non-AQ conferences and teams. The senior senator from Utah held hearings on the BCS last year and has raised the prospect of Congressional involvement. Brigham Young has been, but is no longer, is in the MWC and Utah State is in the WAC, with Utah now in what has become the Pacific 12. The MWC resisted signing onto the new BCS agreement, which runs for three more years, arguing that it disadvantaged them relative to the AQ conferences, but eventually did so, believing it had no other reasonable option. The other non AQ conferences believed and did the same. The junior senator from Idaho is concerned that Boise State, which competed in the WAC and is entering the MWC upon Utah's departure, will be frozen out of the championship game, even if undefeated, given they are perceived to play a weaker schedule than teams from the AQ conferences.

The financial situations of the AQ conferences and non-AQ conferences—and the programs within them—are quite different. Television contracts in FBS football are negotiated and signed by conferences. The leading AQ conferences can generate figures approaching $20 million per member institution annually from league broadcasting rights deals, with individual programs having the ability to sell other media rights. For instance, the SEC contracts signed in 2009 with CBS and ESPN-ABC were worth $205 million annually in their first year, with the figure increasing in subsequent years, with institutions able to negotiate their own local packages, as with Florida having its own deal with Sun Sports for 10 years and $100 million. (The NFL, in comparison, splits $4 billion in television revenue annually among its 32 franchises.) The other AQ conferences earn less from broadcast deals—sometimes one-half or even one-third, with these numbers presently in flux as they aggressively pursue better packages. The non-AQ conferences earn closer to $1 million per year per team (if that), with little interest in their individual media rights. Athletic program budgets parallel these television figures. The leading programs in the top AQ conferences have revenue in the $100 million range, with other AQ conference programs in the $50 to $60 million neighborhood. A typical non-AQ conference program has a budget of $15 to $25 million, with Sun Belt members such as Louisiana-Monroe below $10 million.

The Senate Subcommittee on Antitrust, Competition Policy, and Consumer Rights, with the senior senator from Utah as its ranking minority member, has called a hearing on antitrust issues associated with the BCS. The concern is that the agreement and practices among the AQ conferences unduly limits competition, effectively freezing out the non-AQ conferences from the resources connected with the BCS—and simply the realistic chance to compete for the national championship. There is not a concern that the six AQ conferences (and Notre Dame) that control the BCS have driven out competition to increase prices, but the senator and others are troubled that they have colluded to keep the revenue for themselves and away (at least significantly) from the nonautomatic qualifying conferences and programs.

There are two or three panels appearing before the subcommittee. The first includes the president of Globo University, the commissioner of the SEC, the executive director of the BCS, and a senior representative of ESPN. The second has the president of Fresno State (a non-AQ conference university), the commissioner of the non-AQ Sun Belt Conference (which essentially has no broadcasting revenue and member institutions with budgets in the $10 to $20 million range), and the alumni association president from Boise State. The third (if participating merited by the size of the group), is comprised of a *New York Times* sportswriter critical of the BCS, a law professor who has written a paper arguing that the BCS violates antitrust law; and a student-athlete from a nonautomatic qualifying team (Texas Christian) that went undefeated last season but was not invited to the championship game. The senate panel consists of the senior senator from Utah; the chair, who represents Wisconsin and is indifferent to the issue; and the junior senator from Alabama, who is an ardent BCS supporter.

The simulation begins with the members of each panel convening privately for 20–30 minutes to discuss the arguments in support of their position, develop a list of talking points, and then organize how they want to present them in a three-minute opening statement. The senators should convene to discuss what questions they individually intend to ask. The hearing begins with a representative of the first panel making its opening statement and the senators having 15 minutes to question them, with the chair allotting time as he or she sees fit. The panelists should remember their talking points and refer back to them, even if not entirely responsive to the question. (They risk the senators viewing such behavior as disrespectful.) The arguments of the first panel are likely to focus on the financial disparities present across athletic programs, especially between the AQ conference members and others. The second and third panels are likely to concentrate on anticompetitive behavior and basic fairness.

Conclusion

At the entrepreneurial university and college, traditional values such as advancing public purposes, academic freedom and tenure, and deference to academic decisions continue to be important, but are no longer solely determinative. Institutions across types are additionally influenced by neoliberal ideas that stress efficiency and prompt competition, framing higher education as being about individual gain. These universities and colleges continue to be interested in advancing their missions through effective teaching and advancing knowledge. But their aspirations, particularly to reach the next level of prestige, are also important. The reputational needle tends to be moved by attracting more accomplished students, and institutions intend for various academic and collegiate approaches to enhance their appeal, as with developing attractive degree programs or constructing luxurious student residences (O'Meara, 2007; Toma, 2010a).

Prestige provides a measure akin to shareholder values or other more concrete metrics available to corporations, as well as the legitimacy and security—and the prospect of increased resources—perceived to accompany isomorphic behavior. Institutions are also attempting to reduce costs, primarily by shifting to temporary labor in the instructional budget, while seeking to enhance revenue through various entrepreneurial ventures that extend the boundaries of the institution. But there remains the need to consider access and demonstrate accountability. Even as state support declines at public universities, demonstrating public purposes remains crucial. Additionally, faculty governance continues, especially at the most local levels, but the center of gravity has shifted to professional managers in many areas.

In concluding the discussion of legal issues and commercial realities in managing the entrepreneurial university or college, I address six notions suggestive of the intersection of these and indicative of what the law enables and demands in the context of contemporary higher education. As higher education has become more corporate in nature, it has become more reasonable for legislatures and courts to question the traditional prerogatives such as academic deference long afforded it.

Relationships

Contracts increasingly frame relationships in higher education, with formal agreements important in more uncertain and less communal institutional environments. The greater number of contractors and consultants retained by universities and colleges exist in an essentially contractual context, with their rights effectively limited to receiving compensation for the performance of established duties. For instance, academic freedom may technically apply to all researchers and instructors, but nonrenewal of a contract that is soon to expire offers managers an easy escape if they come to view a temporary employee as difficult. In addition, as teaching shifts to adjunct faculty and graduate assistants, those involved in faculty governance are providing increasingly less of the instruction at institutions.

Even the situations of those with traditional faculty positions have become more particularized and transactional. Those with leverage can negotiate their own arrangements, especially at research universities, no longer having to accommodate communal norms or even collegial relationships. Similarly, the relationship between institutions and students has also evolved into a commercial one, embodying the reasonable expectations that come with having purchased a good, with these only increasing as the product becomes more expensive. Institutions are coming to realize the realities of a neoliberal approach to higher education, emphasizing public purposes and individual gain alike and balancing traditional educational values with more pragmatic interests such as efficiency and agility.

Less clear is the cost of a more contractual approach. Within universities and colleges, the academic freedom balance has shifted to protecting institutional rights when they conflict with the prerogatives of individual faculty members. Additionally, the autonomy and deference that society has afforded higher education is attributable, at least significantly, to the norm within it of making decisions based on educational values through collegial means. But educational values are no longer the sole consideration of entrepreneurial institutions existing increasingly in a commercialized and privatized environment, just as a stratified faculty with divergent interests is hardly collegial in the classical sense. The custom and practice that provides the means to interpret gaps in contracts is thus more complicated—and less likely to afford privilege to institutions. It is increasingly reasonable for courts to treat universities and colleges instead, at least to some degree, as just another business, which has justified judges becoming involved in matters they once would have avoided. If nothing else, common law precedents developed in a different, more traditional environment are increasingly less relevant. But have institutions and courts fully realized these changed circumstances across higher education? There continues to be deference to academic decisions, but for how long?

Agility

The entrepreneurial university or college requires agility, both in seeking strategic advantage and in ensuring its mere survival. In conjunction with public policy, the law enables needed flexibility, as with allowing the shift to temporary faculty and developing academic programs at the institutional periphery. Public institutions are not constrained by civil service laws. Even in unionized settings, absent contractual obligations, there is the autonomy needed to maneuver by transitioning to more use of adjunct faculty and graduate assistants. State-level coordination has also not prevented them from establishing an academic presence in nontraditional settings, whether at satellite campuses or online. Similarly, students have come to take advantage of the options that they have in a competitive market. Even faculty with tenure, while continuing to maintain their privileges, are subject to dismissal under appropriate (albeit extreme) circumstances, whether for cause or due to program reduction. But institutions impose upon themselves limits to their agility in the culture that persists in making it difficult to dismiss ineffective at-will employees.

Intellectual property policy, as interpreted by courts, also illustrates the latitude that institutions have to be entrepreneurial. Rights have broadened, with fair use challenged and the public domain contracting. Academic work has come to be regarded as property, when it is performed by those in online environments, through universities and colleges applying the work-made-for-hire rule to faculty. In this way, institutions get the best of both worlds, with continued deference based on perceptions of them acting in the public interest, but also the ability to exploit commercial advantage as possibilities present themselves. The Bayh-Dole Act (1980) provides an example, formally requiring universities and colleges to frame technology transfer as providing social utility, but enabling institutions to commercialize products for their own sometimes considerable financial gain. Additionally, the continued presence of both governmental and charitable immunity in some areas, as well as federal and state subsidies, allows universities and colleges to assume risks, as in commercial ventures, without always experiencing possible negative repercussions. Finally, the decision in *Grutter* (2003) enables institutions the flexibility needed to implement affirmative action programs to advance diversity in admissions—and perhaps, by extension, in employment.

Process

Those leading and managing universities and colleges are likely to avoid exposure when they simply follow their own reasonable rules. Perhaps the heightened expectations of students or parents require additional process, while the same may be true of rights derived from contracts, whether with employees or connected with commercial transactions. But even in a more contested space with more aggressive assertion of rights, institutions owe limited notice and hearing, especially on purely academic matters, on which there continues to be judicial deference. But what at the entreprenurial university or college is not in some way influenced by commercial realities? Temporary faculty members have neither constitutional nor contractual due process rights, due only what they are owed under their agreement. The situation in admissions is similar, with applicants having no real rights beyond institutions not discriminating against them, with affirmative action programs upheld when they are sufficiently narrowly tailored.

Denials of requests for accommodations by students with disabilities or religious needs tend to be upheld when universities and colleges made a reasoned determination. Academic deference also continues in areas such as granting tenure, even when standards for applicants have changed midstream. Although plaintiffs have the means under Title VII and otherwise to bring discrimination cases, institutions have the clear advantage in litigation, as disparate impact actions are difficult to prove, given the particularized nature of decisions in academe. Even when process rights are most pronounced, as in removing tenured faculty, doing so is still possible in extreme circumstances, provided institutions follow their own reasonable rules and do not discriminate.

But there are also challenges for universities and colleges associated with process requirements. Courts are more willing to review behavioral matters, with individuals being afforded more process rights than in academic matters. There is also the perennial question of what process is due, which is inherently case specific and depends at a state institution on the liberty and property interests implicated. Answers only become more of a challenge as purposes at universities and colleges become more expansive, incorporating not only educational ends but also commercial aspirations. Such lack of clarity poses risks, whether in doing too little and being exposed or too much and suffering inefficiencies.

Autonomy

There are greater external demands upon especially public universities and colleges to be accountable, but there continues to be significant autonomy within higher education. States have not connected appropriations with performance, with meaningful measures difficult to determine. But they do require more reporting. Institutions have also taken to connecting state support less with broad societal benefits, as with generally advancing knowledge, and more with a return on investment, as through local economic development. State coordinating boards continue to regulate matters such as program offerings, and there is occasional chatter from legislators about imposing regulation such as bills of rights to protect conservative students, but public institutions otherwise tend to have significant autonomy in strategy and management.

Additionally, there are various compliance and integrity concerns that accompany federal research grants, as well as general rules in areas such as bioterrorism, human and animal subjects, and taxation. The USA PATRIOT Act also applies, with requirements to provide designated information to federal authorities, as with international students working in areas with national security relevance. There is also increasing emphasis on transparency and accountability in federal policy associated with higher education. These efforts require a significant administrative infrastructure devoted to compliance, especially in sponsored research. And there is the need to simply manage such a complex and regulated enterprise, as with ensuring that efforts in areas such as technology transfer do not compromise the tax-exempt status of institutions. But even with such regulations and requirements, federal support comes with few strings attached, with institutions even able to capture rights to patents developed through funded research. It also essentially amounts to a subsidy that mitigates the risk insitutions assume in acting as entrepreneurs.

As faculty members and institutions have become involved in efforts to commercialize research, the potential for research integrity breaches has increased, especially conflicts of interest, posing both reputation risk and potential financial penalty. The situation is akin to more prominent athletics programs, which are regulated by a private association, the NCAA. Significant competitive and commercial pressures associated with aspects of the enterprise require complex rules over recruiting and eligibility, with meaningful penalties for lack of compliance. Institutions have ceded considerable autonomy to the NCAA, allowing it to impose minimum standards in areas such as admissions and academic programs. Through the application of Title IX, federal policy has regulated gender equity in athletics, but it is the only area of higher education subject to such external influence, despite continuing disparities in areas such as salary equity connected with gender among faculty members and administrators. As in research commercialization, continuing exempt status from taxation requires that institutions maintain some degree of "amateurism," even though sports such as football at larger universities function in many ways that are essentially professional in character.

Reputation

As marketing becomes an increasingly important component in the success of universities and colleges, reputational risk is an essential consideration, accompanying most discussions of legal possibilities or exposure. Institutions are competing aggressively with one another for the most accomplished students, concerned about a scandal or tragedy weakening their position. Universities and colleges tend not to directly regulate expression, even when potentially embarrassing, but have professionalized public relations and are more careful in managing perceptions, seeking to dodge situations that may compromise their messaging. They have responded to the increased possibility of liability, as in tort actions, by emphasizing risk management, even going so far as to initiate threat assessment teams to identify, monitor, and refer students and others identified as risks to themselves or the community.

Universities and college are more subject to tort liability for foreseeable harm, a departure from the *in loco parentis* and bystander eras during which they were at risk only when directly assuming a responsibility. Institutions are deemed to have a special relationship with their students, amounting to logic similar to contractual obligations, with duties to protect them from harm, as reasonable. Nevertheless, liability only attaches when a defendant causes an injury or was negligent in creating the situation for it to occur, as with not doing what was reasonably necessary to become aware of a dangerous condition. Hazing and suicide present particular challenges, but institutions can argue a lack of necessary foreseeability, with defenses such as assumption of risk and contributory negligence continuing. But areas of possible liability have only become broader and more diffuse as the boundaries of entrepreneurial universities and colleges move outward, as with study abroad programs and internships.

Values

Finally, universities and colleges cannot be mercenary, even when the law allows it, and expect to continue to enjoy various advantages that society has traditionally granted to higher education. Much continues to depend upon institutions living up to a set of long established values. Formal protections are minimal, as with the federal Family and Medical Leave Act and institutional progressive discipline policies connected with the dismissal of at-will employees, and even these do not apply to adjunct faculty. Student privacy is also shielded by statute, although there are broad exceptions in areas such as for risks to health and welfare. The First Amendment continues to apply at public institutions, with expression, assembly, and publication protected, especially when it occurs in public forums. Prior restraints and content-based restrictions are disfavored, although reasonable time, place, and manner are permitted. Private universities and colleges tend to have long since voluntarily institutionalized such principles, extending rights through contract theory. Universities and colleges also tend to accommodate religious diversity, making accommodations as merited. Norms such as academic freedom also continue to provide some measure of security to those who perceive themselves to be in a position to assert it.

Perhaps even more important than various formal rules, there is also a well-developed sense of integrity within the culture associated with higher education. Institutions tend to support diversity initiatives, knowing there are strategic benefits, but also because the concept aligns with values. Additionally, commercialization has little effect on institutions enforcing antidiscrimination policies, both based on avoiding reputational risk and because they simply believe it is right. Universities and colleges, despite what the law may allow and even amidst competitive pressures, continue to operate according to traditional values. These may be challenged, but continue to be quite relevant. Managing the entrepreneurial university or college is a matter of balancing legal principles, commercial realities, and these longstanding principles.

References

Acero, G. (2006). Title VII: The duty to make religious accommodations. In R. A. Weitzner, ed., *Religious Discrimination and Accommodation Issues in Higher Education: A Legal Compendium* (pp. 99–120). Washington, DC: National Association of College and University Attorneys.

Adams, K. A. (2005). Negotiating clinical trial agreements. In T. J. Colecchia, ed., *Legal Issues in Sponsored Research Programs: From Contracting to Compliance* (pp. 183–92). Washington, DC: National Association of College and University Attorneys.

Adarand v. Pena, 515 U.S. 200 (1995).

Age Discrimination in Employment Act of 1967 (ADEA) (Pub.L. No. 90-202, 81 Stat. 602).

Alford, D. E. (2002). Negotiating and analyzing electronic license agreements. *Law Library Journal*, 94, 621–44.

Alger, J. R. (2007). Distance education and IP: Contracts and policies. In D. C. Brown, J. R. Przypyszny, and K. R. Tromble, eds., *Legal Issues in Distance Education* (pp. 37–58). Washington, DC: National Association of College and University Attorneys.

Alger, J. R. (2008). As the workplace turns: Affirmative action in employment. In D. C. Brown, ed., *Employment Issues in Higher Education: A Legal Compendium*, 3d ed. (pp. 159–78). Washington, DC: National Association of College and University Attorneys.

Alger, J. R. and M. Krislov (2004). You've got to have friends: Lessons learned from the role of amici in the University of Michigan cases. *Journal of College and University Law*, 30(3), 503–29.

Ambash, J. W. (2005). *Federal Record-Keeping and Reporting for Independent and Public Colleges and Universities*. Washington, DC: National Association of College and University Attorneys.

Ambash, J. W. and S. J. Avila (2008). Snooping, spying, and surveillance of employees. In D. C. Brown, ed., *Employment Issues in Higher Education: A Legal Compendium,* 3d ed. (pp. 457–94). Washington, DC: National Association of College and University Attorneys.

American Association of Universities, Association of American University Presses, Association of Research Libraries, and Association of American Publishers (2005). *Campus Copyrights and Responsibilities: A Basic Guide to Policy Considerations*. Washington, DC: American Association of Universities, Association of American University Presses, Association of Research Libraries, and Association of American Publishers.

American Association of University Professors (AAUP) (1940). *Statement of Principles on Academic Freedom and Tenure*. Washington, DC: American Association of University Professors.

American Association of University Professors (AAUP) (1967). *Joint Statement on the Rights and Freedoms of Students*. Washington, DC: American Association of University Professors.

American Association of University Professors (AAUP) (1983). *Affirmative Action Plans: Recommended Procedures for Increasing the Number of Minority Persons and Women on College and University Campuses*. Washington, DC: American Association of University Professors.

American Association of University Professors (AAUP) (1989). *Statement on Procedural Standards in the Renewal or Nonrenewal of Faculty Appointments*. Washington, DC: American Association of University Professors.

American Association of University Professors (AAUP) (1990). *Statement on Conflicts of Interest*. Washington, DC: American Association of University Professors.

American Association of University Professors (AAUP) (1993). *Statement on Collective Bargaining*. Washington, DC: American Association of University Professors.

American Association of University Professors (AAUP) (1995a). *Nonreappointment and Full-Time Renewable Term Appointments*. Washington, DC: American Association of University Professors.

American Association of University Professors (AAUP) (1995b). *Sexual Harassment: Suggested Policy and Procedures for Handling Complaints*. Washington, DC: American Association of University Professors.

American Association of University Professors (1999a). *Statement on Distance Education*. Washington, DC: American Association of University Professors.

American Association of University Professors (AAUP) (1999b). *On Collegiality as a Criterion for Faculty Evaluation*. Washington, DC: American Association of University Professors.

American Association of University Professors (AAUP) (2000). *Statement on Graduate Students*. Washington, DC: American Association of University Professors.

American Association of University Professors (AAUP) (2005a). *Academic Freedom and Electronic Communications*. Washington, DC: American Association of University Professors.

American Association of University Professors (AAUP) (2005b). *Faculty Handbooks as Enforceable Contracts: A State Guide*, 5th ed. Washington, DC: American Association of University Professors.

American Association of University Professors (AAUP) (2006a). *AAUP Unionism: Principles and Goals*. Washington, DC: American Association of University Professors.

American Association of University Professors (AAUP) (2006b). *AAUP Policy Documents and Reports*, 10th ed. Baltimore, MD: Johns Hopkins University Press.

American Association of University Professors (AAUP) (2009). *Conversion of Appointment to Tenure Track*. Washington, DC: American Association of University Professors.

American Council on Education (ACE) (2002). *Where Credit is Due: Approaches to Course and Credit Recognition Across Borders in U.S. Higher Education*. Washington, DC: American Council on Education.

Americans with Disabilities Act (ADA) (1990) (Pub. L. No. 101-336).

Ancheta, A. N. (2008). *Bakke*, antidiscrimination jurisprudence, and the trajectory of affirmative action law. In P. Marin and C. L. Horn, eds., *Realizing* Bakke's *Legacy: Affirmative Action, Equal Opportunity, and Access to Higher Education* (pp. 15–40). Sterling, VA: Stylus.

Anderson, F. A. (2005). Sophisticated technology transfer and licensing. In J. L. Curry, ed., *Technology Transfer Issues for Colleges and Universities: A Legal Compendium* (pp. 253–64). Washington, DC: National Association of College and University Attorneys.

Animal Welfare Act and Health Research Extension Act (1985). (Pub. L. No. 99-15).

Armstrong, J. R. (2004). Bayh-Dole under siege: The challenge of federal patent policy as a result of *Madey v. Duke University*. *Journal of College and University Law*, 30(3), 619–40.

Araujo, R. J. (2006). *Ex Corde Ecclesia* and mission-centered hiring in Roman Catholic colleges and Universities. In R. A. Weitzner, ed., *Religious Discrimination and Accommodation Issues in Higher Education: A Legal Compendium* (pp. 331–60). Washington, DC: National Association of College and University Attorneys.

Astle, R. (2005). Equity interests in faculty start-ups. In J. L. Curry, ed., *Technology Transfer Issues for Colleges and Universities: A Legal Compendium* (pp. 601–20). Washington, DC: National Association of College and University Attorneys.

Babbitt, E. M. (2004). *Accommodating Students with Learning and Emotional Disabilities*. Washington, DC: National Association of College and University Attorneys.

Babbitt, E. M. (2006). Judicial evaluation of tenure termination arising from financial exigency, program discontinuance, or affiliation. In S. G. Olswang and C. A. Cameron, eds., *Academic Freedom and Tenure: A Legal Compendium* (pp. 1157–71). Washington, DC: National Association of College and University Attorneys.

Babbitt, E. M. and Z. B. Silverstein (2006). Emerging issues in tenure litigation: Does tenure protect salary and other "incidents of tenure." In S. G. Olswang and C. A. Cameron, eds., *Academic Freedom and Tenure: A Legal Compendium* (pp. 809–22). Washington, DC: National Association of College and University Attorneys.

Baker, T. R. (2003). Construing the scope of student conduct codes: Recent federal rulings suggest heightened court scrutiny ahead. *West's Education Law Reporter*, 174, 555–88.

Band, J. (2007). The Google library project: Both sides of the story. In G. K. Harper, ed., *Copyright Law and Policy in a Networked World* (pp. 867–85). Washington, DC: National Association of College and University Attorneys.

Barber, C. K. (1991). *What to Do When OSHA Comes Calling*. Washington, DC: National Association of College and University Attorneys.

Barnes, M., K. G. Heffernan, and C. Hermes (2005). Making sense of uses of human biologic materials: Cadaver and human tissue donations, and secondary research uses of human tissues and data. In T. J. Colecchia, ed., *Legal Issues in Sponsored Research Programs: From Contracting to Compliance* (pp. 369–90). Washington, DC: National Association of College and University Attorneys.

Barnett, M. J. (2008). Troubleshooting the troubled or troubling employee: Psychiatric disabilities in the workplace and dealing with the persistent troublemaker. In D. C. Brown, ed., *Employment Issues in Higher Education: A Legal Compendium*, 3d ed. (pp. 769–94). Washington, DC: National Association of College and University Attorneys.

Bayh-Dole Act of 1980 (University and Small Business Patent Procedures Act) (Pub.L. 96-517, 94 Stat. 3015).

Bazluke, F. and Nolan, J. (2006). "Because of sex": The evolving legal riddle of sexual vs. gender identity. *Journal of College and University Law*, 32(2), 361–410.

Bearby, S. and B. Siegal (2002). From the stadium parking lot to the information superhighway: How to protect your trademark from infringement. *Journal of College and University Law*, 28(3), 633–62.

Bender, K. C. (2007). Copyright and plagiarism in the digital world: Those cunning students. In G. K. Harper, ed., *Copyright Law and Policy in a Networked World* (pp. 659–68). Washington, DC: National Association of College and University Attorneys.

Berger, C. J. and V. Berger (1999). Academic discipline: A guide to fair process for the university student. *Columbia Law Review*, 99(2), 289–364.

Bernard, D. J. (2003). Sexual harassment: The developing case law. In E. K. Cole, ed., *Sexual Harassment on Campus: A Legal Compendium*, 4th ed. (pp. 247–64). Washington, DC: National Association of College and University Attorneys.

Bernstein, D. E. (2003). Defending the First Amendment from antidiscrimination laws. *North Carolina Law Review*, 82, 223-48.

Biancamano, J. J. (2005). Dealing with faculty owned start-up companies: A policy development checklist. In J. L. Curry, ed., *Technology Transfer Issues for Colleges and Universities: A Legal Compendium* (pp. 559–72). Washington, DC: National Association of College and University Attorneys.

Bianchi, M. (2006). *The HIPPA Privacy Regulations and Student Health Centers*. Washington, DC: National Association of College and University Attorneys.

Bickel, R. D. (2007). Confronting the mythology and fear of tort law and liability: Understanding the basic principles of tort law and facilitating the management of risk in the campus environment. In K. M. Novak and A. M. Lee, eds., *Student Risk Management in Higher Education: A Legal Compendium* (pp. 39–52). Washington, DC: National Association of College and University Attorneys.

Bienstock, R. E. (2004). Anti-bioterrorism research post-9/11 legislation: The USA PATRIOT Act and beyond. *Journal of College and University Law*, 30(2), 465–92.

Bienstock, R. E. and T. J. Colecchia (2005). The fundamentals of sponsored research in the university setting. In T. J. Colecchia, ed., *Legal Issues in Sponsored Research Programs: From Contracting to Compliance* (pp. 3–18). Washington, DC: National Association of College and University Attorneys.

Bills, K. (2005). A guide to licensing biotechnology. In J. L. Curry, ed., *Technology Transfer Issues for Colleges and Universities: A Legal Compendium* (pp. 321–30). Washington, DC: National Association of College and University Attorneys.

Bioterrorism Preparedness and Response Act of 2002 (Pub.L. 107-188, 116 Stat. 594).

Bird, L. E. and M. B. Mackin (2006). Campus scenarios and commentary. In L. E. Bird, M. B. Mackin, and S. K. Schuster, eds., *The First Amendment on Campus: A Handbook for College and University Administrators* (pp. 73–128). Washington, DC: NASPA: Student Affairs Administrators in Higher Education.

Bird, L. E., M. B. Mackin, and S. K. Schuster (2006). A practical guide to First Amendment analysis. In L. E. Bird, M. B. Mackin, and S. K. Schuster, eds., *The First Amendment on Campus: A Handbook for College and University Administrators* (pp. 51–72). Washington, DC: NASPA: Student Affairs Administrators in Higher Education.

Birnbaum, R. (2004). The end of shared governance: Looking ahead or looking back. In W. G. Tierney and V. M. Lachuga (Eds.), *Restructuring Shared Governance in Higher Education* (pp. 5–22). San Francisco, CA: Jossey-Bass.

Blakeslee, W. D. and H. A. Bakalyar (2005). Fundamentals of technology transfer and intellectual property licensing. In J. L. Curry, ed., *Technology Transfer Issues for Colleges and Universities: A Legal Compendium* (pp. 241–52). Washington, DC: National Association of College and University Attorneys.

Blakeslee, W. D. and Gallitano, D. J. (2007). *Contracting for Large Computer Software Systems. Journal of College and University Law*. Washington, DC: National Association of College and University Attorneys.

Blau, M. L. (2005). Impact of HIPAA on university research activity. In T. J. Colecchia, ed., *Legal Issues in Sponsored Research Programs: From Contracting to Compliance* (pp. 317–35). Washington, DC: National Association of College and University Attorneys.

Blum, A., D. Cahr, and S. J. McDonald (2007). The halls are alive with the sound of music: The law and policy of file sharing. In G. K. Harper, ed., *Copyright Law and Policy in a Networked World* (pp. 1059–78). Washington, DC: National Association of College and University Attorneys.

Board of Curators of the University of Missouri v. Horowitz, 435 U.S. 214 (1978).

Board of Regents of the University of Alabama v. Garrett, 531 U.S. 356 (2001).

Board of Regents of the University of Wisconsin v. Southworth, 529 U.S. 217 (2000).

Bob Jones University v. United States, 461 U.S. 574 (1983).

Bodensteiner, I. E. (2005). Review of David E. Bernstein's "You Can't Say That!: The Growing Threat to Civil Liberties from Antidiscrimination Laws." *Journal of College and University Law*, 32(2), 437–50.

Bok, D. C. (2002). *Universities in the Marketplace: The Commercialization of Higher Education.* Princeton, NJ: Princeton University Press.

Bollier, D. (2007). Why the public domain matters: The endangered wellspring of creativity, commerce, and democracy. In G. K. Harper, ed., *Copyright Law and Policy in a Networked World* (pp. 235–60). Washington, DC: National Association of College and University Attorneys.

Boswell, D. A. and B. L. Barefoot (2005). *HIPPA and Research*. Washington, DC: National Association of College and University Attorneys.

Bousquet, M. (2008). *How the University Works: Higher Education and the Low-Wage Nation.* New York: New York University Press.

Bowen, W. G. and S. A. Levin (2005). *Reclaiming the Game: College Sports and Educational Values*. Princeton, NJ: Princeton University Press.

Boyle, J. (2003). The second enclosure movement and the construction of the public domain. *Journal of Law and Contemporary Problems*, 66, 33–74.

Boy Scouts of America v. Dale, 530 U.S. 640 (2000).

Brady, P. A. (2008). Whose organization is this? Institutional liability for student organizations. In D. P. Langhauser, R. M. O'Neil, and W. E. Thro, eds., *Free Speech in Higher Education: Important Protections and Permissible Regulations* (pp. 287–94). Washington, DC: National Association of College and University Attorneys.

Brake, D. (2008). The invisible pregnant athlete and the promise of Title IX. *Harvard Journal of Law and Gender*, 31(2), 323–66.

Brewer, D., S. M. Gates, and C. A. Goldman (2002). *In Pursuit of Prestige: Strategy and Competition in U.S. Higher Education*. New Brunswick, NJ: Transaction Press.

Broccolo, B. and H. T. Lutz (2005). Managing research conflicts of interest: Issues and challenges. In T. J. Colecchia, ed., *Legal Issues in Sponsored Research Programs: From Contracting to Compliance* (pp. 391–442). Washington, DC: National Association of College and University Attorneys.

Brooks, A. and D. Davies (2008). Exploring student-athlete compensation: Why the NCAA cannot afford to leave athletes uncompensated. *Journal of College and University Law*, 34(3), 747–61.

Browne, K. R. (2001). Zero tolerance for the First Amendment: Title VII's regulation of employee speech. *Ohio Northern University Law Review*, 27, 563–603.

Bruton, D. P. (2002). At the busy intersection: Title VI and NCAA eligibility standards. *Journal of College and University Law*, 28(3), 569–604.

Buchanan, J. N. and Beckham, J. C. (2006). A comprehensive academic honor policy for students: Ensuring due process, promoting academic integrity, and involving faculty. *Journal of College and University Law*, 33(1), 97–120.

Bulman-Pozen, J. (2006). *Grutter* at work: A Title VII critique of constitutional affirmative action. *Yale Law Journal*, 115, 1408–48.

Bunting, E. C. (2004). Admissions issues: Mental disabilities: Requirements of the ADA. In E. M. Babbitt, ed., *Accommodating Students with Learning and Emotional Disabilities* (pp. 271–90). Washington, DC: National Association of College and University Attorneys.

Bunting, E. C. (2008). Intersection of FMLA, ADA, and workers' compensation laws. In D. C. Brown, ed., *Employment Issues in Higher Education: A Legal Compendium*, 3d ed. (pp. 713–16). Washington, DC: National Association of College and University Attorneys.

Burgan, M. (2006). *What Ever Happened to the Faculty? Drift and Decision in Higher Education*. Baltimore, MD: Johns Hopkins University Press.

Burgoyne, R., S. McNabb, and F. Robinson (1998). *Understanding Attorney-Client Privilege Issues in the College and University Setting*. Washington, DC: National Association of College and University Attorneys.

Burling, P. (2003). *Crime on Campus: Analyzing and Managing the Increasing Risk of Institutional Liability*, 2d ed. Washington, DC: National Association of College and University Attorneys.

Burlington Industries, Inc. v. Ellerth, 524 U.S. 742 (1998).

Burlington Northern and Santa Fe Railway Company v. White, 548 U.S. 53 (2006).

Burtchaell, J. T. (1999). Out of the heartburn of the church. *Journal of College and University Law*, 25(4), 653–95.

Butler, K. C. (2003). Shared responsibility: The duty to legal externs. *West Virginia Law Review*, 106, 51–120.

Byrne, J. P. (2001). Academic freedom of part-time faculty. *Journal of College and University Law*, 27(3), 583–94.

Byrne, J. P. (2004). The threat to constitutional academic freedom. *Journal of College and University Law*, 31(1), 31–88.

Callison, J. C. and Varady, T. S. (2008). Hiring the head coach: Drafting and negotiating the coach's contract. In D. C. Brown, ed., *Employment Issues in Higher Education: A Legal Compendium*, 3d ed. (pp. 27–84). Washington, DC: National Association of College and University Attorneys.

Caltrider, S. P. and P. Davis (2004). The experimental use defense: Post-*Madey v. Duke* and *Integra Lifesciences Ltd. v. Merck*. *Journal of the Patent and Trademark Office Society*, 86, 1011–1037)

Cameron, C. A., L. E. Meyers, and S. G. Olswang (2005). Academic bills of rights in the classroom. *Journal of College and University Law*, 31(2), 243–90.

Cameron, C. A., S. G. Olswang, and E. Kamai (2006). Post-tenure review in higher education. In S. G. Olswang and C. A. Cameron, eds., *Academic Freedom and Tenure: A Legal Compendium* (pp. 1215–34). Washington, DC: National Association of College and University Attorneys.

Cantalupo, N. C. (2009). Campus violence: Understanding the extraordinary through the ordinary. *Journal of College and University Law*, 35(3), 613–90.

Capone, L. (2005). The college, the community, and college students: "When worlds collide." In J. E. Faulkner and N. E. Tribbensee, eds., *Students' Disciplinary Issues: A Legal Compendium* (pp. 27–34). Washington, DC: National Association of College and University Attorneys.

Capone, L. (2008). Politics, religion and culture on campus: Legal issues at the crossroads. In D. P. Langhauser, R. M. O'Neil, and W. E. Thro, eds., *Free Speech in Higher Education: Important Protections and Permissible Regulations* (pp. 865–77). Washington, DC: National Association of College and University Attorneys.

Carey, B. M. (2005). Diversity in higher education: Diversity's lack of a "compelling" nature, and how the Supreme Court has avoided applying true strict scrutiny to racial classifications in college admissions. *Oklahoma City University Law Review*, 30, 329–62.

Carlson, R. B. (2001). Romantic relationships between professors and their students: Morality, ethics, and law. *South Texas Law Review*, 42, 493–508.

Carney, S. (2005). Faculty start-ups: The tangled web. In J. L. Curry, ed., *Technology Transfer Issues for Colleges and Universities: A Legal Compendium* (pp. 543–58). Washington, DC: National Association of College and University Attorneys.

Carpenter, L. and V. Acosta (2007). Title IX—two for one: A starter kit of the law and a snapshot of Title IX's impact. *Cleveland State Law Review*, 55(4), 503–12.

Carr, C. T. (2006). *Negotiating the Mine Field: The Conduct of Academic Research in Compliance with Export Controls*. Washington, DC: National Association of College and University Attorneys.

Cerny, M. (2005). Supporting foundations and technology transfer: Scientific research and development. In J. L. Curry, ed., *Technology Transfer Issues for Colleges and Universities: A Legal Compendium* (pp. 82–98). Washington, DC: National Association of College and University Attorneys.

Chacon, J. M. (2008). Race as a diagnostic tool: Latina/os and higher education in California, Post-209. *California Law Review, 96*, 1215–57.

Chase, M. (2007). Gender discrimination, higher education, and the seventh circuit: Balancing academic freedom with protections under Title VII, case note: *Ferrell v. Butler University*. *Wisconsin Women's Law Journal*, 22(Spring), 153–75.

Chemerinsky, E. (1998). More speech is better. *UCLA Law Review*, 45, 1635–51.

Chin, G. J. and S. Rao (2003). Pledging allegiance to the Constitution: The First Amendment and loyalty oaths for faculty at private universities. *University of Pittsburgh Law Review*, 64, 431–82.

Christian Legal Society v. the University of California, Hastings College of the Law (2010, citation pending).

City of Richmond v. J. A. Crowson Co., 488 U.S. 469 (1989).

Civil Rights Act of 1964 (Pub.L. 88-352, 78 Stat. 241).

Civil Rights Act of 1991, Section 1981 (Pub.L. 88-352, 78 Stat. 241, amended by Pub.L. 102-166).

Clark v. Community for Creative Non-Violence, 468 U.S. 288 (1984).

Classen, H. W. (2005). Fundamentals of software licensing, Parts I, II, and III. In J. L. Curry, ed., *Technology Transfer Issues for Colleges and Universities: A Legal Compendium* (pp. 383–420). Washington, DC: National Association of College and University Attorneys.

Claus, R. (2005). Fundamental research and the international traffic in arms regulations. In T. J. Colecchia, ed., *Legal Issues in Sponsored Research Programs: From Contracting to Com-*

pliance (pp. 657–66). Washington, DC: National Association of College and University Attorneys.

Clotfelter, C. T. (1996). *Buying the Best: Cost Escalation in Elite Higher Education.* Princeton, NJ: Princeton University Press.

Cochran, A. (2005). Copyrights, trademarks, and trade secrets. In J. L. Curry, ed., *Technology Transfer Issues for Colleges and Universities: A Legal Compendium* (pp. 43–68). Washington, DC: National Association of College and University Attorneys.

Cochran, A. (2007). Copyrights, trademarks, and trade secrets. In G. K. Harper, ed., *Copyright Law and Policy in a Networked World* (pp. 37–60). Washington, DC: National Association of College and University Attorneys.

Colbert, S. I. and O. R. Griffin (2007). The TEACH Act: Recognizing its challenges and overcoming its limitations. *Journal of College and University Law*, 33(3), 499–520.

Cole, E. K. (2003). Foul play: Sexual harassment by coaches of student-athletes. In E. K. Cole, ed., *Sexual Harassment on Campus: A Legal Compendium*, 4th ed. (pp. 265–71). Washington, DC: National Association of College and University Attorneys.

Cole, E. K., T. P. Hustoles, and J. R. McClain (2006). *How to Conduct a Sexual Harassment Investigation.* Washington, DC: National Association of College and University Attorneys.

Colecchia, T. J. (2005). A primer on issues for universities engaged in international human subject research studies. In T. J. Colecchia, ed., *Legal Issues in Sponsored Research Programs: From Contracting to Compliance* (pp. 717–22). Washington, DC: National Association of College and University Attorneys.

Coleman, A. L. and J. R. Alger (1996). Beyond speech codes: Harmonizing rights of free speech and freedom from discrimination on university campuses. *Journal of College and University Law*, 23(1), 91–131.

Coleman, A. L., S. R. Palmer, and S. Y. Winnick (2007). *Echoes of* Bakke*: A Fractured Supreme Court Invalidates Two Race-Conscious K-12 Student Assignment Plans but Affirms the Compelling Interest in the Educational Benefits of Diversity.* New York: The College Board.

Collis, D. J. (2004). The paradox of scope: A challenge to the governance of higher education. In W. G. Tierney (Ed.), *Competing Conceptions of Academic Governance: Navigating the Perfect Storm* (pp. 33–76). Baltimore, MD: Johns Hopkins University Press.

Connell, M. A. and D. Euben (2004). Evolving law in same-sex sexual harassment and sexual orientation discrimination. *Journal of College and University Law*, 31(1), 193–238.

Connell, M. A. and D. Gurley (2005). The right of educational institutions to withhold or revoke academic degrees. *Journal of College and University Law*, 32(1), 51–74.

Connell, M. A., R. G. Harris, and B. E. Ledbetter (2005). *What to Do When the NCAA Comes Calling.* Washington, DC: National Association of College and University Attorneys.

Connell, M. A. and F. G. Savage (2001). The role of collegiality in higher education tenure, promotion, and termination decisions. *Journal of College and University Law*, 27(4), 833–58.

Connell, M. A. and F. G. Savage (2003). Releases: Is there still a place for their use by colleges and universities. *Journal of College and University Law*, 29, 579–617.

Connick v. Myers, 461 U.S. 138 (1983).

Cooley, A. H. and A. Cooley (2009). From diploma mills to for-profit colleges and universities: Business opportunities, regulatory challenges, and consumer protection in higher education. *Southern California Interdisciplinary Law Journal*, 18, 505–25.

Cooperative Research and Technology Enhancement Act of 2004 (Pub.L. 108-453, 118 Stat. 3596).

Cope, K. L. (2007). Defending the ivory tower: A twenty-first century approach to the Pickering-Connick doctrine and public higher education faculty after *Garcetti. Journal of College and University Law*, 33(2), 313–60.

Crews, K. D. (2000). Distance education and copyright law: The limits and meaning of copyright policy. *Journal of College and University Law*, 27(1), 15–52.

Crime Awareness and Campus Security Act of 1990 (Pub.L. 102-26, 105 Stat. 128),

Crockett, R. B. (2004). From diagnosis to remedy: Responding to student claims of learning, psychological and emotional disabilities. In E. M. Babbitt, ed., *Accommodating Students with Learning and Emotional Disabilities* (pp. 237–48). Washington, DC: National Association of College and University Attorneys.

Crosset, T. and L. Masteralexis (2008). The changing collective definition of collegiate sport and the potential demise of Title IX protections. *Journal of College and University Law*, 34(3), 671–94.

Crow, R. B. and S. R. Rosner (2002). Institutional and organizational liability for hazing in intercollegiate and professional team sports. *St. John's Law Review*, 76, 87–114.

Daane, R. (1985). The role of university counsel. *Journal of College and University Law*, 12(3), 399–414.

Daggett, L. (2006). Doing the right thing: Disability discrimination and readmission of academically dismissed law students. *Journal of College and University Law*, 32(3), 505–77.

Dall, J. A. (2003). Determining duty in collegiate tort litigation: Shifting paradigms of the college-student relationship. *Journal of College and University Law*, 29(2), 485–524.

Davis v. Monroe County Board of Education, 529 U.S. 629 (1999).

Davis, T. J. (2004). Assessing Constitutional challenges to university free speech zones under public forum doctrine. *Indiana Law Journal*, 79, 267–96.

DeGeorge, R. T. (2001). Academic freedom and academic tenure. *Journal of College and University Law*, 27(3), 595–602.

de Haven, H. H. (2009). The elephant in the ivory tower: Rampages in higher education and the case for institutional liability. *Journal of College and University Law*, 35(3), 503–612.

Dellaverson, J. (2003). Trial techniques: The employer's viewpoint in defending sexual harassment and other discrimination lawsuits. In E. K. Cole, ed., *Sexual Harassment on Campus: A Legal Compendium*, 4th ed. (pp. 305–18). Washington, DC: National Association of College and University Attorneys.

DeMitchell, T. A. (2002). Academic freedom—whose rights: The professor's or the university's? *West's Education Law Reporter*, 168, 1–22.

Denner, K. (2004). Taking one for the team: The role of assumption of the risk in sports torts cases. *Seton Hall Journal of Sports and Entertainment Law*, 14, 209–38.

Dennie, C. (2007). White out full grant-in-aid: An antitrust action the NCAA cannot afford to lose. *Virginia Sports and Entertainment Law Journal*, 7(1), 97–126.

Dickerson, D. (2008). Background checks in the university admissions process: An overview of legal and policy considerations. *Journal of College and University Law*, 34(2), 419–505.

Digital Millennium Copyright Act (1998) (Pub.L. 105-304, 112 Stat. 2860).

DiMaggio, P. J. and W. W. Powell (1983). The iron cage revisited: Institutional isomorphism and collective rationality in organizational fields. *American Sociological Review*, 48,147–60.

DiMaggio, P. J. and W. W. Powell (1991). Introduction. In W. W. Powell and P. J. DiMaggio, *The New Institutionalism in Organizational Analysis* (pp. 1–38). Chicago, IL: University of Chicago Press.

DiNardo, L. C., J. A. Sherrill, and A. R. Palmer (2001). Specialized ADR to settle faculty employment disputes. *Journal of College and University Law*, 28(1), 129–51.

Dixon v. Alabama State Board of Education, 294 F.2d 150 (5th Cir. 1961).

Dobkin, L. J. (2005). Institutional research compliance programs: A user's guide. In T. J. Colecchia, ed., *Legal Issues in Sponsored Research Programs: From Contracting to Compliance* (pp. 615–26). Washington, DC: National Association of College and University Attorneys.

Donley, E. and G. Nelson (2005). Trade secrets law and confidentiality disclosure agreements. In J. L. Curry, ed., *Technology Transfer Issues for Colleges and Universities: A Legal Compendium* (pp. 179–90). Washington, DC: National Association of College and University Attorneys.

Donley, E. and B. Wingo (2005). Research foundations: Establishment, activities, and affiliated entities. In J. L. Curry, ed., *Technology Transfer Issues for Colleges and Universities: A Legal Compendium* (pp. 69–81). Washington, DC: National Association of College and University Attorneys.

Donohue, K. and C. Wright (2005). The university becomes a shareholder: Negotiating equity licenses. In J. L. Curry, ed., *Technology Transfer Issues for Colleges and Universities: A Legal Compendium* (pp. 585–600). Washington, DC: National Association of College and University Attorneys.

Dowling, D. C. (2006). Exporting—and translating—employee handbooks and codes of conduct. In D. C. Brown, ed., *Employment Issues in Higher Education: A Legal Compendium*, 3d ed. (pp. 537–46). Washington, DC: National Association of College and University Attorneys.

Doyle, W. E. (2005). Implications of *Smith v. City of Jackson* on equal pay act claims and sex-based pay discrimination claims under Title VII. *Labor Lawyer*, 21, 183–98.

Dreyfuss, R. (2004). Biotechnology patents get special treatment protecting the public domain of science: Has the time for an experimental use defense arrived. *Arizona Law Review*, 46, 457–72.

Drier, A. E. and M. Michaelson (2006). *A Guide to Updating the Board's Conflict of Interest Policy.* Washington, DC: Association of Governing Boards of Universities and Colleges.

Drooz, D. T. (2007). Copyright updates: TEACH Act implementation and downstream controls. In D. C. Brown, J. R. Przypyszny, and K. R. Tromble, eds., *Legal Issues in Distance Education* (pp. 641–52). Washington, DC: National Association of College and University Attorneys.

Dunkle, J. H., Z. B. Silverstein, and S. L. Warner (2008). Managing violent and other troubling students: The role of threat assessment teams on campus. *Journal of College and University Law*, 34(3), 585–637.

Durant, P. H. and A. Hammersla (2005). University collaborations with small businesses. In T. J. Colecchia, ed., *Legal Issues in Sponsored Research Programs: From Contracting to Compliance* (pp. 131–56). Washington, DC: National Association of College and University Attorneys.

Dutile, F. N. (2001). Students and due process in higher education: Of interests and procedures. *Florida Gulf Coast Law Journal*, 2, 243–90.

Dutile, F. N. (2003). Disciplinary versus academic sanctions in higher education: A doomed dichotomy? *Journal of College and University Law*, 29(3), 619–54.

Dyer, E. (2001). Collegiality as a factor in faculty employment: Decisions at public colleges and universities: A selective review of the case law. *West's Education Law Reporter*, 152, 455–69.

Dyer, E. (2002). The authority to assign grades in public higher education: A "third essential freedom" for instructors or institutions. *West's Education Law Reporter*, 162, 654–67.

Dyer, E. (2003). Faculty dismissals for financial reasons in public higher education: Federal due process requirements. *West's Education Law Reporter*, 172, 13–22.

Ecker, L., J. M. Gagliardo, and H. R. M. Becker (2008). Retaliation and whistleblower claims: Recent developments in the law and guidelines on prevention. In D. C. Brown, ed., *Employment Issues in Higher Education: A Legal Compendium*, 3d ed. (pp. 953–87). Washington, DC: National Association of College and University Attorneys.

Eckert, J. (2006). Student-athlete contract rights in the aftermath of *Bloom v. NCAA. Vanderbilt Law Review*, 59(3), 905–36.

Eckes, S. E. (2005). Diversity in higher education: The consideration of race in hiring university faculty. *BYU Education and Law Journal*, 2005, 33–50.

Economic Espionage Act of 1996 (Pub. L. No. 104-294, 110 Stat. 3488).

Ehrenberg, R. (2002). *Tuition Rising: Why College Costs So Much.* Cambridge, MA: Harvard University Press.

Ehrenberg, R. G. (2003). Reaching for the brass ring: The *U.S. News and World Report* rankings and competition. *Review of Higher Education*, 26(2), 145–162.

Electronic Frontier Foundation (2006). Unintended consequences: Seven years under the DMCA. In G. K. Harper, ed., *Copyright Law and Policy in a Networked World* (pp. 1027–42). Washington, DC: National Association of College and University Attorneys.

Electronic Communications Privacy Act of 1986. (Pub.L. 99-508, 100 Stat. 1848).

Elson, A. S. (2009). Disappearing without a case: The constitutionality of race-conscious scholarships in higher education. *Washington University Law Review*, 86, 975–1024.

Employee Retirement Income Security Act of 1974 (Pub.L. 93-406, 88 Stat. 829).

Equal Pay Act of 1963 (Pub.L. No. 88-38, 77 Stat. 56).

Erwin, S. M. (2007). When the troops come home: Returning reservists, employers, and the law. *Health Lawyer*, (April), 1–15.

Estes, N. (2000). State university presidential searches: Law and practice. *Journal of College and University Law*, 26(3), 485–509.

Euben, D. (2000). *Faculty Rights and Responsibilities in Distance Education*. Washington, DC: American Association of University Professors.

Euben, D. R. (2006a). Academic freedom of individual professors and higher education institutions. In S. G. Olswang and C. A. Cameron, eds., *Academic Freedom and Tenure: A Legal Compendium* (pp. 225–59). Washington, DC: National Association of College and University Attorneys.

Euben, D. R. (2006b). Political and religious belief discrimination on campus: Faculty and student academic freedom and the First Amendment. In S. G. Olswang and C. A. Cameron, eds., *Academic Freedom and Tenure: A Legal Compendium* (pp. 331–62). Washington, DC: National Association of College and University Attorneys.

Euben, D. R. and B. A. Lee (2006). *Legal and Policy Issues in Disciplining College Faculty*. Washington, DC: National Association of College and University Attorneys.

Euben, D. R. and S. R. Thornton (2002). *The Family and Medical Leave Act: Questions and Answers*. Washington, DC: National Association of College and University Attorneys.

Eule, J. N. and J. D. Varat (1998). Transporting first amendment norms to the private sector: With every wish there comes a curse. *UCLA Law Review*, 45, 1537–1634.

Fair Labor Standards Act of 1938. (Pub.L. 75-718, 52 Stat. 1060).

Family Educational Rights and Privacy Act (FERPA; 1974) (Pub.L. 93-380, 88 Stat. 571).

Family and Medical Leave Act (FMLA) (1993) (P.L. 103-3, 107 Stat. 6).

Faragher v. City of Boca Raton, 524 U.S. 775 (1998).

Farmer, K. and S. Scally (2005). Entrepreneurial activities and UBIT. In J. L. Curry, ed., *Technology Transfer Issues for Colleges and Universities: A Legal Compendium* (pp. 667–82). Washington, DC: National Association of College and University Attorneys.

Federal Grant and Co-Operative Agreement Act (1977) (P.L. 95-224).

Ferguson, A. (2005). You want to do what? With whom? Where?: Educational exports. In N. E. Tribbensee, ed., *Study Abroad in Higher Education: Program Administration and Risk Management* (pp. 151–54). Washington, DC: National Association of College and University Attorneys.

Fields, S. K. (2007). Intramural and club sports: The Impact of Title IX. *Journal of College and University Law*, 33(3), 521–46.

Finkin, M. W. (2008). Verification and trust: Background investigations preceding faculty appointment. In D. C. Brown, ed., *Employment Issues in Higher Education: A Legal Compendium*, 3d ed. (pp. 117–20). Washington, DC: National Association of College and University Attorneys.

Flanders, J. M. (2007). Academic student dismissals at public institutions of higher education: When is academic deference not an issue? *Journal of College and University Law*, 34(1), 21–78.

Fliegel, R. M. and Curley, J. T. (2006). Evaluating eligibility for FMLA leave: Federal case law underscores the need for informed decision making. *Labor Lawyer*, 22, 1–18.

Flygare, T. J. (1999). *What to Do When the U.S. Department of Labor Comes to Campus: Wage and Hour Law in Higher Education*. Washington, DC: National Association of College and University Attorneys.

Flygare, T. J. (2002). *Students with Learning and Psychiatric Disabilities: New Challenges for Col-*

leges and Universities. Washington, DC: National Association of College and University Attorneys.

Fossey, R. and N. M. Roberts. (2003). Academic freedom and uncivil speech: When may a college regulate what an instructor says in the classroom. *West's Education Law Reporter*, 168, 549–64.

Foster, S. B. and A. M. Moorman (2003). *Gross v. Family Services Agency, Inc.*: The internship as special relationship in creating negligence liability. *Journal of Legal Aspects of Sport*, 11, 245–64.

Fox, L. E. (2006). Tenure policies and process: Who gets tenure; dealing with those who don't. In S. G. Olswang and C. A. Cameron, eds., *Academic Freedom and Tenure: A Legal Compendium* (pp. 823–40). Washington, DC: National Association of College and University Attorneys.

Franke, A. H. (2006). Faculty misconduct, discipline, and dismissal. In S. G. Olswang and C. A. Cameron, eds., *Academic Freedom and Tenure: A Legal Compendium* (pp. 969–81). Washington, DC: National Association of College and University Attorneys.

Franke, A. H. (2007). Grief management vs. risk management: Dealing with student tragedies. In K. M. Novak and A. M. Lee, eds., *Student Risk Management in Higher Education: A Legal Compendium* (pp. 673–86). Washington, DC: National Association of College and University Attorneys.

Franke, A. H. (2008a). Do your employment policies pass the test? In D. C. Brown, ed., *Employment Issues in Higher Education: A Legal Compendium*, 3d ed. (pp. 3–14). Washington, DC: National Association of College and University Attorneys.

Franke, A. H. (2008b). Retaliation claims after *Burlington Northern*: Managing on campus to avoid a train wreck at trial. In D. C. Brown, ed., *Employment Issues in Higher Education: A Legal Compendium*, 3d ed. (pp. 987–94). Washington, DC: National Association of College and University Attorneys.

Friedl, J. (2000). Punishing students for non-academic misconduct. *Journal of College and University Law*, 26(4), 701–29.

Fuehmeyer, K. A. (2009). Taxing the great academic divorce. *Journal of College and University Law*, 35(3), 721–46.

Fullilove v. Klutznick, 448 U.S. 448 (1980).

Fung, J. (2007). Pushing the envelope on higher education: How states have coped with federal legislation limited postsecondary education benefits to undocumented students. *Whittier Journal of Child and Family Advocacy*, 6, 415–35.

Gaal, J., M. S. Glazier, and T. S. Evans (2002). Gender-based pay disparities in intercollegiate coaching: The legal issues. *Journal of College and University Law*, 28(3), 519–68.

Gaal, J. and P. A. Jones (2003). Disabilty discrimination in higher education. *Journal of College and University Law*, 29(2), 435–46.

Gaal, J. S., Kaplan, and T. H. Murphy (2008). Labor law primer: An A to Z overview of labor relations issues under the NLRA for in-house counsel. In D. C. Brown, ed., *Employment Issues in Higher Education: A Legal Compendium*, 3d ed. (pp. 1037–80). Washington, DC: National Association of College and University Attorneys.

Garcetti v. Ceballos, 547 U.S. 410 (2006).

GarnerG2 and the Berkman Center for the Internet and Society (2005). *Copyright and Digital Media in a Post-Napster World.* Cambridge, MA: Harvard Law School.

Gay Rights Coalition of Georgetown University Law Center v. Georgetown University, 536 A.2d 1 (DC 1987).

Geiger, R. (2004). *Knowledge and Money: Research Universities and the Paradox of the Marketplace.* Stanford, CA: Stanford University Press.

Geller, R. (2007). *Criminal Conduct by Students—The Institution's Response.* Washington, DC: National Association of College and University Attorneys.

Genetic Information Nondiscrimination Act of 2008 (GINA). (Pub.L. 110-233, 122 Stat. 881).

Giroux, H. A. (2007). *The University in Chains: Confronting the Military-Industrial-Academic Complex*. Boulder, CO: Paradigm.

Golden, D. (2007). *The Price of Admission: How America's Ruling Class Buys Its Way into Elite Colleges—and Who Gets Left Outside the Gates*. New York: Three Rivers Press.

Golden, N. (2008). Access this: Why institutions of higher education must provide access to the Internet to students with disabilities. *Vanderbilt Journal of Entertainment and Technology Law*, 10, 363–411.

Goldgeier, E. S. (2007). ADA and Section 504: Technology, distance learning and accommodation of student disabilities. In D. C. Brown, J. R. Przypyszny, and K. R. Tromble, eds., *Legal Issues in Distance Education* (pp. 845–52). Washington, DC: National Association of College and University Attorneys.

Gonzaga University v Doe, 536 U.S. 273 (2002).

Gordon, H. (2008). The Robinson Rule: models for addressing race discrimination in the hiring of NCAA head football coaches. *Sports Lawyers Journal*, 15(1), 1–20.

Gordon, J. D. (2003). Individual and institutional academic freedom at religious colleges and universities. *Journal of College and University Law*, 30(1), 1–45.

Gordon, M. L. (2004). University controlled or owned technology: The state of commercialization and recommendations. *Journal of College and University Law*, 30(3), 641–72.

Gould, J. (1999). Title IX in the classroom: Academic freedom and the power to harass. *Duke Journal of Gender Law and Policy*, 6, 61–81.

Gratz v. Bollinger, 539 U.S. 244 (2003).

Green, R. S. (2005). Privacy in the government workplace: Employees' Fourth Amendment and statutory rights to privacy. *Cumberland Law Review*, 35, 639–69.

Greenup, J. S. (2005). The First Amendment and the right to hate. *Journal of Law and Education*, 4, 605–13.

Greenwood, R., C. Oliver, K. Sahlin, and R. Suddaby (2008). Introduction. In R. Greenwood, C. Oliver, K. Sahlin, and R. Suddaby, eds., *The SAGE Handbook of Organizational Institutionalism* (pp. 1–46). Thousand Oaks, CA: SAGE.

Griffin, O. R. (2002). *Giving a Deposition: A Witness Guide*. Washington, DC: National Association of College and University Attorneys.

Griffiths, B. (2005). Industry sponsored research and university/industry relations. In T. J. Colecchia, ed., *Legal Issues in Sponsored Research Programs: From Contracting to Compliance* (pp. 157–74). Washington, DC: National Association of College and University Attorneys.

Griggs v. Duke Power, 401 U.S. 242 (1971).

Griswold v. Connecticut, 381 U.S. 479 (1965).

Grossman, J. L. (2000). The first bite is free: Employer liability for sexual harassment. *University of Pittsburgh Law Review*, 61, 671–740.

Grutter v. Bollinger, 539 U.S. 306 (2003).

Guenther, J. P. (2006). Religion in the workplace. In R. A. Weitzner, ed., *Religious Discrimination and Accommodation Issues in Higher Education: A Legal Compendium* (pp. 293–305). Washington, DC: National Association of College and University Attorneys.

Hall, J. T. and R. Ferguson (2000). Case study: University of Anyplace: Strategic legal risk review. *Journal of College and University Law*, 27(1), 119–50.

Hamilton, N. W. (2001). Academic tradition and the principles of professional conduct. *Journal of College and University Law*, 27(3), 609–68.

Hammersla, A. M. and W. D. Blakeslee (2005). Software licensing ins and outs. In J. L. Curry, ed., *Technology Transfer Issues for Colleges and Universities: A Legal Compendium* (pp. 369–82). Washington, DC: National Association of College and University Attorneys.

Hanlon, S. (2006). Athletic scholarships as unconscionable contracts of adhesion: Has the NCAA fouled out? *Sports Lawyers Journal*, 13(1), 41–78.

Harding, B. M. (2000). Federal tax issues raised by international study abroad programs. *Journal of College and University Law*, 27(1), 207–22.

Harding, B. M. (2005a). Patent royalties paid to investors: Tax consequences. In J. L. Curry, ed., *Technology Transfer Issues for Colleges and Universities: A Legal Compendium* (pp. 661–66). Washington, DC: National Association of College and University Attorneys.

Harding, B. M. (2005b). Conversations with bond counsel. In J. L. Curry, ed., *Technology Transfer Issues for Colleges and Universities: A Legal Compendium* (pp. 683–88). Washington, DC: National Association of College and University Attorneys.

Harper, G. K. (2005). *Copyright Issues in Higher Education, 2005 Ed.* Washington, DC: National Association of College and University Attorneys.

Harper, G. K. (2007a). Fair use of copyrighted materials. In G. K. Harper, ed., *Copyright Law and Policy in a Networked World* (pp. 597–612). Washington, DC: National Association of College and University Attorneys.

Harper, G. K. (2007b). Google this. In G. K. Harper, ed., *Copyright Law and Policy in a Networked World* (pp. 885–92). Washington, DC: National Association of College and University Attorneys.

Harper, G. K. (2007c). Developing a comprehensive copyright policy to facilitate online learning. In G. K. Harper, ed., *Copyright Law and Policy in a Networked World* (pp. 898–908). Washington, DC: National Association of College and University Attorneys.

Harrington, P. J. (2001). Faculty conflicts of interest in an age of academic entrepreneurialism: An analysis of the problem, the law, and selected university policies. *Journal of College and University Law,* 27(4), 775–831.

Harris, A-M. and K. B. Grooms (2000). A new lesson plan for educational institutions: Expanded rules governing liability under Title IX of the Education Amendments of 1972 for student and faculty sexual harassment. *American University Journal of Gender, Race, and Justice,* 8, 575–621.

Harrison, D. (2006). The P2P file sharing war: It feels like Belgium over here. *Journal of College and University Law,* 32(3), 681–708.

Harrison, D. L. (2002). *Overview of a lawsuit.* Washington, DC: National Association of College and University Attorneys.

Hart, M. (2007). Disparate impact discrimination: The limits of litigation, the possibilities for internal compliance. *Journal of College and University Law,* 33(3), 547–58.

Hartley, R. C. (2001). Enforcing federal civil rights against public entities after *Garrett. Journal of College and University Law,* 28(1), 41–96.

Hawke, C. S. (2001). *Computers and Internet Use on Campus: A Legal Guide to Issues of Intellectual Property, Free Speech, and Privacy.* San Francisco, CA: Jossey-Bass.

Hayward, F. M. (2004). *Internationalization of U.S. Higher Education: Preliminary Status Report.* Washington, DC: American Council on Education.

Health Insurance Portability and Accountability Act of 1996 (Pub.L. 104-193, 110 Stat. 2105).

Healy v. James, 408 U.S. 169 (1972).

Heckman, D. (2003). Educational athletics and freedom of speech. *West's Education Law Reporter,* 177(1), 15–49.

Heins, M. and T. Beckles (2005). *Will fair use survive? Free expression in the age of copyright control.* New York: Brennan Center for Justice, New York University.

Heller, D. E. (2008). Educational attainment in the states: Are we progressing through equity in 2028. In P. Marin and C. L. Horn, eds., *Realizing* Bakke's *Legacy: Affirmative Action, Equal Opportunity, and Access to Higher Education* (pp. 87–109). Sterling, VA: Stylus.

Heller, J. S. (2008). Corporate investigations training manual: A sample. In D. C. Brown, ed., *Employment Issues in Higher Education: A Legal Compendium,* 3d ed. (pp. 387–444). Washington, DC: National Association of College and University Attorneys.

Henning, H. (2005). Negotiating the materials transfer agreement. In T. J. Colecchia, ed., *Legal Issues in Sponsored Research Programs: From Contracting to Compliance* (pp. 193–214). Washington, DC: National Association of College and University Attorneys.

Hiers, R. H. (2002). Institutional academic freedom vs. faculty academic freedom in public colleges and universities: A dubious dichotomy. *Journal of College and University Law,* 29(1), 35–109.

Hiers, R. H. (2003). Institutional academic freedom—A constitutional misperception: Did *Grutter v. Bollinger* perpetuate the confusion? *Journal of College and University Law,* 30(3), 531–81.

Higher Education Act Amendments of 1998 (Pub.L. 105-244, 112 Stat. 1581).

Hirsch, M. (2005). What's in a name?: The definition of an institution of higher education and its effect on for-profit postsecondary education. *NYU Journal of Legislation and Public Policy,* 9, 817–32.

Hirschfeld, S. J. (2008a). College and university codes of conduct. In D. C. Brown, ed., *Employment Issues in Higher Education: A Legal Compendium,* 3d ed. (pp. 15–26). Washington, DC: National Association of College and University Attorneys.

Hirschfeld, S. J. (2008b). Investigating discrimination and harassment claims: How to stay out of hot water and do the right thing. In D. C. Brown, ed., *Employment Issues in Higher Education: A Legal Compendium,* 3d ed. (pp. 445–56). Washington, DC: National Association of College and University Attorneys.

Hirtle, P. B. (2007). Copyright term and the public domain in the United States. In G. K. Harper, ed., *Copyright Law and Policy in a Networked World* (pp. 231–34). Washington, DC: National Association of College and University Attorneys.

Hochel, S. and C. E. Wilson (2007). *Hiring Right: Conducting Successful Searches in Higher Education.* San Francisco, CA: Jossey-Bass.

Hoke, J. R. (2006). *The Campus as Creditor: A Bankruptcy Primer on Educational Debts.* Washington, DC: National Association of College and University Attorneys.

Hoon, P. E. (2007). Recent copyright law developments: Digitalizing text, image collections, and audio materials. In G. K. Harper, ed., *Copyright Law and Policy in a Networked World* (pp. 481–502). Washington, DC: National Association of College and University Attorneys.

Hoon, P. and D. Drooz (2007). Copyright conflicts in higher education and the TEACH Act. In G. K. Harper, ed., *Copyright Law and Policy in a Networked World* (pp. 659–68). Washington, DC: National Association of College and University Attorneys.

Hoon, P. E., E. Kaplan, and G. K. Harper (2007). Topics in copyright law: The library, the university press, and the college of fine arts is here to see you, counselor. In G. K. Harper, ed., *Copyright Law and Policy in a Networked World* (pp. 555–66). Washington, DC: National Association of College and University Attorneys.

Horn, C. L. and P. Marin (2008). Realizing the legacy of *Bakke.* In P. Marin and C. L. Horn, eds., *Realizing Bakke's Legacy: Affirmative Action, Equal Opportunity, and Access to Higher Education* (pp. 1–14). Sterling, VA: Stylus.

Horwitz, P. (2007). Universities as first amendment institutions: Some easy answers and hard questions. *UCLA Law Review,* 54, 1498–58.

Hoye, W. P. (2005). Dealing with overseas risks in a globalized post 9/11 world. In N. E. Tribbensee, ed., *Study Abroad in Higher Education: Program Administration and Risk Management* (pp. 293–304). Washington, DC: National Association of College and University Attorneys.

Hoye, W. P. (2007). In pursuit of excellence: Integrating pro-active risk management into the campus culture. In K. M. Novak and A. M. Lee, eds., *Student Risk Management in Higher Education: A Legal Compendium* (pp. 17–38). Washington, DC: National Association of College and University Attorneys.

Hoye, W. P. and G. M. Rhodes (2000). An ounce of prevention is worth…the life of a student: Reducing risk in international programs. *Journal of College and University Law,* 27(1), 151–86.

Hoye, W. P., P. J. Rypkema, and R. Zerr (2005). Legal and risk management issues involving student foreign travel. In N. E. Tribbensee, ed., *Study Abroad in Higher Education: Program*

Administration and Risk Management (pp. 437–64). Washington, DC: National Association of College and University Attorneys.

Huang, K. Y. (2007). Reimaging and redefining the dream: A proposal for improving access to higher education for undocumented immigrants. *Seattle Journal for Social Justice*, 6, 431–64.

Hubbard, A. (2001). Understanding and implementing the ADA's direct threat defense. *Northwestern University Law Review*, 95, 1279–1355.

Huebinger, A. J. (2008). "Progression" since Charles Whitman: Student mental health policies in the 21st century. *Journal of College and University Law*, 34(3), 695–715.

Hulsey, W. (2005). Establishing and operating an effective university technology transfer office. In J. L. Curry, ed., *Technology Transfer Issues for Colleges and Universities: A Legal Compendium* (pp. 141–48). Washington, DC: National Association of College and University Attorneys.

Humphries, S. (2008). Institutes of higher education, safety swords, and privacy shields: Reconciling FERPA and the common law. *Journal of College and University Law*, 35(1), 145–215.

Hustoles, T. P. (2006a). A study of the law and practice of academic tenure. In S. G. Olswang and C. A. Cameron, eds., *Academic Freedom and Tenure: A Legal Compendium* (pp. 841–71). Washington, DC: National Association of College and University Attorneys.

Hustoles, T. P. (2006b). Examining tenure from a legal and administrative viewpoint. In S. G. Olswang and C. A. Cameron, eds., *Academic Freedom and Tenure: A Legal Compendium* (pp. 3–24). Washington, DC: National Association of College and University Attorneys.

Hustoles, T. P. (2006c). The unionized professorate: Key issues in negotiating faculty collective bargaining agreements: Preserving institutional rights. In S. G. Olswang and C. A. Cameron, eds., *Academic Freedom and Tenure: A Legal Compendium* (pp. 937–55). Washington, DC: National Association of College and University Attorneys.

Hustoles, T. P. (2008). Criminal misconduct by employees: Discipline and discharge issues. In D. C. Brown, ed., *Employment Issues in Higher Education: A Legal Compendium*, 3d ed. (pp. 613–26). Washington, DC: National Association of College and University Attorneys.

Hustoles, T. P. and N. DiGiovanni, Jr. (2005). *Negotiating a Faculty Collective Bargaining Agreement*. Washington, DC: National Association of College and University Attorneys.

Hustoles, T. P. and O. R. Griffin (2000). Employment discrimination in higher education. *Journal of College and University Law*, 27(2), 341–65.

Hutchens, N. H. (2009). Preserving the independence of public higher education: An examination of state constitutional autonomy provisions for public colleges and universities. *Journal of College and University Law*, 35(2), 271–322.

Hutson, T. A. (2006). Pedagogy and social justice: Race and gender bias in higher education: Could faculty course evaluations impede further progress toward parity? *Seattle Journal of Social Justice*, 4(Spring-Summer), 591–605.

Hyde, T (2005). Restrictions on the use of tax-exempt bond financed facilities. In J. L. Curry, ed., *Technology Transfer Issues for Colleges and Universities: A Legal Compendium* (pp. 689–98). Washington, DC: National Association of College and University Attorneys.

Illegal Immigration Reform and Immigrant Responsibility Act (IIRIRA) of 1996. (Pub.L. 104-208, Div. C, 110 Stat. 3009-546).

Individuals with Disabilities Education Act of 1975 (Pub.L. 94-142, 89 Stat. 796).

Irwin, K. S. (2005). University research activities. In T. J. Colecchia, ed., *Legal Issues in Sponsored Research Programs: From Contracting to Compliance* (pp. 19–32). Washington, DC: National Association of College and University Attorneys.

Irwin, K. S. and S. Dries (2005). Research contracting with industry. In T. J. Colecchia, ed., *Legal Issues in Sponsored Research Programs: From Contracting to Compliance* (pp. 73–86). Washington, DC: National Association of College and University Attorneys.

Jabaily, A. (2008). Color me colorblind: Difference, discretion, and voice in higher education after *Grutter*. *Cornell Journal of Law and Policy*, 17, 515–77.

Jacobs, G. (2006). Curbing their enthusiasm: A proposal to regulate offensive speech at public university basketball games. *Catholic University Law Review*, 55(2), 547–82.

Janosik, S. M. (2005). Expectations of faculty, parents, and students for process in campus disciplinary hearings. In J. E. Faulkner and N. E. Tribbensee, eds., *Students Disciplinary Issues: A Legal Compendium* (pp. 41–48). Washington, DC: National Association of College and University Attorneys.

Jed Foundation (2007). Framework for developing institutional policies for the acutely depressed or suicidal college student. In K. M. Novak and A. M. Lee, eds., *Student Risk Management in Higher Education: A Legal Compendium* (pp. 691–720). Washington, DC: National Association of College and University Attorneys.

Jensen, C. (2003). The more things change the more they stay the same: Copyright, digital technology, and social norms. *Stanford Law Review*, 56, 531–70.

Jewett, C. L. and L. H. Rutherford (2005). *What to Do When the U.S. Department of Education, Office of Civil Rights Comes to Campus*. Washington, D.C.: National Association of College and University Attorneys.

Johnson v. Transportation Agency, 480 U.S. 616 (1987).

Johnson, C. (2006). Degrees of deception: Are consumers and employers being duped by online diploma mills and universities? *Journal of College and University Law*, 32(2), 411–90.

Johnson, L. T. and L. C. Schoonmaker (2004). *What to Do When the EEOC Comes Knocking on Your Campus Door*. Washington, DC: National Association of College and University Attorneys.

Johnson, V. R. (2006). Americans abroad: International educational programs and tort liability. *Journal of College and University Law*, 32(2), 309–60.

Jones, E. O. (2007). The Fourth Amendment and dormitory searches. *Journal of College and University Law*, 33(3), 597–623.

Kaminer, D. N. (2000). When religious expression creates a hostile work environment: The challenge of balancing competing fundamental rights. *New York University Journal of Legislation and Public Policy*, 4, 81–142.

Kanter, A. S. (2003). The presumption against extraterritoriality as applied to disability discrimination laws: Where does it leave students with disabilities studying abroad? *Stanford Law and Policy Review*, 14, 291–318.

Kaplin, W. A. and B. A. Lee (2006). *The Law of Higher Education*, 4th ed. (2 vol.). San Francisco: Jossey-Bass.

Kaplin, W. A. and B. A. Lee (2009). *Year 2009 Cumulative Supplement to the Law of Higher Education*, 4th ed. Washington, DC: National Association of College and University Attorneys. Chapters 1–3, 15.

Kaufman, C. (2009). Unsportsmanlike conduct: 15-yard penalty and loss of free speech in public university sports stadiums. *Kansas Law Review*, 57(5), 1235–74.

Kaufman, H. E. (2005). *Access to Institutions for Students with Disabilities*. Washington, DC: National Association of College and University Attorneys.

Kaufman, M. J. (2007). (Still) constitutional school desegregation strategies: Teaching racial literacy to secondary school students and preferencing racial literate applicants to higher education. *Michigan Journal of Race and Law*, 13, 147–76.

Kaveeshvar, J. (2008). Kicking the rock and the hard place to the curb: An alternative and integrated approach to suicidal students in higher education. *Emory Law Journal*, 57, 651–93.

Keaney, C. C. (2007). Expanding the protectional scope of Title VII "because of sex" to include discrimination based on sexuality and sexual orientation. *Saint Louis University Law Review*, 51, 581–605.

Kearney, J. K. (2005). Export control regulations and participation by foreign nationals in university research. In T. J. Colecchia, ed., *Legal Issues in Sponsored Research Programs: From Contracting to Compliance* (pp. 627–56). Washington, DC: National Association of College and University Attorneys.

Keen, K. (2007). The Equity in Athletics Disclosure Act: Does it really improve the gender equity landscape. *Journal of College and University Law*, 34(1), 227–46.

Keith, J. K. (2004). The war on terrorism affects the academy: Principle post-September 11, 2001 federal anti-terrorism statutes, regulations, and policies that apply to colleges and universities. *Journal of College and University Law*, 30(2), 239–336.

Keith, J. L. (2005a). Export controls compliance programs: How colleges and universities can best cope with the complexity, comply and foster the best research and teaching. In T. J. Colecchia, ed., *Legal Issues in Sponsored Research Programs: From Contracting to Compliance* (pp. 667–72). Washington, DC: National Association of College and University Attorneys.

Keith, J. L. (2005b). Creative structures for international and joint research and education transactions: The sublimely simple to the unavoidably complex. In T. J. Colecchia, ed., *Legal Issues in Sponsored Research Programs: From Contracting to Compliance* (pp. 677–708). Washington, DC: National Association of College and University Attorneys.

Keller, G. (2004). *Transforming a College: The Story of a Little-Known College's Strategic Climb to National Distinction*. Baltimore, MD: Johns Hopkins University Press.

Kelly, W. (2005). Establishing university seed and venture capital funds and affiliated research foundations. In J. L. Curry, ed., *Technology Transfer Issues for Colleges and Universities: A Legal Compendium* (pp. 651–60). Washington, DC: National Association of College and University Attorneys.

Kenney, R. J. (2005a). Federal reimbursement problems: Time/effort reporting and the charging of direct costs. In T. J. Colecchia, ed., *Legal Issues in Sponsored Research Programs: From Contracting to Compliance* (pp. 33–48). Washington, DC: National Association of College and University Attorneys.

Kenney, R. J. (2005b). Federal regulation of personnel payments under research grants. In T. J. Colecchia, ed., *Legal Issues in Sponsored Research Programs: From Contracting to Compliance* (pp. 49–72). Washington, DC: National Association of College and University Attorneys.

Kettner, D. M. and W. J. Decker (2005). Fundamentals of technology transfer and IP licensing. In J. L. Curry, ed., *Technology Transfer Issues for Colleges and Universities: A Legal Compendium* (pp. 3–18). Washington, DC: National Association of College and University Attorneys.

Keyishian v. Board of Regents of the University of the State of New York, 345 F.2d 236.

Khatcheressian, L. (2003). FERPA and the Immigration and Naturalization Service: A guide for university counsel on federal rules for collecting, maintaining, and releasing information about foreign students. *Journal of College and University Law*, 29(2), 457–84.

Kimel v. Florida Board of Regents, 528 U.S. 62 (2000).

Kincaid, J. M. (2004a). Implementing the ADA on college campuses: Legal trends in serving students with disabilities. In E. M. Babbitt, ed., *Accommodating Students with Learning and Emotional Disabilities* (pp. 167–74). Washington, DC: National Association of College and University Attorneys.

Kincaid, J. M. (2004b). The perfect story: Navigating the sea of student disability laws. In E. M. Babbitt, ed., *Accommodating Students with Learning and Emotional Disabilities* (pp. 175–211). Washington, DC: National Association of College and University Attorneys.

Kirp, D. (2003). *Shakespeare, Einstein, and the Bottom Line: The Marketing of Higher Education*. Cambridge, MA: Harvard University Press.

Klein, M. K. (2004). "The equitable rule": Copyright ownership of distance-education courses. *Journal of College and University Law*, 31(1), 143–92.

Klein, M. K. (2009). Declaring "financial exigency": Comparing faculty layoffs in the 1970s and today. Paper presented at the Association for the Study of Higher Education Annual Meeting, Vancouver, British Columbia.

Konopasky, A. (2008). Eliminating harmful suicide policies in higher education. *Stanford Law and Policy Review*, 19, 328–58.

Kraatz, M.S. and E. J. Zajac (1996). Exploring the limits of the new institutionalism: The causes and consequences of illegitimate organizational change. *American Sociological Review*, 61(5), 812–836.

Kronman, A. T. (2007). *Education's End: Why Our Colleges and Universities Have Given Up on the Meaning of Life*. New Haven, CT: Yale University Press.

Kurlaender, M. and E. Felts (2008). *Bakke* beyond college access: Investigating racial/ethnic differences in college completion. In P. Marin and C. L. Horn, eds., *Realizing Bakke's Legacy: Affirmative Action, Equal Opportunity, and Access to Higher Education* (pp. 110–44). Sterling, VA: Stylus.

Kwall, R. R. (2000). Moral rights for university employees and students: Can educational institutions do better than the U.S. copyright law? *Journal of College and University Law*, 27(1), 53–82.

LaGrand, A. (2009). Narrowing the tailoring: How *Parents Involved* limits the use of race in higher education admissions. *National Black Law Journal*, 21, 53–80.

Lake, P. F. (2005). Private law continues to come to campus: Rights and responsibilities revisited. *Journal of College and University Law*, 31(3), 621–63.

Lake, P. F. (2008). Still waiting: The slow evolution of the law in light of the ongoing students' suicide cases. *Journal of College and University Law*, 34(2), 252–84.

Lake, P. F. and J. C. Epstein (2000). Modern liability rules and policies regarding college student alcohol injuries: Reducing high-risk alcohol use through norms of shared responsibility and environmental management. *Oklahoma Law Review*, 53, 611–30.

Lake, P. F. and N. Tribbensee (2002). The emerging crisis of college students' suicide: Law and policy responses to serious forms of self-inflicted injury. *Stetson Law Review*, 32, 125–57.

Langford, L. (2007). Preventing violence and promoting safety in higher education settings: Overview of a comprehensive approach. In K. M. Novak and A. M. Lee, eds., *Student Risk Management in Higher Education: A Legal Compendium* (pp. 125–35). Washington, DC: National Association of College and University Attorneys.

Langhauser, D. P. (2005). Free and regulated speech on campus: Using forum analysis for assessing facility use, speech zones, and related expressive activity. *Journal of College and University Law*, 31(3), 481–512.

Langhauser, D. P. (2006). Faculty religious expression on the public campus: The convergence of free speech, academic freedom, and religion. In S. G. Olswang and C. A. Cameron, eds., *Academic Freedom and Tenure: A Legal Compendium* (pp. 451–64). Washington, DC: National Association of College and University Attorneys.

LaNoue, G. and K. L. Marcus (2008). Serious consideration of race-neutral alternatives in higher education. *Catholic University Law Review*, 57, 991–41.

Larche, S. (2008). Pink-shirting: Should the NCAA consider a maternity and paternity waiver. *Marquette Sports Law Review*, 18(2), 393–412.

Larose, C. J. (2004). International money laundering abatement and anti-terrorism financing act of 2001. *Journal of College and University Law*, 30(2), 417–434.

Lasson, K. (1999). Controversial speakers on campus: Liberties, limitations, and common-sense guidelines. *St. Thomas Law Review*, 12, 39–94.

Latourette, A. W. (2006). Copyright implications for online distance education. *Journal of College and University Law*, 32(3), 613–54.

Laughlin, G. K. (2000). Who owns the copyright to faculty-created web sites: The work for hire doctrine's applicabilty to Internet resources created from distance learning and traditional classroom courses. *Boston College Law Review*, 41, 549–84.

Lee, B. A. (2006). Who are you? Fraudulent credentials and background checks in academe. *Journal of College and University Law*, 34(3), 655–80.

Lee, B. A. and G. E. Abbey (2008). College and university students with mental disabilities: Legal and policy issues. *Journal of College and University Law*, 34(2), 349–392.

Lee, B. A. and P. H. Ruger, (2003). *Accommodating Faculty and Staff with Psychiatric Disabilities*. Washington, DC: National Association of College and University Attorneys.

Lee, B. A. and D. Ziegler (2003). In search of an understandable line: The clash of academic freedom with sexual harassment law. In E. K. Cole, ed., *Sexual Harassment on Campus: A Legal Compendium*, 4th ed. (pp. 273–88). Washington, DC: National Association of College and University Attorneys.

Lee, D. (2006). *University Students Behaving Badly.* Sterling, VA: Trentham Books.

LeMay, C. A. and R. C. Cloud (2007). Student debt and the future of higher education. *Journal of College and University Law*, 34(1), 79–110.

Lemley, M. A. (2007). Property, intellectual property, and free riding. In G. K. Harper, ed., *Copyright Law and Policy in a Networked World* (pp. 147–154). Washington, DC: National Association of College and University Attorneys.

Levine, J. M (2006). Stigma's opening: *Grutter's* diversity interest(s) and the new calculus for affirmative action in higher education. *California Law Review*, 94, 457–530.

Lewis, H. R. (2006). *Excellence Without a Soul: How a Great University Forgot Education.* New York: Public Affairs.

Lindsay, N. (2007). Deciphering distance education accreditation: A balance of obstacles and opportunities. In D. C. Brown, J. R. Przypyszny, and K. R. Tromble, eds., *Legal Issues in Distance Education* (pp. 209–28). Washington, DC: National Association of College and University Attorneys.

Llewellyn, M. (2006). Student work: Citizens without statehood: Denying domicile to fund public higher education. *West Virginia Law Review*, 108, 775–97.

Louis, D. (2007). Nationally televised segregation: The NCAA's inability to desegregate college football's head coaching position. *Rutgers Race and the Law Review*, 9(1), 167–208.

Lupu, I. C. and R. W. Tuttle (2008). The cross at the college: Accommodation and acknowledgement of religion at public colleges. *William and Mary Bill of Rights Journal*, 16, 939–97.

MacLachlan, J. (2000). Dangerous traditions: Hazing rituals on campus and university liability. *Journal of College and University Law*, 26(3), 511–48.

Majeed, A. (2009). The misapplication of peer harassment law on college and university campuses and the loss of student speech rights. *Journal of College and University Law*, 35(2), 385–462.

Maki, J. L. (2005). The three R's: Reading, 'riting, and rewarding illegal immigrants: How higher education has acquiesced in the illegal presence of undocumented aliens in the United States. *William and Mary Bill of Rights Journal*, 13, 1341–73.

Mansfield, M-T. (2007). Academic accommodations for learning disabled college and university students: Ten years after *Guckenberger. Journal of College and University Law*, 34(1), 203–26.

Marchese, T. J. and J. F. Lawrence (2006). *The Search Committee Handbook: A Guide to Recruiting Administrators*, 2d ed. Sterling, VA: Stylus.

Marcus, K. L. (2008). Higher education, harassment, and First Amendment opportunism. *William and Mary Bill of Rights Journal*, 16, 1025–58.

Massy, W. F. and R. Zemsky (1994). Faculty discretionary time: Departments and the "academic ratchet." *Journal of Higher Education*, 65(1), 1–22.

Mathieu, D. (2008). Legal restrictions and liabilities associated with criminal background checks. In D. C. Brown, ed., *Employment Issues in Higher Education: A Legal Compendium*, 3d ed. (pp. 91–116). Washington, DC: National Association of College and University Attorneys.

Mawdsley, R. D. and S. Permuth (2008). The Supreme Court upholds mandatory student fees. In D. P. Langhauser, R. M. O'Neil, and W. E. Thro, eds., *Free Speech in Higher Education: Important Protections and Permissible Regulations* (pp. 339–52). Washington, DC: National Association of College and University Attorneys.

McCabe, D. and L. K. Trevino (2002). Honesty and honor codes. *Academe*, 88(1), 37–41.

McCart, W. (2008). *Simpson v. University of Colorado*: Title IX crashed the party in college athletic recruiting. *DePaul Law Review*, 58(1), 153–84.

McCarthy, S. (2007). The legal and social implications of the NCAA's pregnancy exception—Does the NCAA discriminate against male student-athletes? *Villanova Sports and Entertainment Law Journal*, 14(2), 327–62.

McCormick, B. (2006). The times they are a-changin': How current provisions of the Digital Millennium Copyright Act, recent developments in indirect copyright law and the growing popularity of student peer-to-peer file sharing could "chill" academic freedom and technological innovation in academia. *Journal of College and University Law*, 32(3), 709–25.

McCreath, R. (2005). Managing oversees employees: The impact of employment law in England. In N. E. Tribbensee, ed., Study Abroad in Higher Education: Program *Administration and Risk Management* (pp. 251–64). Washington, DC: National Association of College and University Attorneys.

McDonald, J. N. (2002). *Brister v. Faulkner* and the clash of free speech and good order on the college campus. *Journal of College and University Law*, 28(2), 467–94.

McDonald, S. J. (2007). Copyright 101 (and 106, 107, 110, 201, 202, 302, 504…). In G. K. Harper, ed., *Copyright Law and Policy in a Networked* World (pp. 3–16). Washington, DC: National Association of College and University Attorneys.

McElwee, T. P. (2007). Yours? Mine? Ours? Research collaborations in drafting effective intellectual property sharing agreements. In D. C. Brown, J. R. Przypyszny, and K. R. Tromble, eds., *Legal Issues in Distance Education* (pp. 779–88). Washington, DC: National Association of College and University Attorneys.

McGuinness, A. C. (2005). The states and higher education. In P. G. Altbach, R. O. Berdahl, and P. J. Gumport (Eds.), *American Higher Education in the Twenty-First Century: Social, Political, and Economic Challenges* (pp. 198–225). Baltimore, MD: Johns Hopkins University Press.

McKanders, K. A. (2004). ADA and Sec. 504: Application and impact on study abroad programs and clinical and other internships. In E. M. Babbitt, ed., *Accommodating Students with Learning and Emotional Disabilities* (pp. 971–80). Washington, DC: National Association of College and University Attorneys.

McLain, J. (2002). Discrimination in the workplace: Should it be allowed to continue? *Labor Lawyer*, 17(3), 517–40.

McLendon, M. (2003). State governance reform of higher education: Patterns, trends, and theories of the public policy process. In J. C. Smart, ed., *Higher Education: Handbook of Theory and Research*, Vol. 17 (pp. 57–144). London: Kluwer.

McPherson, M. S. and M. O. Shapiro (1998). *The Student Aid Game: Meeting Need and Rewarding Talent*. Princeton, NJ: Princeton University Press.

McSherry, C. (2001). *Who Owns Academic Work? Battling for Control of Intellectual Property*. Cambridge, MA: Harvard University Press.

Meers, E. and W. Thro (2004). *Race-Conscious Admissions and Financial Aid Programs*. Washington, D.C.: National Association of College and University Attorneys.

Melear, K. B. (2003). The contractual relationship between student and institution. Disciplinary, academic, and consumer contexts. *Journal of College and University Law*, 30(1), 175–208.

Melear, K. B. (2007). The First Amendment and freedom of press on the public university campus: An analysis of *Hosty v. Carter*. *West's Education Law Reporter*, 216, 1–18.

Meredith, M. (2004). Why do universities compete in the ratings game? An empirical analysis of the effects of the U.S. News and World Report college rankings. *Research in Higher Education*, 45(5), 443–461.

Meritor Savings Bank v. Vinson, 477 U.S. 57 (1986).

Metro Broadcasting v. Federal Communications Commission, 497 U.S. 547 (1990).

Metzger, W. P. (1988). Profession and constitution: The two definition of academic freedom in America. *Texas Law Review*, 66, 1265–1322.

Meyer, J. W. and B. Rowan (1977). Institutionalized organizations: Formal structure as myth and ceremony. *American Journal of Sociology*, 83(2), 340–63.

Michaelson, M. (2001). Should untenured as well as tenured faculty be guaranteed academic freedom? A few observations. *Journal of College and University Law*, 27(3), 565–72.

Miller, C. and W. Warren (2005). The CREATE Act of 2004: Sharing information with joint research partners just became safer for public institutions. In J. L. Curry, ed., *Technology Transfer Issues for Colleges and Universities: A Legal Compendium* (pp. 195–98). Washington, DC: National Association of College and University Attorneys.

Miller, J. and A. Gillentine (2006). An analysis of risk management policies for tailgating activities at selected NCAA Division I football games. *Journal of Legal Aspects of Sport*, 1, 197–215.

Miller, K. E. and J. D. Toma (forthcoming). Diversity as a strategic imperative in higher education. In M. Baxter-Magolda and P. Magolda, eds., *Contested Issues in Student Affairs*. Sterling, VA: Stylus.

Milligan, R. G. (2008). Financial band-aid: Reactionary fixes to federal family education loan program inducement guidelines solve some problems, raise others. *Journal of College and University Law*, 34(3), 717–46.

Misinec, M. (2005). When the game ends, the pandemonium begins: University liability for field rushing injuries. *Sports Law Journal*, 12, 181–229.

Mississippi University for Women v. Hogan, 458 U.S. 718 (1982).

Monopoli, P. A. (2008). In a different voice: Lessons from Ledbetter. *Journal of College and University Law*, 34(3), 555–84.

Moran, R. F. (2006). Of doubt and diversity: The failure of affirmative action in higher education. *Ohio State Law Journal*, 67, 201–43.

Morgan, J. M. (2009). Consumer-driven reform of higher education: A critical look at the new amendments to the Higher Education Act. *Journal of Law and Policy*, 17, 531–78.

Morphew, C. C. (2002). A rose by any other name: Which colleges became universities. *Review of Higher Education*, 25(2), 207–24.

Morphew, C. C. and Huisman, J. (2002). Using institutional theory to reframe research on academic drift. *Higher Education in Europe*, 27(4), 491–506.

Munsch, M. H. and S. P. Schupansky (2003). *The Dismissal of Students with Mental Disabilities*. Washington, DC: National Association of College and University Attorneys.

Munsch, M. H. and J. D. Verdi (2006). Administration of tenure policies. In S. G. Olswang and C. A. Cameron, eds., *Academic Freedom and Tenure: A Legal Compendium* (pp. 889–900). Washington, DC: National Association of College and University Attorneys.

Murphy, T. H. and C. Kaesebier (2008). Drafting and presenting separation agreements. In D. C. Brown, ed., *Employment Issues in Higher Education: A Legal Compendium*, 3d ed. (pp. 627–44). Washington, DC: National Association of College and University Attorneys.

Murray, K. and L. B. Helms (2001). The buck stops here: Graduate level disability services and the 1998 Rehabilitation Act Amendments. *Journal of College and University Law*, 28(1), 1–39.

Musselman, J. L. (2007). Federal income tax deductibility of higher education expenses: The good, the bad, and the ugly. *Capital University Law Review*, 35, 923–81.

National Institute of Health (NIH). (December 1, 2003). *Grants Policy Statement*. Washington, DC: National Institute of Health.

National Labor Relations Act (NLRA) of 1935 (Pub.L. 74-198, 49 Stat. 449).

National Research Council (2000). *The Digital Dilemma: Intellectual Property in the Information Age*. Washington, DC: National Academy Press.

NCAA v. Board of Regents of the University of Oklahoma, 468 U.S. 85 (1984).

NCAA v. Tarkanian, 488 U. S. 179 (1988).

Nelson, E. S. (2005). What price *Grutter*? We may have won the battle, but are we losing the war? *Journal of College and University Law*, 32(1), 1–50.

Netanel, N. W. (2001). Locating copyright within the First Amendment skein. *Stanford Law Review*, 54, 1–86.

Newfield, C. (2008). *Unmaking the Public University: The Forty-Year Assault on the Middle Class*. Cambridge, MA: Harvard University Press.

Newman, F., L. Couturier, and J. Scurry (2004). *The Future of Higher Education: Rhetoric, Reality, and the Risks of the Marketplace*. San Francisco, CA: Jossey-Bass.

Niehoff, L. (2008). *Garcetti v. Caballos*: The case, its progeny, and its implications for higher education law. In D. C. Brown, ed., *Employment Issues in Higher Education: A Legal Compendium*, 3d ed. (pp. 1025–36). Washington, DC: National Association of College and University Attorneys.

NLRB v. Yeshiva University, 444 U.S. 672 (1980).

Novak, K. J. and K. Jackson (2007). A briefing for President Robert Gates, Texas A&M University. In K. M. Novak and A. M. Lee, eds., *Student Risk Management in Higher Education: A Legal Compendium* (pp. 3–16). Washington, DC: National Association of College and University Attorneys.

Novak, K. J. and A. M. Lee, eds. (2007). *Student Risk Management in Higher Education: A Legal Compendium*. Washington, DC: National Association of College and University Attorneys.

O'Donnell, M. L. (2003). FERPA: Only a piece of the privacy puzzle. *Journal of College and University Law*, 29(3), 679–717.

Office of Management and Budget (May 10, 2004). *OMB circular A-21*. Washington, DC: Office of Management and Budget.

Office of Science and Technology Policy, Executive Office of the President (2000), *Federal Policy on Research Misconduct*, Federal Register: December 6, 2000 (Vol. 65, No. 235), 76260-64.

O'Meara, K. (2007). Striving for what? Exploring the pursuit of prestige. In J. C. Smart, ed., *Higher Education: Handbook of Theory and Research*, Vol. 22 (pp. 121–179). Dordrecht, The Netherlands: Springer.

Oncale v. Sundowner Offshore Services, Inc., 523 U.S. 75 (1998).

Olivas, M. A. (2004a). IIRIRA, the DREAM Act, and undocumented student residency. *Journal of College and University Law*, 30(2), 435–64.

Olivas, M. A. (2004b). Introduction: The war on terrorism touches the ivory tower—Colleges and universities after September 11. *Journal of College and University Law*, 30(2), 233–38.

Olivas, M. A. (2009). An essay on friends, special programs, and pipelines. *Journal of College and University Law*, 35(3), 463–74.

Olswang, S. G. (2006). College and university faculty: Academic freedom and tenure. In S. G. Olswang and C. A. Cameron, eds., *Academic Freedom and Tenure: A Legal Compendium* (pp. 721–46). Washington, DC: National Association of College and University Attorneys.

Olswang, S. G., E. M. Babbitt, C. A. Cameron, and E. K. Kamai (2003). Retrenchment. *Journal of College and University Law*, 30(1), 47–74.

O'Neil, R. M. (2001). Alternatives to tenure. *Journal of College and University Law*, 27(3), 573–82.

O'Neil, R. M. (2008a). Limits of freedom: The Ward Churchill case. In D. P. Langhauser, R. M. McNeil, and W. E. Thro, eds., *Free Speech in Higher Education: Important Protections and Permissible Regulations* (pp. 523–31). Washington, DC: National Association of College and University Attorneys.

O'Neil, R. M. (2008b). Academic research and free expression. In D. P. Langhauser, R. M. McNeil, and W. E. Thro, eds. *Free Speech in Higher Education: Important Protections and Permissible Regulations* (pp. 725–43). Washington, DC: National Association of College and University Attorneys.

O'Neil, R. M. (2008c). Free expression and electronic communications: Campus and cyberspace. In D. P. Langhauser, R. M. O'Neil, and W. E. Thro, eds., *Free Speech in Higher Education: Important Protections and Permissible Regulations* (pp. 943–65). Washington, DC: National Association of College and University Attorneys.

O'Neil, R. M. (2008d). Free expression and artistic freedom in the academic world. In D. P. Langhauser, R. M. O'Neil, and W. E. Thro, eds., *Free Speech in Higher Education: Impor-*

tant Protections and Permissible Regulations (pp. 1177–99). Washington, DC: National Association of College and University Attorneys.

O'Neil, R. M. (2008e). What's so special about academic speech? In D. P. Langhauser, R. M. O'Neil, and W. E. Thro, eds., *Free Speech in Higher Education: Important Protections and Permissible Regulations* (pp. 3–7). Washington, DC: National Association of College and University Attorneys.

O'Neil, R. M. and L. White (2006). Understanding tenure: History, purpose, and relationship to academic freedom. In S. G. Olswang and C. A. Cameron, eds., *Academic Freedom and Tenure: A Legal Compendium* (pp. 3–24). Washington, DC: National Association of College and University Attorneys.

Oregon v. Smith, 494 U.S. 872 (1990).

Osborne, B. (2007). No drinking, no drugs, no lesbians: Sexual orientation discrimination in intercollegiate athletics. *Marquette Sports Law Journal*, 17(2), 481–502.

Oxholm, C. (2005). Sarbanes-Oxley in higher education: Bringing corporate America's best practices to academia. *Journal of College and University Law*, 31(2), 351–76.

Papish v. Board of Curators of the University of Missouri, 410 U.S. 667 (1973).

Parents Involved in Community Schools v. Seattle School District No. 1, 551 U.S. 701 (2007).

Parker, D. M., E. J. Kelly, G. A. Goldsmith, and S. L. Carney (2005). IP clauses in action. In T. J. Colecchia, ed., *Legal Issues in Sponsored Research Programs: From Contracting to Compliance* (pp. 87–130). Washington, DC: National Association of College and University Attorneys.

Parrish, D. M (2006). Religious misconduct and plagiarism. *Journal of College and University Law*, 33(1), 65–96.

Parrot, S. J. (2006). The ADA and reasonable accommodation of employees regarded as disabled: Statutory fact or bizarre fiction. *Ohio State Law Review*, 67, 1495–1532.

Patti, C. M. (2005). Managing the difficult research misconduct case. In T. J. Colecchia, ed., *Legal Issues in Sponsored Research Programs: From Contracting to Compliance* (pp. 245–54). Washington, DC: National Association of College and University Attorneys.

Pennsyl, B. (2008). Whistling a foul on the NCAA: How NCAA recruiting bylaws violate the Sherman Antitrust Act. *Syracuse Law Review*, 58(2), 397-426.

Perez-Arrieta, A. M. (2005). Defenses to sex-based wage discrimination claims at educational institutions: Exploring "equal work" and "any other factor other than sex" in the faculty context. *Journal of College and University Law*, 31(2), 393–415.

Peri, J. (2008). The wisdom of employed general counsel in higher education. *Widener Law Journal*, 18, 191–202.

Perry Education Association v. Perry Local Educators' Association, 460 U.S. 37 (1983).

Personal Responsibility and Work Opportunity Reconciliation Act (PRWORA) of 1996. (Pub.L. 104-193, 110 Stat. 2105).

Pfeffer, J. and G. R. Salancik (1978). *The External Control of Organizations: A Resource Dependence Perspective*. New York: Harper and Row.

PGA Tour, Inc. v. Martin, 532 U.S. 661 (2001).

Pickering v. Board of Education, 391 U.S. 563 (1968).

Pieronek, C. (2000). Title IX and intercollegiate athletics in the federal courts: Myth versus reality. *Journal of College and University Law*, 27(2), 447–518.

Pieronek, C. (2003). Title IX beyond thirty: A review of recent developments. *Journal of College and University Law*, 30(1), 75–174.

Pieronek, C. (2005). Title IX and gender equity in science, technology, engineering and mathematics education: No longer an overlooked application of the law. *Journal of College and University Law*, 31(2), 291–350.

Pike, A. D. (2007). Low-income workers and their federal tax system: No wealthy parent left behind: An analysis of the tax system for higher education. *American University Law Review*, 56, 1229–60.

Pitts, J. (2008). Why wait: An antitrust analysis of the National Football League and National Basketball Association's draft eligibility rules. *Howard Law Journal*, 51(2), 433–78.

Plylar v. Doe, 457 U.S. 202 (1982).

Podberesky v. Kirwan, 64 F.Supp. 364 (D.Md. 1991).

Porter, N. B. (2006). Victimizing the abused? Is termination the solution when domestic violence comes to work. *Michigan Journal of Gender and Law*, 12, 275–330.

Porter, P. D. (2005). Critical issues in clinical trial agreements. In T. J. Colecchia, ed., *Legal Issues in Sponsored Research Programs: From Contracting to Compliance* (pp. 175–82). Washington, DC: National Association of College and University Attorneys.

Porto, B. (2008). Halfway home: An update on Title IX and college sports. *Vermont Bar Journal and Law Digest*, 34, 1–17.

Pregnancy Discrimination Act of 1978. (P.L. 95-555, 92 Stat. 2076).

Price Waterhouse v. Hopkins, 490 U.S. 228 (1989).

Przypyszny, J. R. (2007). ADA and Section 504: Technology, distance learning and accommodation of student disabilities. In D. C. Brown, J. R. Przypyszny, and K. R. Tromble, eds., *Legal Issues in Distance Education* (pp. 837–44). Washington, DC: National Association of College and University Attorneys.

Ravitch, F. S. (2008). Higher education and the First Amendment: Intelligent design in public university science departments: Academic freedom or establishment of religion. *William and Mary Bill of Rights Journal*, 16, 1061–90.

Reaves, R. (2001)."There's no crying in baseball:" Sports and the legal and social construction of gender. *Journal of Gender, Race and Justice*, 4, 283–319.

Regents of the University of California v. Bakke, 438 U.S. 265 (1978).

Regents of the University of Michigan v. Ewing, 474 U.S. 214 (1985).

Rehabilitation Act of 1973 (Pub.L. No. 93-112, 87 Stat. 355).

Rendleman, D. (2002). Academic freedom in *Urofsky's* wake: Post September 11 remarks on "who owns academic freedom." *Washington and Lee Law Review*, 59, 361–69.

Rhoades, G. (2005). Capitalism, academic style, and shared governance. *Academe*, 91(3), 38–42.

Rhoads, M. B. and H. L. Konrad (2007). *Immigration Law: Faculty and Staff Issues, 2007 Update.* Washington, DC: National Association of College and University Attorneys.

Ricci v. DiStefano, 557 U.S. __ (2009).

Rice, N. R. (2005). Human subjects research: The basics. In T. J. Colecchia, ed., *Legal Issues in Sponsored Research Programs: From Contracting to Compliance* (pp. 279–302). Washington, DC: National Association of College and University Attorneys.

Ritchie, M. A. (2005). Risk management in study abroad: Lessons from the wildnerness. In N. E. Tribbensee, ed., *Study Abroad in Higher Education: Program Administration and Risk Management* (pp. 417–28). Washington, DC: National Association of College and University Attorneys.

Robben, P. D. (2008). No cookie cutters, please: How to draft effective noncompete agreements. In D. C. Brown, ed., *Employment Issues in Higher Education: A Legal Compendium*, 3d ed. (pp. 85–90). Washington, DC: National Association of College and University Attorneys.

Roberts, K. (2007). Correcting culture: Extraterritoriality and U.S. employment discrimination law. *Hofstra Labor and Employment Law Journal*, 24, 295–331.

Robinson, J. H. (2000). The extraterritorial application of American law: Preliminary reflections. *Journal of College and University Law*, 27(1), 187–206.

Rooksby, J. H. (2007). Rethinking student press in the "marketplace of ideas" after *Hosty*: The argument for encouraging professional journalistic practices. *Journal of College and University Law*, 33(2), 429–72.

Rose, A. D. (2004). ADA and Section 504: Policies and procedures for accommodating student claims on disabilities. In E. M. Babbitt, ed., *Accommodating Students with Learning and Emotional Disabilities* (pp. 227–35). Washington, DC: National Association of College and University Attorneys.

Rose, B. T. (2006). Accommodation of student religious beliefs. In R. A. Weitzner, ed., *Religious Discrimination and Accommodation Issues in Higher Education: A Legal Compendium* (pp. 425–50). Washington, DC: National Association of College and University Attorneys.

Rosenberg, J. L. and G. Skoning (2006). Current issues in age discrimination. In D. C. Brown, ed., *Employment Issues in Higher Education: A Legal Compendium*, 3d ed. (pp. 917–51). Washington, DC: National Association of College and University Attorneys.

Rosenburger v. Rector and Visitors of the University of Virginia, 515 U.S. 819 (1995).

Rothstein, L. (2007). Millennials and disability law: Revisiting *Southeastern Community College v. Davis*. *Journal of College and University Law*, 34(1), 169–202.

Rothstein, L. (2009). Disability law issues for high risk students: Addressing violence and disruption. *Journal of College and University Law*, 35(3), 691–720.

Ruge, T. R. and A. D. Iza (2005). Higher education for undocumented students: The case for open admission and in-state tuition rates for students without lawful immigration status. *Indiana International and Comparative Law Review*, 15, 257–78.

Russo, C. J. and D. L. Gregory (2001). *Ex Corde Ecclesiae* and American Catholic Higher Education: Dead on Arrival? *Religion and Education*, 28(1), 58–74.

Russo, C. J. and W. E. Thro (2007). The constitutional rights of politically incorrect groups: *Christian Legal Society v. Walker* as an illustration. *Journal of College and University Law*, 33(2), 361–87.

Ryan, K. A. (2008). Access assured: Restoring progressivity in the tax and spending programs for higher education. *Seton Hall Law Review*, 38, 1–62.

Santoro, T. M. (2006). Key innovative, creative, or essential provisions for your next collective bargaining agreement. In S. G. Olswang and C. A. Cameron, eds., *Academic Freedom and Tenure: A Legal Compendium* (pp. 903–35). Washington, DC: National Association of College and University Attorneys.

Sarbanes-Oxley Act of 2002 (Pub.L. 107-204, 116 Stat. 745).

Scaraglino, P. (2003). Complying with HIPPA: A guide for the university and its counsel. *Journal of College and University Law*, 29(3), 525–78.

Schimelfenig, M., C. D. Beckenhauer, and R. Yanikoski (2006). Hiring, tenure, and activities of faculty at religiously affiliated institutions. In R. A. Weitzner, ed., *Religious Discrimination and Accommodation Issues in Higher Education: A Legal Compendium* (pp. 267–92). Washington, DC: National Association of College and University Attorneys.

Schmidt, P. (2007). *Color and Money: How Rich White Kids Are Winning the War over College Affirmative Action*. New York: Palgrave Macmillan.

Schmit, J. (2007). Fresh set of downs: Why recent modification to the Bowl Championship Series still draw a flag under the Sherman Act. *Sports Lawyers Journal*, 14(1), 219–54.

Schulman, E. P. (2006). Challenges by religious student groups to university nondiscrimination policies. In R. A. Weitzner, ed., *Religious Discrimination and Accommodation Issues in Higher Education: A Legal Compendium* (pp. 451–66). Washington, DC: National Association of College and University Attorneys.

Schultz, K. L. (2005). Contracting with foreign entities. In N. E. Tribbensee, ed., *Study Abroad in Higher Education: Program Administration and Risk Management* (pp. 111–50). Washington, DC: National Association of College and University Attorneys.

Sciscoe, T. S. (2006). *Should I Stay or Should I Go? Early Retirement Incentive Programs in Higher Education*. Washington, DC: National Association of College and University Attorneys.

Secunda, P. M. (2007). The Solomon Amendment, expressive associations, and public employment. *UCLA Law Review*, 54, 1767–1813.

Sermersheim, M. D. (2003). *Computer Access: Selected Legal Issues Affecting Higher Education*. Washington, DC: National Association of College and University Attorneys.

Shamloo v. Mississippi State Board of Trustees, 620 F.2d 516 (5th Cir. 1980).

Shea, L., F. Robinson, and L. Parkin (2004). *Managing Financial Conflicts of Interest in Human*

Subjects Research. Washington, DC: National Association of College and University Attorneys.

Shekleton, J. F. (2005). The campus as agora: The constitution, commerce, gadfly stonecutters, and irreverent youth. *Journal of College and University Law*, 31(3), 513–620.

Shiels, B. L. (2005). Animal research under siege. In T. J. Colecchia, ed., *Legal Issues in Sponsored Research Programs: From Contracting to Compliance* (pp. 255–66). Washington, DC: National Association of College and University Attorneys.

Shulman, J. L. and W. G. Bowen (2002). *The Game of Life: College Sports and Educational Values*. Princeton, NJ: Princeton University Press.

Sidbury, B. F. (2003). *Gonzaga University v. Doe* and its implications: No right to enforce student privacy rights under FERPA. *Journal of College and University Law*, 29(3), 655–77.

Simon, C. S. and D. B. Simon (2006). Bully for you; full steam ahead: How Pennsylvania employment law permits bullying in the workplace. *Widener Law Journal*, 16, 141–64.

Simonelli, J. (2005). Service learning abroad: Liability and logistics. In N. E. Tribbensee, ed., *Study Abroad in Higher Education: Program Administration and Risk Management* (pp. 429–36). Washington, DC: National Association of College and University Attorneys.

Slaughter, S. and L. L. Leslie (1997). *Academic Capitalism: Power, Politics and the Entrepreneurial University*. Baltimore, MD: Johns Hopkins University Press.

Slaughter, S. and G. Rhoades (2004). *Academic Capitalism and the New Economy*. Baltimore, MD: Johns Hopkins University Press.

Small, L. (2008). *Meredith*, colorblind constitutionalism, and the impact on higher education. *Journal of Law and Education*, 37, 453–60.

Smith v. City of Jackson, 544 U.S. 228 (2005).

Smith, P. C. (2008). The elusive cap and gown: The implications of tax policy on access to higher education for low-income individuals and families. *Berkeley Journal of African-American Law and Policy*, 10, 181–225.

Snow, B. A. and W. E. Thro (2001). The significance of Blackstone's understanding of sovereign immunity for America's public institutions of higher education. *Journal of College and University Law*, 28(1), 97–128.

Sokolow, B. A., W. S. Lewis, J. A. Keller, and A. Daly (2008). College and university liability for violent campus attacks. *Journal of College and University Law*, 34(2), 319–48.

Somers, N. (2007). College and university liability for the dangerous yet time-honored tradition of hazing in fraternities and student athletics. *Journal of College and University Law*, 33(3), 653–80.

Southwest Community College v. Davis, 442 U.S. 397 (1979).

Spellings Commission (2006). *Report of the Commission on the Future of Higher Education*, U.S. Department of Education, Washington, DC.

Spies, J. (2006). Winning at all costs: An analysis of a university's potential liability for sexual assaults committed by its student athletes. *Marquette Sports Law Review*, 16(2), 429–60.

Sprague, R. (2007). Fired for blogging: Are there legal protections for employees who blog? *University of Pennsylvania Journal of Labor and Employment Law*, 9, 355–87.

Springer, A. (2008). Political viewpoint and religious belief discrimination. In D. P. Langhauser, R. M. McNeil, and W. E. Thro, eds. *Free Speech in Higher Education: Important Protections and Permissible Regulations* (pp. 459–88). Washington, DC: National Association of College and University Attorneys.

Springer, F. J. and K. W. Gage (2006). Tenure evaluation policies and processes: Advancing institutional interests while creating the appearance of fact and fairness. In S. G. Olswang and C. A. Cameron, eds., *Academic Freedom and Tenure: A Legal Compendium* (pp. 873–88). Washington, DC: National Association of College and University Attorneys.

Spurgeon, L. D. (2007). A transcendent value: The quest to safeguard academic freedom. *Journal of College and University Law*, 34(1), 111–68.

Stegmaier, S. M. (2008). Incentives for higher education in the internal revenue code: Education tax expenditure reform and the inclusion of refundable tax credits. *Southeastern University Law Review*, 37, 135–81.

Stevens, E. (1999). *Due Process in Higher Education: A Systematic Approach to Fair Decision Making*. ASHE-ERIC Higher Education Report (Vol. 27, No. 2). Washington, DC: The George Washington University, Graduate School of Education and Human Development.

Stoner, E. N. and J. W. Lowrey (2004). Navigating past the "spirit of insubordination": A twenty-first century model student conduct code with a model hearing script. *Journal of College and University Law*, 31(1), 1–79.

Stoner, E. N. and J. M. Showalter (2004). Judicial deference to educational judgment: Justice O'Connor's opinion in *Grutter* reapplies longstanding principles, as shown by rulings involving college students in the eighteen months before *Grutter*. *Journal of College and University Law*, 30(3), 583–618.

Strickland, L. S., M. Minow, and T. Lipinski (2004). Patriot in the library: Management approaches when demands for information are received from law enforcement and intelligence agents. *Journal of College and University Law*, 30(2), 363–416.

Stuart, S. P. (2009). Participatory lawyering and the ivory tower: Conducting a forensic law audit in the aftermath of Virginia Tech. *Journal of College and University Law*, 35(2), 323–84.

Suggs, W. (2005). *A Place on the Team: The Triumph and Tragedy of Title IX*. Princeton, NJ: Princeton University Press.

Sun, J. C. and B. Baez (2009). *Intellectual Property in the Information Age: Knowledge and Commodity and Its Legal Implications for Higher Education*. ASHE Higher Education Reports, 34(4). San Francisco, CA: Jossey-Bass.

Swope, J. (2005). Student or defendant?: How college and university disciplinary proceedings and criminal charges interact. In J. E. Faulkner and N. E. Tribbensee, eds., *Students Disciplinary Issues: A Legal Compendium* (pp. 243–52). Washington, DC: National Association of College and University Attorneys.

Taft-Hartley Act (Labor–Management Relations Act of 1947. (Pub.L. 80-101, 61 Stat. 136).

TEACH Act (the Technology, Education, and Copyright Harmonization Act) of 2002 (Pub.L. 107-273, 116 Stat. 1758).

Thomas, E. C. (2007). Racial classification and the flawed pursuit of diversity: How phantom minorities threaten "critical mass" justification in higher education. *Brigham Young University Law Review*, 2007(January), 813–55.

Thomas, S. M. (2004). Students and disability laws: What's new? In E. M. Babbitt, ed., *Accommodating Students with Learning and Emotional Disabilities* (pp. 257–70). Washington, DC: National Association of College and University Attorneys.

Thornton, S. R. (2006). *Pregnant in the Academy: Questions and Answers*. Washington, DC: American Association of University Professors.

Thro, W. E. (2006a). Talking about religion: Student and employment issues. In R. A. Weitzner, ed., *Religious Discrimination and Accommodation Issues in Higher Education: A Legal Compendium* (pp. 139–50). Washington, DC: National Association of College and University Attorneys.

Thro, W. E. (2006b). The constitutionality and current status of the Solomon Amendment. *NACUA Notes*, 4(4), 1–6.

Thro, W. E. (2007). *Why You Cannot Sue State U: A Guide to Sovereign Immunity*. Washington, DC: National Association of College and University Attorneys.

Thro, W. E. (2008). But that group is offensive: Recognition, facility access, and funding for political and religious groups. In D. P. Langhauser, R. M. O'Neil, and W. E. Thro, eds., *Free Speech in Higher Education: Important Protections and Permissible Regulations* (pp. 277–94). Washington, DC: National Association of College and University Attorneys.

Tiffany, K. (2007). Cheering speech at state university athletic events: How do you regulate bad spectator sportsmanship. *Sports Lawyers Journal*, 14(1), 111–36.

Tiscione, F. (2007). College athletics and workers' compensation: Why the courts get it wrong in denying student-athletes workers' compensation benefits when they get injured. *Sports Lawyers Journal*, 14(1), 137–68.

Title IX of the Educational Amendments of 1972 (Pub.L. 92-318, 86 Stat. 235).

Todd, J. (2007). State university v. state government: Applying academic freedom to curriculum, pedagogy, and assessment. *Journal of College and University Law*, 33(2), 387–27.

Toma, J. D. (2003). *Football U.: Spectator Sports in the Life of the American University*. Ann Arbor: University of Michigan Press.

Toma, J. D. (October 2009). The business of intercollegiate athletics. In D. Siegel and J. Knapp (Eds.), *The Business of Higher Education*, Vol. 3 (pp. 179–216). Santa Barbara, CA: Praeger.

Toma, J. D. (2010a). Strategy and higher education: Differentiation and legitimacy in positioning for prestige. In M. Bastedo, ed., *Organizing Higher Education*. Baltimore, MD: Johns Hopkins University Press.

Toma, J. D. (2010b). *Building Organizational Capacity: Strategic Management in Higher Education*. Baltimore, MD: Johns Hopkins University Press.

Tribbensee, N. (2002a). *The settlement process*. Washington, DC: National Association of College and University Attorneys.

Tribbensee, N. (2002b). *Helping Your Institution's Lawyer Defend You*. Washington, DC: National Association of College and University Attorneys.

Tribbensee, N. (2003). *The Family Educational Rights and Privacy Act: A General Overview*. Washington, DC: National Association of College and University Attorneys.

Tribbensee, N. (2004). Privacy and security in higher education computing after the USA PATRIOT Act. *Journal of College and University Law*, 30(2), 337–62.

Tribbensee, N. (2008). Privacy and confidentiality: Balancing student rights and campus safety. *Journal of College and University Law*, 34(2), 393–417.

U.S. Copyright Office (2007a). Copyright Basics. In G. K. Harper, ed., *Copyright Law and Policy in a Networked World* (pp. 17–28). Washington, DC: National Association of College and University Attorneys.

U.S. Copyright Office (2007b). International Copyright. In G. K. Harper, ed., *Copyright Law and Policy in a Networked World* (pp. 85–86). Washington, DC: National Association of College and University Attorneys.

U.S. Department of Education, Office for Civil Rights (1997). *Sexual Harassment: It's Not Academic*. Washington, DC: U.S. Department of Education.

U.S. Department of Education, Office for Civil Rights (2001). *Revised Sexual Harassment Guidance: Harassment of Students By School Employees, Other Students, or Third Parties*. Washington, DC: U.S. Department of Education.

U.S. Equal Employment Opportunity Commission (EEOC) (1990). *Policy Guidance on Current Issues of Sexual Harassment*. Washington DC: United States Equal Employment Opportunity Commission.

U.S. Equal Employment Opportunity Commission (EEOC) (1999). *Enforcement Guidelines: Vicarious Employer Liability for Unlawful Harassment by Supervisors*. Washington DC: United States Equal Employment Opportunity Commission.

United States v. Paradise, 480 U.S. 149 (1987).

United States v. Virginia, 518 U.S. 515 (1996).

United Steelworkers of America v. Weber, 443 U.S. 193 (1979).

Uniting and Strengthening America by Providing Appropriate Tools Required to Intercept and Obstruct Terrorism Act (USA PATRIOT) Act of 2001. (Pub.L.107-56, 115 Stat. 272).

VanDeusen, D. R. (2006). FMLA checklists for employers and employees. In D. C. Brown, ed., *Employment Issues in Higher Education: A Legal Compendium*, 3d ed. (pp. 691–712). Washington, DC: National Association of College and University Attorneys.

Vercauteren, J. L. (2007). An alternative to prescriptive standards in hazardous waste regulation: Subpart K and performance-based standards for academic labs. *Journal of College and University Law*, 33(3), 681–706.

Vicker, L. A. and H. J. Royer (2006). *The Complete Academic Search Manual: A Systematic Approach to Successful and Inclusive Hiring*. Sterling, VA: Stylus.

Vinik, D. F., E. M. Babbitt and D. M. Friebus (2006). The "quiet revolution" in employment law and its implications for colleges and universities. *Journal of College and University Law*, 33(1), 33–63.

Visual Artists Rights Act 1990 (Pub. L. 101-650, 104 Stat. 5089).

Volokh, E. (2006). Freedom of expressive association and government subsidies. *Stanford Law Review*, 58, 1919–68.

Vullo, S., T. Lewkowicz and M. Rosenbaum (2008). Hot issues in employee benefits in higher education. In D. C. Brown, ed., *Employment Issues in Higher Education: A Legal Compendium*, 3d ed. (pp. 301–54). Washington, DC: National Association of College and University Attorneys.

Wagner Act (National Labor Relations Act [NLRA]) of 1935 (Pub.L. 74-198, 49 Stat. 449).

Ward v. Rock Against Racism, 491 U.S. 781 (1989).

Warner, C. C. (2006). Selected developments and issues in religious discrimination and accommodation. In R. A. Weitzner, ed., *Religious Discrimination and Accommodation Issues in Higher Education: A Legal Compendium* (pp. 39–68). Washington, DC: National Association of College and University Attorneys.

Warren, W. L. and D. C. Holloway (2005). Reach-through licensing: Avoiding a reach too far. In J. L. Curry, ed., *Technology Transfer Issues for Colleges and Universities: A Legal Compendium* (pp. 331–36). Washington, DC: National Association of College and University Attorneys.

Wasserman, H. M. (2005). Cheers, profanity, and free speech. *Journal of College and University Law*, 31(2), 377–92.

Weber v. Kaiser Aluminum Co., 443 U.S. 193 (1979).

Weber, M. C. (2000). Disability discrimination in higher education. *Journal of College and University Law*, 27(2), 417–45.

Weddle, D. B. (2004). Dangerous games: Student hazing and negligent supervision. *West's Higher Education Law Reporter*, 187, 373–82.

Weeks, K. and R. Haglund (2002). Fiduciary duties of college and university faculty and administrators. *Journal of College and University Law*, 29(1), 153–87.

Wei, M. H. (2008). College and university policy and procedural responses to students at risk of suicide. *Journal of College and University Law*, 34(2), 285–318.

Weitzner, R. A. (2006). Religious discrimination and accommodation law in employment. In R. A. Weitzner, ed., *Religious Discrimination and Accommodation Issues in Higher Education: A Legal Compendium* (pp. 3–38). Washington, DC: National Association of College and University Attorneys.

Weyl, S. E. and R. F. Rodgers (2006). *Tax-Exempt Bonds: Considerations for College and University In-House Counsel*. Washington, DC: National Association of College and University Attorneys.

Wheelhouse, M. A. (2009). Second class citizens: Federal limits on state benefits for higher education. *Journal of Gender, Race, and Justice*, 12, 655–86.

White, B. (2007). Student rights: From *in loco parentis* to *sine parentibus* and back again? Understanding the Family and Educational Rights and Privacy Act. *BYU Education and Law Journal*, 2007, 321–50.

White, N. (2005). Taking one for the team: Should colleges be liable for injuries occurring during student participation in club sports? *Vanderbilt Journal of Entertainment Law and Practice*, 7, 193–207.

Widmar v. Vincent, 454 U.S. 263 (1981).

Wilhelm, S. (2003). Accommodating mental disabilities in higher education: A practical guide to ADA requirements. In E. M. Babbitt, ed., *Accommodating Students with Learning and*

Emotional Disabilities (pp. 305–21). Washington, DC: National Association of College and University Attorneys.

Wilhelm, S. (2006). Is someone riding around a golf course from shot to shot really a golfer? *Journal of College and University Law*, 32(3), 579–612.

Williams, C. R. (2007). *FERPA, GLBA, and HIPPA: The Alphabet Soup of Privacy.* Washington, DC: National Association of College and University Attorneys.

Williams, J. C. and C. A. Pinto (2007). Family responsibilities discrimination: Don't get caught off guard. *Labor Lawyer*, 22, 293–327.

Winston, G. (2000). The positional arms race in higher education. Williams Project on the Economy of Higher Education, Discussion Paper 54.

Winston, G. C. (1993). The capital costs conundrum: Why are capital costs ignored by colleges and universities and what are the prospects for change. *Business Officer*, 26(12), 22.

Woltz, R. R. (2006). Religion in the public workplace. In R. A. Weitzner, ed., *Religious Discrimination and Accommodation Issues in Higher Education: A Legal Compendium* (pp. 123–37). Washington, DC: National Association of College and University Attorneys.

Wygant v. Jackson Board of Education, 476 U.S. 267 (1986).

Yamada, D. C. (2002). The employment law rights of student interns. *Connecticut Law Review*, 35, 215–57.

Yun, J. T. and C. Lee (2008). O'Connor's claim: The educational pipeline and *Bakke*. In P. Marin and C. L. Horn, eds., *Realizing Bakke's Legacy: Affirmative Action, Equal Opportunity, and Access to Higher Education* (pp. 61–86). Sterling, VA: Stylus.

Yunus, H. T. (2006). Employment law: Congress giveth and the Supreme Court taketh away: Title VII's prohibition on religious discrimination in the workplace. *Oklahoma Law Review*, 57, 657–85.

Zemsky, R. (2004). On classifying universities: Policy, function and market. In L. E. Weber and J. J. Duderstadt, eds., *Reinventing the Research University* (pp. 109–17). Paris: Economica.

Zemsky, R., G., R. Wegner, and W. F. Massy (2005). *Remaking the American University: Market-Smart and Mission-Centered.* New Brunswick, NJ: Rutgers University Press.

Zemsky, R., S. Shaman, and M. Iannozzi (1997). In search of strategic perspective: A tool for mapping the market in higher education. *Change*, (Nov./Dec.), 23–38.

Zumeta, W. (2001). Public policy and accountability in higher education: Lessons from the past for the new millennium. In D. E. Heller (Ed.). *The States and Public Higher Education Policy: Affordability, Access, and Accountability* (pp. 155–97). Baltimore, MD: Johns Hopkins University Press.

Index

A

Academic deans, 38
Academic freedom
  accountability, 98–99
  employment, 69–70, 95–98
  graduate students, 98
  individuals *vs.* institutions, 96–97
  nontenured faculty, 97–98
  rationale, 95–96
  statements by courts, 96–97
  tenure, 90–91, 95–96
Accommodations, 51
  Americans with Disabilities Act, 49–50
Accountability, 5, 171
  academic freedom, 98–99
Accreditation, 15
Administrative budgets, 2
Administrators
  authority, 20
  increasing influence, 3
Admissions
  athletics, 135
  disability, 126
  discrimination, 133–137
    highly selective admissions simulation, 62–63, *64–67*
    mystery group, 63
  earlier criminal conduct, 143–144
  process, 121, 133
  risk, 147
  safety, 147
Affiliations, 106
Affirmative action, 6
  challenges, 135–136

compelling interest standard, 42, 54
constitutionality, 54
disability, 137
discrimination, 53–55
diversity, 135–137
hiring, 80
race, 133–134
Age Discrimination in Employment Act, 51
  age, 106
  mandatory retirement, 106
Agility, 196–197
Alternative dispute resolution, employment, 77
Americans with Disabilities Act, 49–51, 72
  accommodations, 49–50
  disabled person defined, 49–50
  students, 124–128
Ancillary joint ventures
  liability, 185
  taxation, 185
Antitrust, athletics, simulation, 192–194
Appointment letter, 70–71
Assembly, by students, 157–159
  discrimination, 158
  funding student groups, 157
  religious groups, 157–158
Assumption of risk, 7
Athletics, 1–2
  admissions, 135
  antitrust, simulation, 192–194
  Civil Rights Act Title IX, 190
  codes of conduct, 155
  gender, 190
  hiring, 81

Athletics (*continued*)
    National Collegiate Athletic Association, 8
    regulation, 167
        private regulation, 188–190
    spectators, 150
Attorneys
    litigation, 24–31
    university counsel, 39
At-will employees, wrongful dismissal,
        101–102
Authority
    administrators, 20
    personal liability, 20
    process, 19–22
Autonomy, 5, 198–199
    deference, 15

B
Bayh-Dole Act, 183, 185, 197
Benefits, compliance, 172
Bioterrorism Preparedness and Response Act,
        168
Bona fide occupational qualification
    Civil Rights Act Title VII, 43–44
    hiring, 79
Boundaries
    characterized, 21–22
    partnerships, 22
    process, 21–22
Buckley Amendment, *see* Family Educational
        Rights and Privacy Act

C
Campus crime, 145–147
Charitable immunity, 20–21
Civil Rights Act Title VII, 41
    bona fide occupational qualification,
        43–44
    disparate impact, 47–48
    disparate treatment, 43–47
    failure to accommodate, 45–46
    hostile environment, 45
    religion, 44
    remedies, 48
    retaliation, 45
    sexual harassment, 57–58
Civil Rights Act Title IX
    athletics, 190
    gender, 190
Code of conduct, 140
    athletics, 155

Collaborations, 173
Collective bargaining, 69
    employment, 75–77
Collegiate infrastructure, 1
Commercialization
    conflicts of interest, 85
    deference, 15–16
    discipline, 85
    discrimination, 41
Common law
    employment contracts, 71–72
    less predictable, 5
    process, 11
Compelling interest standard, affirmative
        action, 42, 54
Compensatory damages, 30
Compliance, 168–174, 198–199
    benefits, 172
    salary, 172
    sponsored research regulations, 171–174
    tax exemption, 174
Confidentiality, 184
Conflicts of interest, 173–174
    commercialization, 85
    discipline, 85
    research universities, 8
Consultants, 69
Consumer awareness, 170–171
Consumers of legal services, 4
Continuing education, 3
Contractors, 69
Contracts, 6, 195–196
    students, 7
        contract theory, 122–131
        contractual rights, 122–126
        student fees, 124
        student rights, 122–131
        student services, 123–124
Contributory negligence, 7
Copyright, 167, 178–182
    criticism, 181–182
    distance education, 180
        faculty rights, 180–181
    fair use exception, 179–180
    work-made-for-hire, 179
Corporate disclosures, 170–171
Custom and usage, process, 11–12

D
Deference, 5–6, 198
    autonomy, 15

challenge, 14
commercialization, 15–16
discrimination, 47
history, 14
process, 14–17
   academic-disciplinary distinction, 14–15
   behavioral issues, 14, 16
   weakened, 15
public universities, 15
religion, 44
student discipline, 140
tenure, 89
wrongful dismissal, 103
Development, Relief and Education for Alien
   Minors (DREAM) Act, 169
Digital Millenium Copyright Act, 179,
   181–182
Disability
admissions, 126
affirmative action, 137
assessment, 126–127
characterized, 126
discrimination, 49–51
dismissal, 142
students, 124–128
   discipline, 128
   subject to same rules, 128
student services, 128
Discipline
commercialization, 85
conflicts of interest, 85
employment, 84–86
   progressive discipline, 84–85
process, 141–142
students, 140–144
   concurrent judicial proceedings, 142–143
   deference, 140
   misbehavior off campus, 143
   withholding or revoking degree, 143
Disclosure
governing boards, 20
risk, 146–147
safety, 146–147
Discrimination, 5–6, 41–67
admissions, 133–137
   highly selective admissions simulation,
      62–63, *64–67*
   mystery group, 63
affirmative action, 53–55
age, 51
antidiscrimination measures, 5–6

commercialization, 41
deference, 47
disability, 49–51
diversity, 53–55
federal statutes, 41–51
   scope, 41–43
hiring, 80
hypothetical case, 51–53, 55–57, 60–62
race, 53–55
religion, 44
sexual harassment, 57–60
   hostile work environment, 57–58
   quid pro quo harassment, 57
students, 133–137
tenure, 92
U.S. Equal Employment Opportunity
   Commission, 42
Dismissal, *see also* Wrongful dismissal
Dismissal, disability, 142
Disparate impact
Civil Rights Act Title VII, 47–48
gender disparities in compensation, 47–48
tenure, 92
Disparate treatment
Civil Rights Act Title VII, 43–47
tenure, 92
Distance education, copyright, 180
faculty rights, 180–181
Diversity, 4
affirmative action, 135–137
discrimination, 53–55
recruitment, 4
Drug testing, 130
Duty, 145

E
Economic security guarantee, tenure, 89
Electronic Communications Privacy Act, 86
Employment, 6, 69–120
academic freedom, 69–70, 95–98
alternative dispute resolution, 77
best practices, 69
collective bargaining, 75–77
discipline, 84–86
   progressive discipline, 84–85
hiring, 78–81
hypothetical case, 73–75, 77–78, 81–83,
   86–88, 92–95, 99–101, 106–108
monitoring, 86
   Electronic Communications Privacy Act,
      86

Employment (*continued*)
  performance evaluations, 83–84
    evaluation criteria, 83
  rights, 6
  tenure, 89–92
  wrongful dismissal, 101–106
Employment contracts, 70–72
  common law, 71–72
  elements, 70
  entrepreneurial universities, 71
  federal statutes, 72
  institutional policies overlapping or
    conflicting, 70–71
  principles, 72
  process, 11–12
  religious universities, 71
Entrepreneurial universities, employment
    contracts, 71
Establishment Clause
  Free Exercise Clause, 46–47
  religion, 46
Expulsion, *see* Dismissal

F
Faculty, *see also* Tenured faculty
  decreasing influence, 3
  temporary, 5
    wrongful dismissal, 101–102
  tenure-significant lines *vs.* contingent, 2
  visas, 169–170
Faculty union, 37–38
Failure to accommodate, Civil Rights Act
    Title VII, 45–46
Fair labor standards, 170
Fair use exception, copyright, 179–180
Family and Medical Leave Act, 72
Family Educational Rights and Privacy Act
  privacy, 121, 128–130
  records, 129
  students, 121, 128–130
Federal Grant and Co-Operative Agreement
    Act, 172
Federal policy, 8
Federal statutes, *see also* Specific act
  discrimination, 41–51
    scope, 41–43
  employment contracts, 72
  process, 10–11
Financial exigency
  process, 105

simulation, 108–110, *111–120*
wrongful dismissal, 105–106
Foreseeability, 145
Free Exercise Clause, Establishment Clause,
    46–47
Free expression, 7
  students, 153–156
Fund raising, 3

G
Gender
  athletics, 190
  Civil Rights Act Title IX, 190
  disparities in compensation, disparate
    impact, 47–48
Globalization, 4
Governing boards
  disclosure, 20
  liability, 19–20
  process, 19–22
  responsibilities, 19–20
Governmental immunity, 5, 20–21
Graduate programs, 1
Graduate students, academic freedom, 98
Grants, loans, shift from, 2
Grutter v. Bollinger, 134–136, 140

H
Handbooks, 70
  institutional policies overlapping or
    conflicting, 70–71
Hazing, 147
Health Insurance Portability and
    Accountability Act
  privacy, 129–130
  students, 129–130
Higher education, *see also* Specific type
  as commodity, 1
  private regulation, 8
Hiring
  affirmative action, 80
  athletics, 81
  bona fide occupational qualification, 79
  discrimination, 80
  employment, 78–81
  interviews, 79–80
  public institutions, presidents, 80–81
  screening, 79
Hostile environment
  Civil Rights Act Title VII, 45

students, 144–145
Hostile work environment, 57–58

I
Illegal Immigration Reform and Immigrant
    Responsibility Act, 169
Immigration, 7–8, 168–170
Immorality, 104
Incapacity, 104
Incompetence, 104
Injunctive relief, 30
In loco parentis approach, 122
    transition from, 122
Instructional budgets, 2
Insubordination, 104
Integrity, 198–200
Intellectual property, 8, 167, 178–187, 197
    criticism, 181–182
Internet, 4
Internships, 150

L
Legal issues, 4, 24–31, *see also* Specific type
    academic deference, 5–6
Liability
    ancillary joint ventures, 185
    governing boards, 19–20
    risk, 145–146
    safety, 7, 145
        causation, 145
        duty, 145
        foreseeability, 145
    students, 122–123, 144–150
    threat assessment, 146
    waiver, 21
Litigation, process, 24–31
    attorneys, 24–25
    clients, 24–25
    compensatory damages, 30
    complaint and answer, 25–27
    depositions, 28
    discovery, 27–29
    document requests, 28
    injunctive relief, 30
    interrogatories, 28
    monetary damages, 30
    punitive damages, 30
    remedies, 29–31
    settlement, 27–29
    trial, 29–31

Loans, grants, shift from, 2

M
Mandatory retirement, Age Discrimination in
    Employment Act, 106
Mergers, 106
Misconduct, wrongful dismissal, 103–104
Mismanagement, 19–20
Monetary damages, 30
Monitoring
    employment, 86
        Electronic Communications Privacy Act,
            86
    privacy, 131

N
National Collegiate Athletic Association, 167,
    188–190
    athletics, 8
National Labor Relations Act, 75
Neglect of duty, 104
Nonmanagement, 19–20
Nontraditional students, 3

O
Online, 3

P
Partnerships, boundaries, 22
Patents, 183–185
Performance evaluations, employment, 83–84
    evaluation criteria, 83
Personal liability, authority, 20
Personal Responsibility and Work
        Opportunity Reconciliation Act, 169
Podberesky v. Kirwan, 136–137
Positioning, 1
Pregnancy Discrimination Act, 72
Privacy
    Family Educational Rights and Privacy Act,
        121, 128–130
    Health Insurance Portability and
        Accountability Act, 129–130
    monitoring, 131
    records, 129
    risk, 131
    students, 121, 128–130
    U.S. Constitution, 130–131
Private regulation, 187–190
    athletics, 188–190

Process, 5, 9–40, 197–198
  admissions, 121, 133
  authority, 19–22
  boundaries, 21–22
  common law, 11
  custom and usage, 11–12
  deference, 14–17
    academic-disciplinary distinction, 14–15
    behavioral issues, 14, 16
    weakened, 15
  discipline, 141–142
  employment contracts, 11–12
  federal statutes, 10–11
  formalized and enhanced, 16
  governing boards, 19–22
  how much hearing, 17
  how much notice, 17
  hypothetical case, 12–14, 17–19, 22–23,
      31–36
  law sources, 9–12
  litigation, 24–31
    attorneys, 24–25
    clients, 24–25
    compensatory damages, 30
    complaint and answer, 25–27
    depositions, 28
    discovery, 27–29
    document requests, 28
    injunctive relief, 30
    interrogatories, 28
    monetary damages, 30
    punitive damages, 30
    remedies, 29–31
    settlement, 27–29
    trial, 29–31
  necessity of, 9
  students, 7, 141–142
  tenure
    academic deans, 38
    application process simulation, 33–40
    faculty union, 37–38
    local business and nonprofit partners, 39
    student government, 38
    university counsel, 39
    vice president for academic affairs, 38
  U.S. Constitution, 10
    First Amendment, 10
    Fourteenth Amendment, 10, 16–17
  waiver, 21
  wrongful dismissal, 103

Progressive discipline, 84–85
Psychiatric disabilities, 84
Public institutions
  deference, 15
  hiring, presidents, 80–81
  resources, 2
  return on investment, 2
Punitive damages, 30

Q
Quid pro quo harassment, 57

R
Race
  affirmative action, 133–134
  athletics, 189–190
  discrimination, 53–55
Rampages, students, 146–148
Rankings, 1
  means to increase, 1
  research universities, 1
  resources, 1
Reasonable accommodation, *see*
      Accommodations
Record release, student records, 7
Records
  Family Educational Rights and Privacy
      Act, 129
  privacy, 129
Recruitment, diversity, 4
Reforms, 3
Regents of the University of California v. Bakke,
      134, 136
Regulation, 7–8, 167–194
  athletics, 167
  federal statutes, 41–51
  hypothetical case, 174–178, 185–187,
      190–192
  private regulation, 187–190
    athletics, 188–190
  state regulation, 187
Rehabilitation Act, 49–51
Release of student records, 7
Religion
  characterized, 45
  Civil Rights Act Title VII, 44
  deference, 44
  discrimination, 44
  Establishment Clause, 46
  students, 159–160

accommodation, 159
Religious universities, employment contracts, 71
Remedies, 29–31
    Civil Rights Act Title VII, 48
    sexual harassment, 60
    students, 124
    types, 30
Reputation, 195, 199–200
Research foundations, 183–184
Research misconduct, 173
Research universities, 3
    commercializing university research, 3
    conflicts of interest, 8
    rankings, 1
    sponsored research regulations, 171–174
Resources, public institutions, 2
Retaliation
    Civil Rights Act Title VII, 45
    sexual harassment, 60
    tenure, 90–91
Return on investment
    public institutions, 2
    students, 2
Rights, employment issues, 6
Risk
    admission, 147
    assumption of, 7
    disclosure, 146–147
    liability, 145–146
    privacy, 131
Risk management, 5

S
Safety, 170
    admission, 147
    disclosure, 146–147
    liability, 7, 145
        causation, 145
        duty, 145
        foreseeability, 145
    students, 145
    threat assessment, 146
Salary, compliance, 172
Sarbanes-Oxley Act, 170–171
Satellite campuses, 3
Search and seizure, 130, 143
Self-dealing, 19–20
Settlement decrees, 29
Sexual harassment

affirmative defense against liability, 59–60
    characterized, 58
    Civil Rights Act Title VII, 57–58
    coworker, 59
    discrimination, 57–60
        hostile work environment, 57–58
        quid pro quo harassment, 57
    investigating complaints, 58–59
    remedies, 60
    retaliation, 60
    same-sex harassment, 58
    students, 144
    supervisors, 59
Sexual orientation, 41–42
Shared ownership agreements, 180–181
Single-sex colleges, 137
Special relationship doctrine, students, 123
Sponsored research, regulations, 171–174
State regulation, 187
Statutory rights, students, 124–131
Student fees, 124
Student government, 38
Student organizations, *see* Assembly
Student publications, First Amendment, 156
Students, 121–165
    admissions, earlier criminal conduct, 143–144
    Americans with Disabilities Act, 124–128
    assembly, 157–159
        discrimination, 158
        funding student groups, 157
        religious groups, 157–158
    competition for, 1–2
    contracts, 7
        contract theory, 122–131
        contractual rights, 122–126
        student fees, 124
        student rights, 122–131
        student services, 123–124
    disability, 124–128
        discipline, 128
        subject to same rules, 128
    discipline, 140–144
        concurrent judicial proceedings, 142–143
        deference, 140
        misbehavior off campus, 143
        withholding or revoking degree, 143
    discrimination, 133–137
    Family Educational Rights and Privacy Act, 121, 128–130

Students (*continued*)
  free expression, 153–156
  Health Insurance Portability and
      Accountability Act, 129–130
  hostile environment, 144–145
  hypothetical case, 131–133, 137–139, 151–
      152, 160–161
  liability, 122–123, 144–150
  privacy, 121, 128–130
  process, 7, 141–142
  rampages, 146–148
  reasonable accommodation, 127
  relationship between institutions and
      students, 121–122
  religion, 159–160
    accommodation, 159
  remedies, 124
  return on investment, 2
  safety, 145
  sexual harassment, 144
  special relationship doctrine, 123
  statutory rights, 124–131
  suicide, 147–148
  U.S. Constitution, 121–122, 124–131
    First Amendment, 152–160
    Fourth Amendment, 130
  visas, 169–170
Student services
  contracts, 123–124
  disability, 128
  study abroad programs, 149–150
Study abroad programs, 149–150
Suicide, students, 147–148

T
Taxation, ancillary joint ventures, 185
Tax exemption, compliance, 174
TEACH Act, 180
Technology transfer, 167, 178–187
Tenure
  academic freedom, 90–91, 95–96
  challenge to failure to grant, 91–92
  decisions, 89–92
  deference, 89
  discrimination, 92
  disparate impact, 92
  disparate treatment, 92
  economic security guarantee, 89
  employment, 89–92
  limitations, 89

probationary period, 90
process, 90–92
  academic deans, 38
  application process simulation, 33–40
  faculty union, 37–38
  local business and nonprofit partners, 39
  student government, 38
  university counsel, 39
  vice president for academic affairs, 38
relevant factors, 90
retaliation, 90–91
standards, 90–92
wrongful dismissal, 102–106
Terrorism, 7
Threat management
  liability, 146
  safety, 146
  simulation, 162–165
Trade secrets, 184

U
Undocumented students, 8, 168–169
Unions, 75–77
University counsel, 39
Unrelated business income tax, 173
U.S. Constitution
  privacy, 130–131
  process, 10
    First Amendment, 10
    Fourteenth Amendment, 10, 16–17
  students, 121–122, 124–131
    First Amendment, 152–160
    Fourth Amendment, 130
U.S. Equal Employment Opportunity
      Commission, discrimination, 42
USA PATRIOT Act, 168

V
Values, 195, 200
Vice president for academic affairs, 38
Visas
  faculty, 169–170
  students, 169–170
Voluntary settlement agreement, 29

W
Waiver
  liability, 21
  process, 21
Work-made-for-hire, copyright, 179

Wrongful dismissal
    at-will employees, 101–102
    deference, 103
    employment, 101–106
    financial exigency, 105–106
    misconduct, 103–104
    process, 103
    temporary faculty, 101–102
    tenured faculty, 102–106